Ambitious Appetites

Dining, Behavior, and Patterns of Consumption in Federal Washington

Barbara G. Carson

To Stara
What a fine time we had
with John and Betty.
Do come to Williamsburg
Barbara

Octagon Museum
Kym S. Rice, Guest Exhibition Curator

August 7, 1990–October 30, 1990

The American Institute of Architects Press
Washington, D.C.

Barbara G. Carson teaches in the Art and American Studies departments of George Washington University and in the American Studies Department of the College of William and Mary.

The American Institute of Architects Press
1735 New York Avenue, N.W.
Washington, D.C. 20006

94 93 92 91 90 5 4 3 2 1

Library of Congress Cataloging-in-Publication Data
Carson, Barbara G., 1941–
   Ambitious appetites: dining, behavior, and patterns of consumption in
Federal Washington/Barbara G. Carson.
      p. cm. — (Octagon research series)
   "Octagon Museum Kym S. Rice, guest exhibition curator, August 7,
1990–October 30, 1990."
   Includes bibliographical references and index.
   ISBN 1-55835-026-8 (paperback)
   1. Washington (D.C.)—Social life and customs—Exhibitions. 2. Food
habits—Washington (D.C.)—History—Exhibitions. I. Rice, Kym S. II.
Octagon (Washington, D.C.) III. Title. IV. Series.
F196.C33   1990   90-1156
306.4′074753—dc20   CIP

Designed by Quinn Design, Cabin John, Maryland
Composed in Caslon Old Face No. 2 by Carver Photocomposition, Inc.,
   Arlington, Virginia
Printed by Port City Press, Baltimore, Maryland

Contents

The Octagon

This Federal period house, the winter home of Col. John Tayloe III, was designed by William Thornton, the first architect of the U.S. Capitol, and erected from 1799–1802. After the British burned the President's House during the War of 1812, President and Mrs. James Madison made the Octagon their official residence. Madison ratified the Treaty of Ghent, ending the war, in the second floor study. Today, under the auspices of the American Architectural Foundation, the museum is a lively center of exhibitions and public programs relating to architecture, decorative arts, and American and Washington history.

Octagon Research Series

1. *Creating the Federal City, 1774–1800: Potomac Fever,* by Kenneth R. Bowling (1988).
2. *Building the Octagon,* by Orlando Ridout V (1989).
3. *Ambitious Appetites: Dining, Behavior, and Patterns of Consumption in Federal Washington* (1990), by Barbara G. Carson.

Acknowledgments
This publication and exhibition were made possible by grants from the AIA College of Fellows Fund, The Morris and Gwendolyn Cafritz Foundation, the District of Columbia Community Humanities Council, the Faulkner Catalogue Fund, and the Rohm and Haas Company.

Foreword

Ambitious Appetites: Dining, Behavior, and Patterns of Consumption in Federal Washington, the third book in the
Octagon Research Series, explores the domestic activities of the Octagon in the early nineteenth century through the display and social
use of food. Barbara Carson superbly captures the unique quality of
the Washington environment as reflected in its habits of etiquette,
dining, and entertaining, which shaped many of America's social
and cultural patterns. Documentation of the Tayloe family's participation in these events, as seen in this important book, provides evidence for the delineation of spaces within the Octagon. Such
scholarly research is an extension of the work begun under Orlando
Ridout V in *Building the Octagon*. Barbara Carson sets the Tayloes'
everyday, high style life within the context of the daily experience of
more ordinary people.

We are most appreciative of the support of our sponsors, the AIA
College of Fellows Fund, The Morris and Gwendolyn Cafritz
Foundation, the District of Columbia Community Humanities
Council, the Faulkner Catalogue Fund, and the Rohm and Haas
Company. Significant contributions were made by our guest curator
Kym Rice and research associate Ellen Kirven Donald, who have
given unstintingly to the entire research series. These projects would
not have occurred without their complete dedication. Nancy Klavens
served ably as consultant for the kitchen reinterpretation.

Our gratitude also extends to our exhibition lenders, the AIA
Press staff, the Octagon Committee, and the American Architectural Foundation Board of Regents, and to Nancy Davis, director of
the Octagon, and the American Architectural Foundation staff who
have provided such enthusiastic support.

It is our hope that this research, which has proved so valuable to
the Octagon, will be of great interest to our public and of benefit to
scholars in the field.

Norman Koonce
President, American Architectural Foundation

Introduction

Whether people knew it or not, matters of power embedded in meal-taking affected everyone in the new capital city in the early nineteenth century. Menus, table settings, guest lists, and polite behavior varied according to a person's standing. Examples recorded at the time provide windows that allow us to look at class and gender relationships as they evolved in the Washington social order. One visitor pronounced a dinner given by Secretary of State James Monroe as the most stylish she had ever attended. She particularly noted the width of the table, the plateau with ornamental images and vases of flowers, plentiful candles, silver dishes, and silver utensils.[1] When John Tayloe III, the wealthy planter who commissioned the Octagon, invited William Thornton, its architect, to an afternoon dinner, his guest list did not include Mrs. Thornton.[2] At midnight following a ball at another private house "chocolate in cups with dry toast was handed round among the ladies, and *after that* the gentlemen were regaled in a back parlor with a cold ham, mutton & tongue."[3] A Washington hostess allowed two little girls from an indigent family to stand in a back room during an evening party, watch the guests, and gather up fragments of cake, blanc-mange, and jellies.[4]

This book and its accompanying exhibition describe food, table settings, and social rituals in early nineteenth century Washington, D.C., and investigate issues that emerge from the scenes and events. Both are part of a larger project that aims to develop an interpretive plan for the Octagon, a historic house museum and rare survivor of 200 years of urban development in the capital city. A wealthy and therefore most exceptional man built this luxurious dwelling between 1799 and 1802. He lived there until his death in 1828. However, if John Tayloe's entire household—his large family, white employees, and black slaves—are set within the context of everyday activities in a growing city, his elite residence becomes a platform from which we can scan the population in all its diversity. During

Jelly glass, England, ca. 1800
(Gunston Hall Plantation).
Sweetened and jelled fruit
juice served in glasses, often
grouped on stacked salvers, remained a popular dessert for
many years. This example originally belonged to Georgetown
businesssman John Mason,
who entertained frequently at
his Analostan Island residence
in the Potomac.

the decades between 1800, when the first session of Congress met in
the new Capitol, and 1829, when Andrew Jackson became president, dining and entertaining practices underwent significant transformations that expressed and helped shape new social and cultural
patterns.

Washington was a peculiar city where elected and appointed officials and an exotic corps of foreign diplomats had special reasons for
entertaining each other. Upper class residents of the permanent
community enjoyed their own social activities. Sometimes the
groups blended together; other times they went their separate ways.
Their activities stand out against the variegated behavior of more
ordinary people. The picture of dining and entertaining throughout
these years is never uniform or static. Yet for all that, it is possible
to discern a definite direction in the changing scenes and events.

In the years between the Revolution and the Civil War the hierarchical, male-dominated character of American society became
more equality-conscious, if not more equal. This book stresses the
early years of the nineteenth century, in which these changes become
more noticeable in the historical record. Increasingly people became

attuned to rhetoric appropriate to a democratic republic, and occasionally they behaved accordingly. Elite women, once mere silent functionaries at their husbands' tables, began to share responsibility in a hosting partnership, especially at evening parties. During the same period, some ordinary men and women strove to acquire the possessions and the genteel behavior that might make their families more socially acceptable. Others were little inclined or had few opportunities to share these aspirations.

The story progresses through six chapters from descriptions of simple meals eaten in family settings to accounts of more elegant food and its ritual service at grand social events. The first chapter explores the special character of the city in the early nineteenth century and describes how meal-taking and the concept of gentility can be lenses for examining the workings of the social order. The second chapter begins with a brief glance back through time. Dining has an ancient history that helps explain the diversity of people's experiences at their family tables. A survey of Washington probate inventories from 1818 to 1826 has revealed five distinct groups of implements for meal-taking. This division of tableware corresponds to different patterns of eating among classes of people representing all but the city's slaves and poorest families. The third chapter focuses on differences in the design and production of knives, forks, and spoons and the ways they have changed over time. The distribution and use of these three table utensils among Washington households were sensitive indicators of status. Every object used to take a meal might be similarly studied to reinforce the argument.

The last half of the book deals with high society. The fourth chapter examines prescriptions for the roles of hosts, hostesses, guests, and servants. It stretches the term "family" to include those intimate friends who shared casual, relaxed occasions and contrasts these events with those in "society." The social credentials of people invited to dinner parties and the gender-specific behavior at private, public, and official functions reveal the intricate hierarchies of elite entertainments. In chapter five the private aspects of high society are viewed through two different events, all-male dinners and mixed-gender evening tea parties. Chapter six is devoted to official Washington. During legislative sessions transient congressmen and occasionally their wives and families lived in boardinghouses, ate at "messes," and at best arranged makeshift entertainments. By contrast, members of the executive branch of the government and foreign ministers usually moved their entire families to Washington, where they rented dwellings and kept house. Their parties were conducted with grand style. Both groups were part of the higher levels of Washington society that stepped out to diplomatic dinners, evening tea parties hosted by government officials, and various kinds of presidential receptions.

Although many popular and scholarly books have been written about food, table settings, and mealtime etiquette, they have devoted their attention almost exclusively to the colonial or Victorian years, neglecting the federal era. This project represents an initial effort to sketch changing events during the decades that bridge these two very different periods.[5] The current exhibition program at the Octagon offers an appropriate opportunity to publish these preliminary findings as a basis for further research. Members of the project team have made new material available for public scrutiny and have sought to use it to raise worthwhile issues. The story told here is far from finished. Some of the information, especially that about women's silence, immobility, and lack of participation, leaves unanswered questions and probably needs a broader interpretive context to be fully understood. Likewise, questions concerning the differences between family and formal dining customs among the elite and distinctions between the public and private spheres demand further investigation. Dining practices that distinguished urban from rural tables and Washington from other American cities require comparative study. In addition, it remains for future scholars to explain international influences and the complex nature of the competition between French and English table manners and cuisines. Both affected American practice. In the end, members of the project team hope that both the exhibition and this book will serve as springboards for future research.

It is my pleasure to thank the many people who brought this book to print. Overall planning for the Octagon Research Series, a five-year undertaking, does not give specific direction to each phase. Each exhibit and its accompanying book is conceived and completed within fifteen months, a daunting task if one were working alone. Nancy Davis, director of the Octagon Museum, holds the enterprise together, raises funds, and throughout remains even-tempered. The collaboration to produce volume three gave me responsibility for the research agenda, the interpretation of the material, and the writing of this book. Kym S. Rice took charge of the accompanying exhibition, selected the illustrations, and wrote caption copy. Ellen Kirven Donald organized the inventory study. The three of us ran down relevant published sources and discovered useful manuscript collections. We pooled our findings. As I wrote, they read, corrected, and amplified the text. Their hard work and extraordinary good humor pushed me to complete a book to which they contributed enormously. I thank them very warmly and with a tiny wish that collective enterprise included collective responsibility. It does not; errors are mine.

During six months of the past year I was generously supported by a Henry Francis du Pont Fellowship from Winterthur. Working again with the excellent resources and fine staff of that institution was a pleasure. A long list of colleagues shared information and exchanged ideas about its significance. I would like to thank Jim Cassedy of the Suitland Reference Branch, National Archives and Records Administration; Dean Lahikainen of the Essex Institute; Ardis Beeman, Margaret Piatt, and Caroline Sloat of Old Sturbridge Village; Patricia Gibbs, John Davis, William Graham, Betty Leviner, Lorena S. Walsh, Mark R. Wenger, William E. White, and Mary Wiseman of the Colonial Williamsburg Foundation; Donald Fenimore, E. McSherry Fowble, Pauline Eversman, and Rosemary Krill of Winterthur museum; Bert Denker, Neville Thompson, and the staff of the library at Winterthur; Margaret Cook and Ellen Strong of the rare book collection of Swem Library, the College of William and Mary; Yvonne Carrigan and the staff of the Lloyd House, Alexandria Library; Cynthia Ware and Janet Rumbarger of the AIA Press; Ellen Denker, Richard S. Dunn, Arlene Horvath, David Hosford, Orlando Ridout V, and Susan Williams. The following institutions provided assistance: the Colonial Williamsburg Foundation, the Library of Congress, the Museum of Early Southern Decorative Arts, the Virginia Historical Society, and the Virginia State Archives.

Various individuals commented on all or part of the manuscript at various stages of its development. The work benefited from discussion of preliminary sections prepared for a colloquium of The Institute of Early American History and Culture. Kenneth R. Bowling, A. Purcell Carson, Cary Carson, Nancy Davis, Rhys Isaac, Ann Smart Martin, George Miller, Rodris Roth, and Fredrika J. Teute read drafts and offered sound advice about ways to improve the text. Pamela James Blumgart, who edited the manuscript, kept pushing to improve it when others had given up.

The following participants in graduate seminars at the College of William and Mary and The George Washington University (Smithsonian Affiliated Programs) helped with the preliminary analysis of the inventories and reported on published or manuscript accounts of life in Washington: Richard Brown, Laurie Cook, Colleen Curry, Elizabeth Dalton, Anne Deines, Alicia Delahunty, Diane Devaul, Ywone Edwards, Pie Friendly, Bonnie Garmisa, James Goode, Anthea Hartig, Genny Holterman, Andrea Kerr, Liza Kirwin, Julia Kurdt, Ursula Marcum, Joanne Manwarring, Richard Pickering, Stephen Phillips, Lynne Schaffer, Patrick Sheary, Amy Watson Smith, Suzanne Stallings, Anne Verplanck, Shannon Williams, and Karen Yaffee.

My gratitude to others extends beyond professional circles to a loving family and good friends. Three separate households sustained my efforts and a large number of visitors distracted me entertainingly during the year. It is hard to say which was more important. These people know who they are, how much fun we had even when we were working hard, and how very fond I am of all of them.

F Street, Washington, D.C. by Baroness Hyde de Neuville, watercolor and pencil, 1821 (courtesy, The New-York Historical Society, New York City). With its wide, unpaved streets and picket-fenced yards, Washington looked less like a city and more like a small rural town through the first half of the nineteenth century.

I. A Capital City in a Wilderness: Emergent Structures, Emergent Civility

Early one May morning in 1820 Colonel John Tayloe, his wife Ann, and a party of friends boarded carriages at the Octagon, the Tayloes' Washington residence, and drove out into the countryside. They disembarked at the falls of the Potomac, where they enjoyed the scenery, gathered wildflowers, and listened to "a charming band . . . stationed in the wood." Eventually, the company arrived at the dinner site, enigmatically described as an "elegantly dilapidated mansion," where they found "a sumptuous collation." Everyone became "very sociable and agreeable" under the influence of "the jokes and the sparkling champagne." By and by the guests finished their refreshments, whereupon the coachmen followed "our example [and] took our places." They were less "prudent in quaffing the exhilarating Cup and our ride home was rendered less safe and less pleasant in consequence." Happily, all returned without accident and were pleased with the excursion.

The account of this outing is one of only a handful of descriptions of Washington meals that mention people of different social groups. With help from their domestic staff, a band of musicians, and some coachmen, the Tayloes provided an entertainment suitable to their wealth and station in society. It was an event that only a few privileged people in the nation's capital were entitled to experience. To understand the exercise of power reflected in this and other elegant meals, the Tayloes' party must be set in the social landscape of Washington and the diversity of its people.[1]

A picture of early Washington

In 1800 the government of the United States moved from Philadelphia to a new city laid out on the banks of the Potomac River between Georgetown and the Anacostia River. Holders of executive offices, congressmen, and foreign diplomats, who had grown accustomed to the amenities of the country's largest city, found themselves transported to a farming region, which one optimist pronounced "the best city in the world to live in—in the future."[2] The road south from Baltimore to the capital was so poorly marked in 1800 that Abigail Adams, wife of the president, and her party got lost in the woods. "Fortunately," she recounted, "a straggling black came up with us, and we engaged him as a guide."[3] Twenty years later her daughter-in-law noted the city streets were still "dreadful beyond anything you can conceive." On their way to a ball at the British minister's Louisa Catherine and John Quincy Adams, then secretary of state in the Monroe administration, passed "two carriages overturned nobody hurt fortunately." The experience was all too common.[4] Well into the century the District of Columbia remained a loose collection of urban landmarks lightly laid on an established rural landscape.

Although George Washington's hand-picked engineer and city planner Pierre L'Enfant had drawn a scheme full of potential grandeur, the spatial organization he gave to the infant city combined an inspired architectural dream with the visions of those who had designed a new form of government. Americans' uncertainty about their ability to rule each other wisely and the importance they assigned to a system of checks and balances can be read in the plan of Washington. Over a mile separated Congress on Capitol Hill and the president in the White House. The judiciary was inconspicuously attached to the legislative territory.[5] An attitude of wariness among those in government toward each other and toward their mission encouraged a pattern of living in dispersed settlements that to some extent corresponded to their official responsibilities. The dismal condition of connecting roads, a fact of life no one tried seriously to change, translated the separateness of government units from the map of Washington to the reality of everyday movement around the city.

Washington was not a proper unified urban area, but a series of villages. One settlement grew up around the Capitol, another near the White House, and a third along the shores of the Anacostia River. West across Rock Creek was Georgetown, an eighteenth century commercial center, which became a service satellite to the executive community. Although the town lands of Alexandria on the south shore of the Potomac were included in the original Federal District, this important colonial entrepot was too well-established to surrender its own identity.[6] The major enclaves that composed the district were described in 1818 as "*Alexandria*, which is seven miles from the city, [and] may be considered the seaport. *Georgetown* is the residence of shopkeepers, and *Washington* the depot for office-holders, placehunters, and boarding-house keepers, none of whom would appear to be in possession of too much of this world's goods."[7]

"Look before you leap," prospective British immigrants to the federal city were warned in 1796. They were told not to expect "ideal romantic happiness, in a solitary uncultivated waste, little calculated, and still less capable of conferring the comforts and benefits of society."[8] The anonymous advice-giver was not referring to life among the fashionable set, but to the meager existence that ordinary people might look forward to after they met the expenses of board, lodging, washing, wearing apparel, and other incidentals.[9] The cautionary warning was well taken. Most people in Washington were far from prosperous. The 1800 census counted 14,093 men, women, and children. More than half of these individuals lived in Georgetown or Alexandria, 3,000 to 4,000 were scattered over the open countryside inside the Federal District, and 3,000 lived in the villages that made up Washington proper. Of the latter, 623 were slaves, 123 free blacks, and many more poor whites.[10] In 1802 only 233 males in a "center city" population then numbering between 3,000 and 4,000 owned personal or real property valued, separately or combined, at $100 or more. As early as 1802 poor relief claimed over 42 percent of the town's revenue.[11]

Washington's total population had more than doubled by the 1820s. Not surprisingly, increases were greater in the more urbanized areas.[12] Concentrated there were 22,614 whites, 6,377 slaves, and 4,084 free blacks. Through these years Congress grew, from 138 in 1802 to 273 in 1829. Federal bureaucracies expanded similarly. Most newcomers did not thrive financially, and the need for charitable services continued to expand.

The swelling population was inadequately sheltered. In 1800 the city contained only 109 brick and 263 wooden houses.[13] Not in-

3

In Washington City by Augustus Kollner, pen and ink, 1839 (Library of Congress).
Local farmers carted their produce into the Federal City and frequently sold it in the vicinity of the Central Market, which opened at 7th and Pennsylvania in 1801. Although men and trusted servants usually did the daily marketing, women also purchased food for their households.

cluded in this count were "temporary wooden hovels, somewhat similar to booths . . . erected at country . . . fairs in many parts of England." These were crammed with people, as many as eight in "one apartment partitioned off into two boxes."[14] Even the permanent structures were likely to be small, no more than one or two rooms with a loft or at best a full second story. Taverns and boardinghouses were larger, but they accommodated more people—paying guests, the keeper's family, servants, and slaves. Congressmen, sharing rooms, were also squeezed into crowded quarters, yet their situation was better than most if only because it was temporary.[15] Before 1815 the Tayloes' Octagon was the only private house with rooms large and elegant enough for grand entertaining.

Steady building activity increased the housing stock from 372 in 1800 to 2,346 in 1823. A record-keeper at the time estimated that, no matter what their size (and many still had only one room), each sheltered slightly more than six persons.[16] Larger and better hous-

Scrubwoman by Baroness Hyde de Neuville, watercolor, before 1822 (collection of The New-York Historical Society, New York City). As was true in other cities of the Upper South, Washington's population included a significant number of free African-Americans. In 1820 a little less than half the black residents of the city were free.

ing was available to those who could afford it. Brick houses "three stories high, and decent, without being in the least elegant" lined the streets of Capitol Hill.[17] Similar development could be seen along Pennsylvania Avenue on either side of the White House and north around Lafayette Square.[18] Although these houses might be comfortable for everyday family life, many were inadequate for entertaining. One New England gentleman attended an evening party and reported to his wife that his host's heart was "bigger than his house." Eighteen people, enjoying good food and drink, felt both "a hearty welcome and a close squeeze."[19] On the other hand, the Octagon was no longer the city's only large, elegant private dwelling. Benjamin Latrobe, William Thornton, and other architect-builders provided the city's wealthiest citizens with houses appropriate to their wealth and entertaining style. The Van Ness mansion was under construction by 1815, and Stephen Decatur moved into his grand residence in 1819. In the same year the British minister rented a house with a dining room "about 40 feet long and of a handsome width with a fire place at each end but it is miserably low." He and his wife could seat between thirty and forty people but he recommended that his successor follow his example and "contemplate 24 persons as the outside."[20]

Emergent social order

Whether they lived in shanties or houses, most newly transplanted residents of Washington were employed by government agencies or supplied the city with goods and services. During congressional sessions the pace of life quickened. "All of Washington is now jumping alive," one participant noted in 1815. "Strangers & members of Congress and gentlemen are daily arriving, and the Tavern Keepers and boarding House people Laugh for joy . . . every body, and everything seems to hang upon the Government."[21] Very little is known about the local farming community, although in the 1820s it was still substantial enough to retain its own identity.[22]

The procurement of food on the one hand and its preparation on the other must have provided jobs for many people and support for their families. The Central Market opened in 1801, followed by other markets as the city grew.[23] In 1818 a British traveler counted "three market-houses in Washington, and I believe, four market days per week. Negroes are the chief sellers. The supplies at this time are neither good nor various."[24] Another writer approved of the supplies but not the culinary results, "We have good markets and high prices and bad cooks."[25] The inventory of John Krause, taken on the third of October 1820, hints at how purveyors went to market. Krause owned "Weights & Scales & Butchers Work Tools" valued at $15, "1 Cart & Gear" at $20, and another "old cart" at $2. His appraisers valued a lease on a "Stall in market House" at $20 and "2 meat Stands & tops" at $4.[26] Poor whites and blacks are known to have gathered wild mushrooms and fruits and sold them on the streets or at the markets. More prosperous citizens like John Tayloe had outlying farms or more distant plantations that supplied much of their food. Sometimes they sent their surplus to be sold at market.[27]

The Capitol at Washington . . . from the Pennsylvania Avenue by Philip John Banbrigge, watercolor, ca. 1837 (National Archives of Canada, acc. 1948.77.44). "The appearance of the metropolis rising gradually into life and splendour," visitor Frances Trollope commented in 1831, "is a spectacle of high historic interest." Lower Pennsylvania Avenue, lined with hotels, boardinghouses, and shops of all varieties, was the city's major commercial district.

Newspapers advertised grocery stores and the sale at auction of produce from ships. They reveal that a wide range of food was imported. Between 1806 and 1809 Thomas Jefferson's maitre d'hotel Etienne Lemaire recorded purchasing many different meats, fowl, fish, vegetables, fruits, nuts, and spices for the White House table.[28] Washington city directories for 1822 and 1830 do not reveal much change in the numbers or types of purveyors of food. The number of grocers increased from eighty-eight to 100, the bakers from five to ten, wine merchants from two to five. Confectioners held constant at seven, but the number of butchers declined from seventeen to fifteen. The earlier directory listed a "col'd man" as a cook. The single pastry cook was probably white. One free black is listed as running an oyster house and another as an "oyster man." Plenty of food was available so long as customers could pay for it.

Aside from these local planters and purveyors, those in the building trades and those who provided support services to the government and its personnel dominated the city. Artisans, mechanics, laborers, free blacks, and slaves who fed, housed, furnished, clothed, transported, and waited on the ranks of executives, bureau-crats, legislators, judges, and military personnel made up the bulk of Washington's population. Just above that deep bottom layer of society were tradespeople, storekeepers, and specialized retailers.[29] Washington had few merchants and fewer manufacturers. It did attract an unusual number of professionals, architects, educators, physicians, lawyers, and newspapermen—all "citizens of fair character and suitable appearance," as one writer termed them.[30] Men of business, depending upon their wealth, were counted either in the professional ranks or among the elite.

Boardinghouse keepers posed a special classification problem for Washington society. Because transient congressmen, sometimes accompanied by their wives and families, took rented lodgings during the legislative session and social season, the men and women who cared for them were "in the habit of seeing, doing, and associating with genteel and distinguished strangers." This regular contact made the business "more respectable [in Washington] than in any other place." This according to the author of an etiquette book who further observed in 1829 that most of the widows who kept board-inghouses had "more or less grown daughters . . . decidedly more accomplished than the daughters of any business class of people with which I have ever been acquainted."[31] Even so, fashionable society often ruled against them. When Benjamin W. Crowninshield was secretary of the navy in the Monroe administration and he and his wife were living in a boardinghouse, Mary Crowninshield was frustrated in her desire to give a genteel party. She explained that it was "impossible in this house, for I must invite all the boarders, and what would be worse, Mrs. Willson and her daughters; but this I would not do."[32]

At the top of the social hierarchy in Washington were two elites, those with political status and those who, like John Tayloe III, had no personal involvement with politics but whose wealth, education, and social bearing entitled them to a place in fashionable or genteel society. A small percentage of the residents of each village enclave tended to be associated with the nearby branch of government. Congressmen were less settled than members of the executive branch and the diplomatic corps. Even officeholders seldom had the sense of rootedness that gradually became a hallmark of the city's affluent

Marcia Burns Van Ness (1782–1832) by James Peale, watercolor on ivory, 1797 (Corcoran Gallery of Art). One of the first native "Washingtonians," Marcia Burns inherited her large landholdings at seventeen, and before her marriage in 1802, she was, for her looks, wealth, and independence, "more talked of than any other female in the District of Columbia."

permanent population. A few of these residents were holdovers from the original farming community, men such as Daniel Carroll of Duddington and women like Marcia Burns, who inherited the holdings of her father and married New Yorker John Van Ness. Some, like Thomas Law, an Englishman who married Martha Washington's granddaughter Eliza Custis, and John Tayloe III, whose great wealth came initially from tobacco lands on Virginia's middle peninsula, moved to the new capital by choice.

Establishing gentility

Because Washington was a brand new city with a temporary and transient population and both an official and a private social life, two vexing problems arise for historians. The first concerns the presence or absence of women at social events. Their participation varied with the particular group of people, the season of the year, and whether the time is early or late in the decades under consideration. Even then, the evidence is contradictory.

When historians suggest that Washington society had a peculiarly masculine quality because of the absence of families, they are not referring to a sexual imbalance throughout the entire population, but only to those congressmen who resided in the city temporarily and alone.[33] In the first few years, when travel conditions were poor, congressmen who were away for only a few months usually left their wives and children at home. Through the first decades of the nineteenth century, however, they increasingly brought their wives at least for a few weeks during the social season.[34] In 1815 James Kirke Paulding wrote to a friend, "You cannot conceive of what consequence a Batchelor like myself is in this odd City, where there are at least one thousand women."[35] From the beginning wives of government officials and diplomats set up temporary housekeeping and entertaining schedules alongside families in permanent residence. In 1805 Louisa Catherine Adams did not mention the absence of women, but commented, "Society consisted chiefly of the heads of Department and those Families of residents whose independent fortunes enabled them to live handsomely."[36]

The English visitor Frances Trollope may have caught the changing practice at half stride in the late 1820s, when she observed that evening parties in Washington differed from those in other cities in the United States because of "the great majority of gentlemen." She found female society only "among the families of the officers of state [the Cabinet], and of the few members, the wealthiest and most aristocratic of the land, who bring their families with them."[37] Margaret Bayard Smith, who had been a member of Washington society for thirty years and certainly knew it better than Mrs. Trollope, at almost the same time saw the opposite: "The city is thronged with strangers, fashionable ladies from all quarters, a great many mothers with daughters to show off, a great many young ladies coming to see relatives and to be seen by the public."[38] The question of the presence or absence of women is not easily resolved when surviving records exhibit such contradictory views.

The second vexing question arises from the special circumstances of life in the capital city: to what extent did political position guarantee or exclude people from a place in genteel society? Aside from the years when Thomas Jefferson attempted his short-lived and ill-fated innovations in official manners known as "pell mell" etiquette, a formal "Code of Procedure" specified who had access to the official social order and assigned rank based on precedent. Creating rules to govern social acceptability in the private sphere was not so easy. To individuals such decisions are never trivial; in a democratic republic, where all citizens are assumed to be equal, resolution of the problem carries broader philosophical implications, whether on a general or a case-by-case basis. As one modern critic observes, "From its birth, America has badly needed a way to express equality, individual freedom, social mobility, and the dignity of labor in the language of human social behavior."[39] The difficulty arose in part out of a confusion between an individual's social standing in private life and the status attached to his public responsibilities. The distinction was less clear in the late eighteenth century than it later became. In the colonial period both elites—private citizens and high officeholders—were likely to be one and the same. Under the Constitution that correlation became a matter less taken for granted, and "the comparative talents, manners, and respectability of the members of congress, at Washington, [began to] differ as much from each other, as that of their constituents at home."[40]

While all elected officeholders were obviously part of officialdom in Washington, people's opinions about their social status differed markedly. Margaret Bayard Smith, an admirer of Jefferson, thought "the drawing room circle . . . ought to be co extensive with the sovereign power."[41] Louisa Catherine Adams took the opposite position; she remembered the early years when officeholders were not automatically admitted to "the general society," whose members "had not yet clothed themselves in the buffonery of the modern democracy."[42] Perceptions shifted somewhat during the first three decades of the nineteenth century. By 1828 Mrs. Smith observed that social rights had "been somewhat encroached on." She thought it remained "to be seen how far the people will be able to maintain their claims."[43]

The permanent residential elite, comprised largely of town-dwelling southern planters, consistently placed great stock in pedigree and good breeding. Official society, forever renewed through a revolving door of elections and appointments, assigned increasing importance to personal achievement and visible wealth, whether public or private. Most Americans in the federal era seem to have believed in the idea of an open society as long as it pertained to someone else. When faced with hard choices, they backed off. "I suppose," wrote Juliana Seaton, wife of William Seaton, publisher of the *National Intelligencer*, in 1830, "there have never been in the city so many plain women in every sense of the word, as are now here among the families of official personages. I have always heard it asserted without contradiction, that nothing was easier than to learn to be a lady; but I begin to think differently, being morally certain that many among the new-comers will never achieve that status."[44] Writing in a similar vein about the social awareness of congressmen, the author of *A Description of the Etiquette at Washington City* judged that "the want of good sound sense, and a pretty general information, is confined to a very limited number; but many of them figure much better on the floor of congress-hall, then they do on that of a ladies drawing-room."[45]

The judgments meted out to the kind of enterprising person who was successful in exercising his "right to get above his neighbour in wealth, respectability and power" reveal both the humor and the brutality of social one-upmanship in Washington.[46] Cloaked in her own self-assurance, Harriet Otis, half sister of Massachusetts politician Harrison Gray Otis, returned from a gossipy visit with friends "to enliven mother with the runaway match of Miss Laura Senett who has taken a fancy to the genteel son of bricklayer which has proved a most sore mortification to the aristocratic spirit of her democratical father—her mother's father having been a cobler one would suppose it was no great degradation."[47] Miss Otis and her mother undoubtedly enjoyed their little laugh, but presumably they would not have accepted the couple as social equals. A description of the prospective bride and groom in another match expressed distinctions in dietary terms. They were "your *good* old-fashioned hog and hominy people who have not been dressed clean but once a week in their lives, who never took a bath except in the puddles of a corn field, . . . and whose taste is so exquisite that they prefer a bed of cabbages before their parlor windows to a *parterre*."[48] Unfortunately, not all social assessments were so benign and amusing.

The standards for acceptance into genteel society and the all important matter of who established and maintained them developed into a political controversy over the fate of Peggy Eaton. The story can be read as one of human pettiness, the importance of moral judgments, the status of boardinghouse keepers, and the confusion of private and political criteria in the life of a democracy. Peggy's father, William O'Neale, kept one of Washington's better boardinghouses. His pretty, vivacious daughter, who married a naval purser, lived with her father while her husband was at sea. When a close friend of Andrew Jackson, Senator John Eaton, lodged at the tavern he enjoyed Peggy's company. Too much, said some. When her husband died on duty in the Mediterranean in 1828, rumors hinted at suicide. The following year, after John Eaton and the former Peggy O'Neale were married and newly elected President Jackson had appointed him secretary of war, the scene was set for a great clamor. Simply put, the wives of the other cabinet secretaries refused to recognize that Eaton's official position required them to extend basic

The Celeste-al Cabinet by Henry R. Robinson, engraving, 1836 (Library of Congress). Disguised as a popular entertainer, Madame Celeste, Peggy Eaton is depicted dancing before President Andrew Jackson and his cabinet. Accused of various social improprieties including adultery, Mrs. Eaton was completely ostracized by Washington society.

civilities to his wife. Their private social judgment so affected his ability to perform his public responsibilities that Eaton was forced to resign.

In several letters written between January 1829 and August 1831 Margaret Bayard Smith detailed episodes of the "universal topic of conversation." She applied none of her usual democratic sentiments to Mrs. Eaton. Instead she concurred with the ladies of Washington who had taken "a stand, a *noble* stand . . . against power and favoritism." Even though they knew President Jackson and Vice President Van Buren wished it, they refused to "violate the respect due to virtue, by visiting one, who has left her strait and narrow path."[49] She was welcomed only "at the houses of some of the foreigners, the President's and Mr. V. B.'s."[50] On three public occasions at the time of Jackson's inauguration, "she was left along, and kept at a respectful distance from these virtuous and distinguished women, with the sole exception of a seat at the supper-table, where . . . she was not spoken to by them."[51] John Quincy Adams recorded that she received similar treatment at other events.[52] She was not received at any private parties, and because of "marked and universal neglect and indignity" she withdrew from public assemblies.[53]

Senator William Barry from Kentucky analyzed the unfortunate business in a letter to his daughter. He expressed high regard for Major Eaton and found his wife an "artless, sincere and friendly woman [who] may have been imprudent, as most of the ladies here are, but I cannot believe she was ever criminal." He cautioned his daughter about the rumors circulated by disappointed competitors for office, "The truth is, there is an aristocracy here, . . . claiming preference for birth or wealth, and demanding obeisance from others. . . . Mrs. Eaton was the daughter of a Tavern-keeper belonging to the democracy: she has by good fortune (if it may be so considered) moved into the fashionable world. This has touched the pride of the self-constituted great, awakened the jealousy of the malignant and envious, and led to the basest calumny."[54] Altogether it was a sad and sorry affair.

The self-appointed aristocratic ladies who rejected Peggy Eaton never explained their criteria for admission to their select group. They arbitrarily decided she was not "on a footing of equality, real or apparent."[55] Undoubtedly, they would have agreed with the author of *The laws of etiquette* that "the formalities of refined society" are "like the hyphen-marks of grammar, which unite without confusing." This same author went on to say that the standards that were "at first established for the purpose of facilitating the intercourse of persons of the same standing, and increasing the happiness of all to whom they apply," were kept up "both to assist the convenience of intercourse and to prevent too great familiarity."[56] A few references to the Tayloes' social life at the Octagon suggest they received and entertained people like William and Anna Maria Thornton, John Quincy and Louisa Catherine Adams, and Harrison Gray and Sally Otis. However, they do not seem to have made any effort to bridge the social distance they inherited with wealth and family position.

In 1829 one writer identified three seemingly simple requirements a man needed to meet to pass "through the ranks of fashionable society in Washington." He had to pay attention to personal appearance, demonstrate an understanding of etiquette, and obtain introductions "to some few who will take an interest in introducing him to others." The statement confused the social and political realms, a mistake corrected when the author acknowledged a difference between being introduced to someone and making his acquaintance. In Washington the first was easy, the second very difficult.[57] Ten years later another arbiter of etiquette, who had either clarified the distinctions in his own mind or had closely observed changes in the 1830s, first noted that all foreigners and most Americans confound the political with the social system when writing or speaking about American society. He went on to observe, "In remodelling the form of the administration, society remained unrepublican. There is perfect freedom of political privilege, all are the same upon the hustings, . . . but this equality does not extend to the drawing room." He expressed the opinion that American society was more exclusive than that of England or France because in Europe there was "less danger of permanent disarrangement or confusion of ranks by the occasional admission of the low-born aspirant" and hence less need "for a jealous guarding of the barriers."[58]

Although inequities of birth could not be overcome, there was an established, if vaguely mapped, route across social barriers. It was called "gentility." In the early nineteenth century many newly rich and not-so-rich Americans sought the benefits gentility bestowed

15

and went on a quest for it. Writers and publishers of etiquette books attempted to help them through the thickets of social niceties. Americans used the word over and over as they energetically pursued the ideal, because only with gentility could they achieve socially what they had already gained politically. The term indicated an "ease and freedom of manners which distinguish persons in the higher walks of fashionable life."[59] It was related to politeness, to the art of pleasing, and to a sense of propriety. Explained etiquette writer Charles Day, "Gentility is neither in birth, manner, nor fashion—but in *the* MIND. A high sense of honor—a determination never to take a mean advantage of another—an adherence to truth, delicacy, and politeness, toward those with whom you may have dealings—are the essential and distinguishing characteristics of a GENTLEMAN."[60]

Although these definitions lack the simplicity of a checklist, the bridge of gentility was built of several recognizable components— material goods, educational attainments, behavioral practices, and the "je ne sais quoi" of polite society. By the early nineteenth century the clothing, houses, and furnishings that were the essential equipment for social life could be purchased readily, although admittedly one needed sufficient disposable income. Also available for a fee were established schools that opened the doors to book learning and offered lessons in the polite accomplishments of music, dancing, art, and foreign languages. These educational services did not help uninitiated adults as much as they benefited their children. The third component, the behavioral aspect of gentility, changed in several significant ways during these years.

Members of polite society began to pay closer attention to the formalities that governed personal relationships and to the little rules regulating the use of paraphernalia associated with specific ceremonies. For instance, formal visiting acquired an elaborate code of procedure with respect to the appropriate time of day for the type of call, duration of stay, the offering of refreshments, and above all the presentation of cards. Simple pieces of good paper printed with the caller's name and stuffed into an all-purpose wallet were insufficient. There were cases for carrying, trays for receiving, racks for displaying, and rules and more rules. At the same time the publishing industry, which previously had regarded manners as a minor aspect of the general subjects of conduct-of-life and morality, began

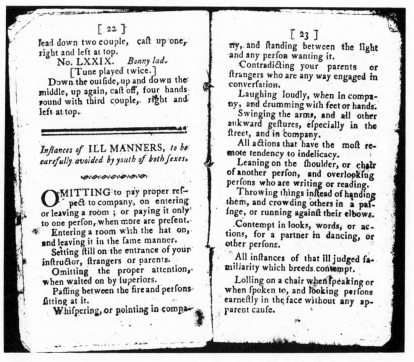

"Instances of ILL MANNERS . . ." in *The Gentleman and Lady's Companion*, 1798 (Library of Congress). Adherence to a recognized code of conduct was part of what defined a genteel person. Books that outlined appropriate behavior began to appear at the end of the eighteenth century in America.

to churn out etiquette books that taught persnickety dos and don'ts to the uninformed.

The fourth component of gentility, an easy self-confidence tempered by a generous attitude toward all others, remained the most difficult to express and therefore the hardest for the beginner to master. Expounded one etiquette guide, "Whatever may be the accomplishments necessary to render one capable of reaching the highest platform of social eminence, and it is not easy to define what they are, there is one thing . . . which will enable any man to retain his station there; and that is, GOOD BREEDING."[61]

With sufficient money would-be gentle men and women could pay for material goods, books that taught manners, and other lessons intended to develop academic and social skills. Nevertheless, everyone agreed that wealth alone could not provide gentility. One arbiter of etiquette explained, "All of the merely rich will find that there does exist a small and unchanging circle, whether above or below them 'it is not ours to say' yet completely apart from them, into which they would rejoice to find entrance."[62] With the possession of new wealth, people acquired "a taste for the luxuries of life, expensive furniture, gorgeous plate, and also numberless superfluities," but rarely did they synchronize "the polish of their manners . . . with the rapidity of their advancement."[63] Wealth granted its owner leisure, but without education it became merely free time, a wearisome and heavy burden. Knowledge of music, art, and literature and the ability to converse about them enhanced the use of leisure, making it pleasurable.[64]

If the acquisition of wealth did not automatically provide gentility, a mad dash after fashion made its attainment impossible. "Fashion," according to one writer, was "a system of refined vulgarity" completely at odds with good breeding. Notoriety and desire for influence were characteristics associated with its adherents, good sense and self-respect with gentlemen.[65] Those who misunderstood the true nature of gentility thought, "if you wish to get up in the world" you must obey the law of fashion.[66] Those dedicated to this foolishness drove "four, five, or six miles over miserable roads" to visit "*friends* whom they rejoiced to find from home." In the late afternoon they dressed and drove out again "in storms or darkness" to dinners or evening events "precisely like twenty other parties to which they had been." No wonder they became "wearied to death by the perpetual sameness" of the social treadmill, "but it was the fashion!"[67]

Many books were written on the assumption that readers could learn gentility by rote. E. Cooley, M.D., author of the first etiquette book specifically written for a Washington audience, made it clear that his 1829 work, *A Description of the Etiquette at Washington City*, was not for people who knew "the customs and etiquette of the polite and fashionable society" and would consider his rules trivial, but for those who had not had "their opportunity of seeing and knowing" the customs that prevailed in the nation's capital.[68] His little book was part of a growing trend away from moralistic tracts, which generally discussed character-in-action, toward etiquette books, which gave precise instructions about what to do in social situations.[69] None of the authors made extravagant claims for the probability of their readers' success. "If the publication of this work saves the blush but upon one cheek, or smooths the path into 'society' of only one honest family," wrote Charles Day, "the object of the author will be attained."[70] Elsewhere he wrote, "Although these remarks will not be sufficient in themselves to *make* you a *gentleman*, yet they will enable you to avoid any glaring impropriety, and do much to render you easy and confident in society."[71] Many writers, like good music teachers, stressed the importance of practice. Some maintained that learning what to do was easier than sensing the nuances of what to avoid.[72] As one put it, "Good manners can certainly only be acquired by much usage in good company." Where novices who were not welcomed into genteel drawing rooms could go to perfect their skills remained an unsolved problem.[73]

If the writers were not overly encouraging about their ability to inculcate gentility in their readers, they held out the hope that some people might substitute the natural ease they were born with for acquired and contrived manners. An acceptance of innate or intuitive social grace is the most democratic and in some ways the most appealing aspect of the concept of gentility. "Properly instructed by the Book of Etiquette, a pure and generous heart and cultivated mind will be enabled to supply the omission of any rule required for intercourse with the most refined society," asserted the 1857 book *Etiquette at Washington*.[74] Margaret Hall, an English traveler in the late 1820s, did not credit Americans with gentility, but she did say that "with all their want of polish and refinement they are not vulgar. It appears that want of leisure is what prevents them from becoming polished, they are so constantly hard at work with real business that they have no time to think of the little minor things that constitute refinement. At the same time they are all sufficiently educated and have a want of selfishness that makes them desirous to please."[75] The truly genteel person was never proud or demanding but extended courtesy to all. The old haughty attitudes that permitted members of the upper class to order everyone else about and to accept subservience as their God-given right were mitigated by a newer perception. Although others may not be socially equal, they should be treated politely.

Gentility was a concept that permeated the upper levels of American and European society. Its practice knew no national boundaries.

Bows and curtsies, hat-doffing and handshaking, and the knowledge of how to stand and walk and when and where to sit spoke all languages and communicated personal status wherever one went. The old signifiers of position were neither so portable nor so visible. The land one owned could not be carried about on one's back, and a local reputation was not a glowing badge of acceptability beyond home range. Genteel behavior, although its full expression was intimately bound up with proper dress and experience with certain kinds of household possessions, was completely portable. The code always recognized the priority of regional variations over general practice. The Earl of Chesterfield, author of the most influential book about behavior in the late eighteenth and early nineteenth centuries, put it best. Manners are, he wrote,

personal, local, and temporal; they are modes which vary, and owe their existence to accidents, whim, and humor; all the sense and reason in the world would never point them out; nothing but experience, observation, and what is called knowledge of the world, can possibly teach them. . . . Good sense bids one be civil and endeavor to please; though nothing but experience and observation can teach one the means, properly adapted to time, place, and persons.[76]

Authors of etiquette books were not the only writers who tried to define gentility and teach people about it in the hope of bettering their lives. Some novelists in England and America aspired to realism and professed a desire to instruct as well as entertain their readers. Several published lively accounts of Washington society and its manners during these decades. They sketched characters from all walks of life and presented them to readers with rich detail and insight into motives for their actions. While the historical record occasionally provides this kind of information about real people at the top of society, rarely is it so informative about the lives of people at the bottom. One author assured readers that although the characters were imaginary, "the descriptions of scenery and society, are drawn with truth and fidelity, from the then existing circumstances of place and manners."[77] Close correlation between the fictional events and the historical record confirms this assertion and justifies using references from novels to expand the picture of the early capital.[78]

Margaret Bayard Smith, who married the first publisher of *The National Intelligencer*, answered the question *What is Gentility?* in a novel. Although published in 1828, it was set in Washington some

Margaret Bayard Smith (1778–1844) by Charles Bird King, oil on canvas, 1829 (Redwood Library and Athenaeum). An intelligent and perceptive observer, Mrs. Smith chronicled the manners and customs of the Washington society she knew intimately in several novels published during her lifetime and in her correspondence, an edition of which appeared in 1906.

years earlier. Subtitled "A Moral Tale," the work aimed to demonstrate that gentility was "independent of birth, wealth, or condition" and derived from that "cultivation of mind which imparts elevation to sentiment and refinement to manners in whatever situation of life they may be found." More specifically, through amusing incidents, the author wished to encourage parents "who now lavish their hard earned wealth on dress and equipage, to devote it to the mental improvement of their children."[79]

The story of *What is Gentility?* centers on the social fortunes, misfortunes, and adjustments of the McCarty family. Mr. McCarty has grown rich on the profits of a grocery store and grogshop. Although neither he nor his wife has ever been to a gentleman's house, they begin to acquire better furniture, more servants, and a desire for gentility.[80] Mrs. McCarty thinks "raal gentility" comes with material possessions; her husband senses something more is required. They have three children. One son is destined to take over the family business. Mr. McCarty convinces his wife to send the other son and their daughter away from home for better educations than living at home can provide. At Princeton Charles is to acquire book learning as his stock in trade, and according to his father, "if learning is as profitable as they tell me it is, a good capital it will be."[81] Catherine studies art, music, and French at a Philadelphia boarding school and is expected to marry. The choices the children make after the family is reunited in the "smiling and seducing world" of Washington set up the moral lessons that answer the title question.[82] In the final pages Mrs. McCarty concludes, "I see, now, it is not fine dressing and fine furniture, nor even a fine fortune, nor getting *pushed* up into the *first circle*, that makes people *raal genteel*." She glances at her own daughter and observes that "larning and gentility" have been known to make some folks "proud and unnatural." Her older son acknowledges that he "found by experience that wealth without education cannot make one either happy or genteel." He openly admires his brother's example "that education, even without wealth, can make a man genteel, respectable, and happy."[83]

The novel's rich descriptions detail the social life of Washington as the family experienced it. Two subthemes, the place of women and the dignity of members of the middling class, amplify ideas about social arithmetic. In Margaret Bayard Smith's opinion, "woman is a quantity—man is the denominator, which gives to that quantity its value."[84] The Princetonian brother, addressing his sister and trying to convince her to give up her "foolish desire for the society of those in a rank of life to which you have no pretension," argues that women depend for their status in society on their fathers or their husbands. He assesses their father's condition as low and suggests that, unless she conforms to it, Catherine will make herself ridiculous. When she tries to apply the concept of political equality to the social order, Charles challenges her with her own haughtiness, "If we are all equal, why do you look with such distain, not only on those whom the world thinks lower than you, but even on those whom the world thinks your equal?"[85]

For his part, Charles has renewed several childhood acquaintances and found young men and women like himself "who were neither deficient in good manners or information." He never advocates upward social mobility. Instead, he finds respect and contentment "in what is called the middling class."[86] He is a spokesman for Margaret Bayard Smith's view that people who lived in comfort within their means and chose "their society from their equals" were at an advantage: "When thrown by accident either into the circle above, or the circle below them, the unpretending simplicity and benevolence of their manners, to the one, ensured them kindness and good will; while that dignity, which a cultivated mind always imparts to character, obtained for them esteem and respect from the other."[87]

Charles McCarty understood the ambiguities in the American mind about politics and society and about equality and rank. While he recognized the importance of formal entertainment in general society, he avoided the fashionable world and preferred his own family circle. All of Mrs. Smith's sympathetic characters shared this view. They valued most the warmth of their families, either alone or occasionally enlarged and diversified "by company, conversation, music, and dancing." Though they "sometimes attended the parties, in order to keep up social intercourse," they returned to true happiness around the domestic fire.[88]   The matter-of-fact author of the 1857 edition of *Etiquette at Washington* did not share this sentimentalized view of family life. The events of society, he observed, whether agreeable or disagreeable, were of short duration. "Not so with the domestic circle," which he found "inseparably connected with the long hours of those who compose it." It was "their life of pleasure or of pain."[89]

The novels and etiquette books convey a clear sense of the difference between events in society and the peace or boredom of domestic routine. Against the background of the city's geography and its limited housing amenities, the diverse population of transient officials, permanent residents, and their family members ate their customary breakfasts and dinners. A few either prepared or consumed refreshments on special occasions. The differences in the ways early Washingtonians consumed food and entertained each other sharpen our perceptions of their physical well-being, domestic comforts, and social opportunities.

The Wedding Dinner or Moses and the Magistrate by Charles Williams, engraving, 1812 (Library of Congress). The company in this English print enjoy the kind of dinner available only to a select few. They are at the final course of the meal, a fine dessert of fruits, cakes, and jellies—displayed on stacked salvers—arranged carefully on a table. After "a handsome dinner" at the home of Delaware politician Louis McLane in 1825, a guest reported that "the dessert was arranged on the table in the form of an H joined in the center by two silver wafers containing beautiful Calfsfoot jelly and blancmange, served in elegant cut glass."

II. Ways to Take a Meal: A Ranked Order

Show me the way people dine and I will tell you their rank among civilized beings."[1] The food selected, the utensils owned to serve and eat it, and the manner of consumption are separate elements of dining this mid-nineteenth century writer for *Harpers New Monthly Magazine* would have viewed when judging other diners. In early Washington the top and the bottom of the social ladder looked very different at mealtimes. Louis McLane, congressman from Delaware, recounted a dinner party at the British minister's residence in 1818. The servants were "richly liveried," the plateau or centerpiece ornamented with candlesticks, artificial flowers, and alabaster statues, and the meal literally eaten "off of plate, and of the most splendid kind." McLane appreciated the magnificent display, but he also enjoyed the company, passing his "time very pleasantly till 10 o'clock."[2] At the other end of the hierarchy Margaret Bayard Smith depicted two young boys seated on the ground eating mush and skim milk from a coarse earthenware dish. Her novel conveys their mother's embarrassment as she laments the family's decline in fortune.[3] Between these two extremes people ate different foods, used or did not use a selection of the diverse tableware available in the city, and exhibited a wide range of dining behavior. Some were influenced by the concept of gentility; others undoubtedly had never heard of it.

Meal-taking has a history

Understanding the variety of dining experiences in Washington, D.C., in the first three decades of the nineteenth century requires taking a long look back in time and across the Atlantic. Before colonists arrived in the Chesapeake region most people throughout the world lived very meager material lives. Their shelters and sleeping places gave them little comfort, and often they were hungry and cold. Only members of the tiny ruling class experienced any luxury. Very gradually, over the centuries between roughly 1400 and 1800 Europeans began to produce more food, better shelters, and more consumer goods. The timing and extent of change differed significantly from place to place. Customers' demands for products and manufacturers' abilities to produce them urged each other on. By the middle of the eighteenth century ordinary people in England, other parts of Europe, and the American colonies had increased the quantity of objects—beds, tables, cooking pots, and so forth—with which they lived their everyday lives. However, the industrial revolution that further altered productive capacity and consumer desire had not yet achieved momentum. An examination of the varied ways residents in Washington took their meals in the early nineteenth century captures a single aspect of this long process of material change for one place in one relatively brief period of time.

Today most meal-takers in the western world expect a table to be laid with familiar utensils, each part of a matched set. Their ordered placement allocates a certain space and one set of tools to every diner. Individuals transfer food from large serving platters to their plates with large utensils. They eat with smaller knives and forks. Few dishes are considered finger foods.

Westerners did not always eat this way. Before the sixteenth century, like most other people in the world, they used their fingers and shared utensils. Before dining and between courses members of the ruling class washed their hands with scented water poured from a ewer into a basin and dried them on elegant damask napkins. They used knives with pointed ends to cut helpings of meat off large joints. Since they seldom had plates to use as intermediate staging areas, they put food directly into their mouths on the points of their knives or with their fingers. Bread or spoons were used to ladle up porridge and other foods of a soupy consistency. Lacking individual bowls, diners dipped spoons, bread, or fingers into the common pot. Knives and spoons were personal possessions, carried by the owner and not likely to be provided by the host. Diners did sometimes share their utensils. If one person wanted a taste of something out of reach, he asked a neighbor to help him to a spoonful. A sixteenth century refinement prescribed that the person gathering the morsel not taste it in passing, but give it directly to the diner who had made the request.[4]

For reasons that may seem obvious to our notions of sanitation and propriety, but make less sense from the perspective of the past, elite diners in the sixteenth century began to think that sharing spoons and drinking vessels, eating without plates and bowls, and touching food with the fingers were no longer acceptable table manners. These novel ideas translated into a requirement that each diner have a fork, knife, plate, and drinking glass for his or her own use. These utensils and the new dining practices they made possible spread very slowly throughout the general population.

When the Chesapeake region was first settled in the early seventeenth century, very few immigrants knew about the new ways of eating. Nearly everyone cooked boiled, one-pot meals. The dominant dining patterns were often communal in the age-old tradition. Although by this time prosperous colonists owned individual plates, they continued to drink from communal vessels. Poorer settlers shared plates or bowls. These patterns of simple preparation and meal-taking persisted for quite some time. In the 1740s on his way north from Annapolis, Dr. Alexander Hamilton observed a Susquehanna River ferryman and his wife eating a "homely dish of fish without any kind of sauce." He contrasted their way of living with his expectations of dining. The couple put no cloth on their table. Instead of using "knife, fork, spoon, plate, or napkin," they ate with their hands communally from a deep, wooden dish. By the 1740s Hamilton and others of his class preferred a more elaborate cuisine and a table with a clean cloth, large serving dishes, and individual place settings. To Hamilton the couple's table manners presented "a picture of that primitive simplicity practiced by our forefathers long before the mechanic arts had supplied them with instruments for the luxury and elegance of life." Although they invited Hamilton to share their meal, he "had no stomach" for it.[5]

Farther north, along the Hudson River, Hamilton entered another "clean and neat but poorly furnished" cottage, where he noticed "half a dozen pewter spoons and as many plates, . . . a set of stone tea dishes, and a tea pot." His companion thought this poor family of nine should eat from wood rather than pewter and had no need at all for tea things. He presumed to criticize their personal decision about how to spend their money, saying such people should not have "superfluous things which showed an inclination to finery."[6]

To Hamilton's friend tea-drinking was properly a prerogative of the elite. The tea ceremony he would have known was an elaborate social performance about which many travelers and diarists wrote. When their separate descriptions are pieced together, a distinctive pattern of behavior emerges.[7] Most eighteenth century tea-drinking happened in people's houses. Either exclusively a private occasion or an affair that slightly stretched the family circle to include intimate friends or others deserving warm hospitality, it was an important occasion of polite family life.

By the early nineteenth century tea equipage included a tea table, a tray (sometimes called a waiter or a tea board), a teapot, cream jug, sugar bowl and tongs, cups, saucers, and teaspoons. There might also be a tea urn, a small stand for the urn or pot, a slop bowl, a canister, strainer, spoon tray, and plates for buttered bread or cakes.

Sketch of a groupe for a drawing of Mount Vernon by Benjamin Henry Latrobe, pencil, pen and ink, 1796 (collection of the Maryland Historical Society). By the end of the eighteenth century, the daily serving of tea was an accepted social ritual practiced by Americans at home. Martha Washington's tea equipage included a large silver urn filled with boiling water for making tea on the spot.

Coffee with its own pot and cups and saucers was sometimes offered along with tea. If the family was not large and the guests few, the company gathered around a small table that held everything they needed. If more people were to be served, tea might be poured into cups in another room, placed on trays, and handed round to guests. They then faced the challenge of balancing a cup and saucer and anything else that might be served at the same time they were lifting the cup to drink the hot beverage.[8]

Curiously, despite the growing popularity of tea, the proper methods of serving and drinking it were not discussed in behavioral manuals of the post-Revolutionary era. When writers began to prescribe precise rules to govern table manners, they focused on those pertaining to dinners. They probably overlooked tea because at that time it was a family activity and their objective was to help people perform better in general society. Only when tea parties became large evening events for thirty to a hundred or more guests did writers begin to describe proper behavior associated with them.

Not all families drank tea, and not all who drank tea did so genteelly. Many did not have an appropriate setting, enough of the essential equipment, knowledge of the behavior, or a way to practice it. Their tea was an economical beverage. When diluted and served hot with bread, it could create the illusion of a warm and filling meal. Taking tea meant different things to different people—a hospitable gesture, a bid for gentility, a cup of warmth in a cold room, a draft to quench thirst, or a substitute for a hot meal.[9]

In the thirty years between Hamilton's trip and the Revolution, many families came to share aspirations for ornamental luxuries. They, like the family who lived in the Hudson River cottage, expressed these desires by purchasing tea equipment. In 1774 nearly 50 percent of a large number of probate inventories from Maryland, Virginia, and Massachusetts included some equipment associated with tea-drinking.[10] Whether all these households owned enough of the requisite equipment—at the minimum a teapot, several cups and saucers, teaspoons, and a sugar bowl—to serve tea genteelly is not readily apparent. Even more difficult to sort out is the relationship between people's desire for the beverage, the ever lower price for poorer grades of tea, and the increasing diversity of objects associated with tea-drinking. In the routine of an eighteenth century

Tea canister, mahogany with inlay, ca. 1800 (Gunston Hall Plantation). Regardless of their social or occupational level, many early Americans owned some type of tea paraphernalia. Canisters fulfilled both a decorative and practical purpose on the table and were likely to be owned by someone with a full complement of tea equipment.

day, tea-drinking followed dinner, but among those who reached for a new life of gentility in food and drink, tea led the way.[11]

Although the list of paraphernalia associated with the preparation and serving of tea seems long, its length is insignificant when compared with that for serving an elite dinner. Patterns of ownership of furniture and tableware identified in probate inventories taken in Washington between 1818 and 1826 reveal a hierarchy of family and social dining practice in the city. An inventory, created during the process of settling an individual's estate, identified property to be secured for the benefit of either heirs or creditors. Although the procedure involved some cost, during this period recorded property was not subject to taxation. As part of the assessment of an estate going through probate, appraisers visited the house where the deceased person had lived and wrote out a list of furnishings, item by item, everything from the best bed to an old wine bottle to a silver serving dish. Inventories taken at a particular time and place provide historians with their best opportunity to look at the personal possessions of a broad spectrum of the economic and social order.[12]

A hierarchy reflected in tableware

Based only on the objects they owned and not on income or total wealth, 224 men and women whose lives are represented in the Washington inventories differed markedly in the way they dined. Their possessions fall into five distinct groups that for convenience can be labeled simple, old-fashioned, decent, aspiring, and elite. The history of changing table utensils and manners—the introduction of forks, the increasing importance of individualized service, and the appearance of sets of objects—determined the criteria for the groupings. No knives, forks, or spoons appear in the inventories of simple diners, who presumably ate with their fingers or with utensils in such poor condition or of such low value that they were not worthy of the appraisers' notice. Spoons appear in the inventories of old-fashioned diners. All other inventories list the goods of people who owned knives, forks, and spoons.

The number of inventories in each group provides an estimate of the relative frequency of the different ways of consuming meals and illustrates the elaborate configurations of dining habits only the few at the top could exercise. Of 224 decedents, 20 percent ate with their fingers and 19 percent could be considered old-fashioned diners. Nearly everyone else's habits ranged through various unpretentious but decent practices (48 percent) to the two highest categories, which included nineteen individuals who aspired (9 percent) and eight (the top 4 percent) whose possessions indicated they could set fashionable, elegant tables for large numbers of guests. Since only those who died with property worth securing through the probate process were included, this rough statistical breakdown markedly underrepresents the poor. Slaves, 13 percent of the population in 1820, had no possessions the law recognized as their own. Free blacks, 11 percent of the population at that time, are represented by only one "coloured man."[13] The number or percentage of urban poor similarly left out remains undetermined.

The differences among the objects recorded may relate to choices or limitations of diet; they certainly imply patterns of behavior. The inventories reveal the persistence of traditional performance as well as the lure of gentility and new fashions, especially in urban areas. The dining furnishings and tableware of ordinary folk, those in the simple, old-fashioned, and decent categories, present a significant contrast to the aspiring Washingtonians and the few who can be considered the elite. So much evidence exists for the possessions and behavior of the latter groups that understanding their dining styles requires first a description of the objects they used and then of the settings in which they dined and the prescribed behavior they followed. Behavior changed with the setting, whether a meal was part of family life, private social life, or public and official dinners and entertainments.

Two sources enliven the static pictures that emerge from the inventories. Personal descriptions of real places and events and fictional stories of people's lives told in several novels set in Washington in the early decades of the nineteenth century inject action and emotion. The various characters, both in reality and in fiction, based their judgments of each other at least partly on food preparation, table settings, and dining behavior.

The Cotters Saturday Night by Eunice Pinney, watercolor, ca. 1815 (National Gallery of Art; gift of Edgar William and Bernice Chrysler Garbisch). Like the family seen here, most early nineteenth century Americans lived simply. They owned only a small number of eating and cooking implements and had no knives, spoons, or forks among their possessions.

Many families, perhaps as high as 40 percent of the city's population, appear to have had very limited stocks of equipment. Everyone in the group labeled simple owned tables, and all but a few had a small number of chairs. They had no table linen and no knives, forks, or spoons. Their "crockery ware" or an occasional dish, plate,

32

and bowl mostly was of low value and not counted or described. Amenities, like cups and saucers, a tea kettle, tea chest, a coffee mill, or candlesticks, showed up here and there, but never combined with enough related articles to suggest anything remotely useful for up-to-date sociable occasions.

The value of most of these inventories was less than $150, and although very few of the documents indicate the size of the house where the recently deceased owner or occupant had lived, one-room structures with or without a loft were the most probable family quarters.[14] However, the presence of several inventories with property worth between $500 and $1,000 indicates simple meal-taking could be a matter of choice rather than necessity. Simple standards did not always imply a life without comfort or other amenities. Eating with fingers can be both sanitary and visually attractive, even to those long accustomed to the use of knives, forks, and spoons. A life without these utensils need not be barren emotionally or intellectually or deprived in other material ways.

For instance, before his death in 1823 Jeremiah Hunt, a wheelwright, rented a four-room house and shop on Twentieth Street in the neighborhood near the Octagon. His personal property was worth $394, most of it invested in the tools and products of his trade. Hunt's inventory is unusual for several reasons. First, the appraisers listed each of Hunt's possessions under the names of the rooms where they found them, indicating the house was larger than most. Second, while the appraisers noted a stove, a small pine table, four old chairs, and a variety of cooking utensils in the kitchen, they did not list any dining paraphernalia. And third, Hunt's dining furniture was scattered throughout two of the remaining four rooms. A waiter or tray was in the back parlor, and a mahogany dining table and a little breakfast table were in the front chamber with two beds. The two remaining rooms were furnished as bedrooms only. Nowhere was there the necessary equipment for individual place settings. By this late date most people with five-room houses had separated the functions of dining and sleeping. Hunt seems to have been old-fashioned in his room use and arrangement of furniture and very simple in his conception of dining.[15]

The novel *What is Gentility?* gives a glimpse of a typical poor family's dinner. In the opening scene Mr. McCarty, tending his grocery and grog shop on a winter evening, overhears a "meager looking man," who had drawn a chair close to the stove, talking about his wife and children, who are at home without food or firewood. Mr. McCarty becomes "fidgetty," goes to the counter, cuts

off a large slice of cheese, picks up a loaf of bread, gives them to the man, and sends him home.[16] The author does not follow the man to the "hut" where presumably he lives, so readers do not learn whether his family put the bread and cheese on a table set with a cloth and plates and pulled chairs up before it. However, we do know there was no fuel for warmth, and therefore presumably none for cooking. In another Washington novel a poor woman, who has already burned her table and chairs, is in the process of burning her bedstead to keep her fire going. She eats directly from the cooking pan and explains, "I'se sure my victuals taste every morsel as good, eating it out of that there skillet, as if it was in a plate on a table."[17]

The description of Mr. McCarty's shop tells about laborers' midday meals and the way they combined eating and conviviality. "Grocery" was something of a misnomer for the "very Noah's Ark of comforts and conveniences" where Mr. McCarty sold dry goods as well as a range of food and beverages. On the counter on one side was "a large cheese, with a huge knife beside it, with bread, crackers and gingerbread . . . where the laborer or mechanic could stop for his luncheon, instead of going home to his dinner." These were "baits used for catching customers in a much more profitable commodity, . . . wines and spirits of every description," sold on the other side of the shop. Mr. McCarty kept a kind of club for cartmen and other laborers who seem to have avoided their family circles, if they had any, and ate, drank, smoked, and dozed around the warm stove.[18]

By the late eighteenth century two pastry cooks and confectioners across the river in Alexandria were advertising early versions of carry-out food. They sold hot mutton, beef steak, veal, and chicken pies "for the accommodation of families" who presumably had little time for cooking, no ovens, or little money for fuel. The pies were ready "every day at 1 o'clock" and again "every night from 7 to 9 o'clock." The cooks also advertised that those who prepared their own dinners could have them "baked every day."[19] Perhaps these pies relieved the monotony of a diet of hoe bread and bacon for travelers

Hearth and kitchen scene by John Lewis Krimmel, watercolor, ink and pencil, 1819 (courtesy, Winterthur: Joseph Downs Collection of Manuscripts and Printed Ephemera, No. 59x5.6). In the modest household of an "old-fashioned" diner—without the means or equipment for entertaining—the emphasis was on preparing and serving family meals.

as well as residents. This ordinary diet seems to have been varied only with sweet potatoes and an occasional and expensive cabbage.[20]

The abundance of food in rural areas caused Americans to grow taller than Europeans in only a generation, but dietary plenty was not a feature of city life in the United States in the early nineteenth century. The urban poor were noticeably shorter than their prosperous neighbors and their rural relatives, suggesting they were less well fed.[21] The burden of the poor was especially heavy in the nation's capital. People came to Washington to apply for pensions, press claims, and seek offices. Many had no clear goal except finding a job. Few had any money to sustain them. The winter season, when bad weather made work for day laborers irregular at best and cold increased the need for fuel, made their lives more miserable and uncertain than usual. On December 31, 1822, *The National Intelligencer* announced the opening of a "Soup House . . . in the lower part of Mr. Law's round house" on Capitol Hill for the "relief of the Poor." It was scheduled to operate daily until April. The advertisement instructed the needy to apply for "tickets for Soup" from any of six "curators."[22] How the food was served, how the applicants ate it, and whether similar services were offered in subsequent years are not known. It is, however, extremely unlikely that any of these poverty-stricken people had enough property to list in an inventory. Although they may once have owned cooking and dining equipment, their condition implies that at best they followed the same practices as those whose inventories can be considered evidence of simple meal consumption.

Poverty may explain much about the conditions of simple meal-taking. All but a few of the households represented by these inventories had little wealth and probably less opportunity to choose what they ate or how they consumed it. Cursory examination of the financial values and some of the more expensive possessions of the old-fashioned group, however, suggests that lack of money usually was not the reason these people decided to dine one way rather than another. The single most significant characteristic of old-fashioned dining was the lack of knives and forks and the use of spoons. Often spoons were present in the inventories in significant numbers, for instance, five or eight, and just as frequently they were specified as made of silver. However, old-fashioned diners, like their finger-eating cousins, owned equipment that conveys a sense of haphazardness about their dining habits and suggests they had no notion of laying a well-ordered table with sets of plates or drinking glasses.

Generally, the inventories of these former Washington residents showed they had a greater interest in furniture than in tableware. They all owned several tables. Breakfast tables and those made of mahogany were common. Sideboards or side tables were not universal, but they were part of the furniture of several households. Chairs ranged in number from five to more than thirty; more people owned the larger numbers. Nearly everyone had candlesticks, usually plated ones rather than brass. Lamps were rare. Fewer than a third of the householders had tablecloths and no one had napkins. More owned waiters or trays. Tableware of ceramics and glass was present, but in small quantities and motley assortments that seem random and meager. Only a few sets of anything were mentioned by appraisers. Serving dishes or tureens were more common, but only in enough numbers to present one or two meats or vegetables on the table. Casters and decanters were referred to in about the same number. The

Frugality by Peter Pasquin after J.M. DeLattre, mezzotint, dated 1796 but believed to be later (courtesy, The Colonial Williamsburg Foundation). In addition to a knife and fork, a "decent" diner likely set his or her everyday table with a variety of mismatched wares typical of the array of imported goods widely available in this country.

inventories reveal little about how people drank beverages. Few tumblers and even fewer wineglasses were listed. More surprising was the lack of evidence of tea or coffee drinking in roughly half the households in this group.

The details of the inventory of a professional man illustrate the general preference for furniture and other kinds of personal possessions over tableware. George Hadfield, an English architect who worked on the Capitol and designed the Treasury Building and City Hall, died in 1826. The inventory of his four-room house reflects his status as an old-fashioned diner and the attention he paid to his personal appearance and to his profession. He was probably a bit of a dandy, with a gold watch, a walking cane, and a sword. His drawing table and instruments were valued at $25, more highly than any of his other furniture. Prints, drawings, and books on architecture and other subjects totaled over $100. These were in his "office or study" and his parlor. His other possessions open the door on a daily life with some comforts but no mealtime refinements. The kitchen, with its two pots, three skillets, frying pan, two dutch ovens, and roaster, was more adequately equipped than his table. He owned two silver teaspoons and two silver tablespoons but no sets of knives and forks. He did have two tumblers, three wineglasses, twelve plates, four white dishes, a sugar dish, some bowls, and two coffee mills, one English and one Dutch. Perhaps his cups and saucers were recently broken and not replaced or he and others in the household drank coffee from bowls. His breakfast table was in a bedroom along with his shaving equipment. His parlor was furnished with a writing desk, chairs, and an old sideboard, but no table. Perhaps Hadfield was a bachelor who occasionally invited a friend or associate home for a drink. He certainly was not equipped to give a dinner party, although possibly he borrowed equipment and ordered pre-cooked food for special occasions.[23]

For more than a century the trend at mealtimes had been away from eating with fingers and spoons to dining with a knife and fork. The presence of these utensils indicated a household had abandoned old-fashioned practices and joined the trend toward refinement. Their inclusion in an inventory distinguishes the category labeled "decent," which is the largest of the five, accounting for nearly 50 percent of the inventories. At the upper end of the group people owned a wide range of dining furniture and tableware, including knives and forks, but their inability to seat as many as ten people at table and to host an evening tea party for larger numbers (at least without borrowing or renting equipment) prevented them from joining the ranks of the aspiring social climbers. At the lower end householders met the basic criteria and owned knives and forks, but otherwise most were meagerly equipped. If they entertained at all, their objects suggest it was over a sociable cup of tea or with alcoholic beverages and snacks rather than a full meal. Although the odd mention of tablecloths and serving dishes suggests awareness of proper service, low and random numbers for most items indicate mealtimes were at best family occasions. Generally these unpretentious people exhibited a tendency to acquire better furniture and lighting equipment than teaware and tableware. When they did purchase utensils, they seem to have paid greater attention to and spent more money on ceramics than on glassware.

Five examples, four men and a widow, illustrate the diversity among the 105 former residents categorized as decent or unpretentious diners. In the descriptions ownership of knives, forks, and spoons can be assumed. John Poor is the first case in point. A watchman in the Treasury Department, he lived in the residential and commercial area on F Street.[24] Like the large majority of inventories, the one that records his possessions reveals nothing specific about the size of his house or the number of rooms, but the sequence of the objects, valued at $186.48 in November 1825, vaguely hints at a simple four-room structure—a kitchen and an all-purpose room for sitting and eating below, with two chambers above. When families moved out of one-room houses, the first functional specialization of space they were likely to enjoy was the separation of cooking from other domestic activities. Next they removed their beds to chambers, usually up a flight of stairs, and continued to eat and sit in the same room. At best John Poor may have lived in such a four-room dwelling. He owned eight tables, among them a walnut dining table valued at $2.00 and a circular tea table, also of walnut, valued at 75 cents. To sit on he could offer guests a settee and nineteen chairs. His house contained a lamp (37 1/2 cents), but no candlesticks, a "small domestic diaper tablecloth ($1.00), pots for coffee and tea, a sugar bowl, and a cream jug." No cups and saucers were specifically itemized. Although uncounted, his knives and forks were appraised at 25 cents and "1 Lot [of] dishes" at 50 cents. For his table he had three common decanters (62 1/2 cents), "3 wine glasses & 2 tumblers" (50 cents), "5 blue edged plates" (20 cents), and "7 Blue plates & 1 dish" (87 1/2 cents). The value of this tableware totaled $2.95. Domestic luxuries of two comfortable feather beds, a mahogany desk, and an eight-day clock with a mahogany case offset the unimpressive tableware. Poor's plates were numerous (seven blue and five blue-edged), but these were not enough to lay a table for ten with a matching set.[25]

The butcher John Krause had furnished his house very much like that of Poor, but his tableware was more numerous and included "a lot of Queens Ware" ($4), "20 pieces of old odd, cups & saucers & Tea Pot," (20 cents), and "glass" ($6). However, the uncertain numbers, the lack of specific reference to serving dishes, and the suggestion of casualness in the choice of the words "lot" and "odd" make it likely that Krause's table was respectably but not pretentiously laid. It is worth noting that his "Weights & Scales & Butchers Work Tools" were worth $15 and a "stall in market House on lease" at $20.[26] The total value of Krause's tableware ($10.20) is representative of total values assigned to the possessions of other householders in this group, although some owned more goods with correspondingly higher amounts. In 1819 Abner Ritchie's ceramics and glassware were appraised at $10.82. Much of this ($8.41) was uncounted, simply listed as "Crockery Ware" or "Lot of Wine & Tumblers." His appraisers did note eight common plates at 25 cents, a tureen for 50 cents, four cups and saucers for 20 cents, and twenty-two "edged Plates" for 88 cents and twenty-nine smaller ones for 58 cents. The total value of the wares they counted was $2.41.[27] Henry M. Steiner's possessions showed greater attention to the presentation of a meal, but his glassware was not equal to his crockery. He had a "Lot [of] Queensware" ($1), a "Set [of] Tea China" ($1.50), a dining set of 110 pieces of "Liverpool" ware ($20), nine tumblers (75 cents), and five wineglasses (25 cents). His possessions did not quite stretch to set a table for ten with matching service.[28]

The possessions of the widow Ann T. Woods suggest she once

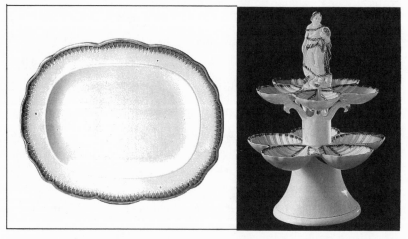

Platter, earthenware, 1800–1840; epergne, earthenware, 1800–1815 (both courtesy, Winterthur). The cheapest form of early nineteenth century decorated ceramics, pearlware has been found by archeologists at sites of differing economic levels. While the platter is more typical of what people owned, to the "aspiring" diner this unusual epergne or center dish communicated status and taste at a reasonable price.

Caster set in *Metal-Work Trade Catalogue*, 1818 (courtesy, Winterthur: Printed Book and Periodical Collection). Technological innovation allowed manufacturers to recreate elite forms from less expensive materials and in the case of tableware to put them within the reach of more ordinary diners.

aspired to a more active social life and had been equipped for party-giving, with dinner sets, tea sets, and glassware, much of which had been broken by the time of her death in 1819. The appraiser divided over two dozen blue-edged plates into four groups of unequal numbers, perhaps according to size. The separation of eleven coffee cups into two smaller groups suggests they did not match. Like a few other decedents at the upper end of the unpretentious category, Mrs. Woods was well supplied with waiters or trays, casters, cruets, decanters for water or wine, and a miscellaneous assortment of serving dishes, in her case tureens for sauce and soup and cream dishes. Mrs. Woods's ceramics held her in the unpretentious rather than the aspiring group. Her glassware was probably better matched. She owned four superior and four common tumblers, nine superior and seventeen common wineglasses, and two jelly glasses.[29]

Ceremonious dining

Among the upper echelons, here designated as "aspiring" and "elite," the whole context of the ceremonious dinner, not just the furniture and table setting, must be considered. These elite households were distinguished from unpretentious ones by the way their allocation of domestic space and purchases of furniture and tableware conformed to standards expressed in prescriptive literature. Most of the houses in which these people lived were not large, three or at most four rooms on each of two floors with perhaps a full third story, garret, or cellar.[30] In addition to several bedrooms and a kitchen, each house had a pair of rooms easily recognized as public spaces by the absence of beds and washstands.[31] A genteel household or one "where affluence abounds" needed these two rooms. "To receive company in a dining-room, is not allowed," stated one etiquette book, "except among those who cannot bear the expense of furnishing a parlour or drawing-room."[32]

The furnishings of these public rooms indicate they were flexible spaces. Dining was more likely to take place in one, but with relative ease they could be adapted to accommodate intimate family gatherings or larger social events, such as dinner parties or evening teas.[33] Usually one of these rooms was furnished with a set of dining tables, the other with tea tables, pairs of card tables, and musical instruments, mainly a harp or piano forte. This arrangement reflects a pattern of formal dinner behavior; after the meal the family usually left the table and retired to another room to drink tea or coffee. In the evening, alone or with guests, they played cards, listened to music, or danced while someone played familiar cotillions or new waltzes. The furnishings of prosperous Washington households conformed to the ambiguous room use described in an English design book of 1788. With only minor variations, Hepplewhite's single fold-out "Plan of a Room shewing the proper distribution of Furniture" applied equally to a drawing room, dining room, or parlor. The author recommended a sofa and a commode to distinguish the drawing room from the dining room, for which a sideboard and a set of dining tables rather than pier tables were intended.[34]

The seemingly random distribution of sofas, settees, and sideboards in either room and the presence of many chairs in both suggests that on other occasions the rooms were used in similar ways. When large numbers of guests were invited to evening parties, several rooms were thrown open, all the furniture was placed against the walls, and people sat around the perimeter or moved from place

A plantation dinner, engraved plate in Mrs. A. French, *Slavery in South Carolina*, 1862 (Library of Congress). Among the well-to-do, meals were served in a separate dining room with servants standing by at attention to wait on family members and guests. In this late example, barefoot slaves serve dinner to a Southern planter and his family.

to place as best they could. Guests helped themselves to refreshments set out on tables or sideboards, and servants carried around trays with other delectables and beverages.

The Octagon was exceptionally well-planned for formal family life and public entertaining. Compared to the narrow side halls and small rooms of most of the city's houses, the entry of the Octagon, with its generous windows, marble floor, brilliant blue paint, and two iron stoves, must have impressed arriving guests. A large stair hall provided a formal approach to both parlor and dining room, and up the stairs a round room above the entry may have been used as an office or for large parties as a second parlor or drawing room.[35] Very little is known about the furnishings of the house, but undoubtedly they matched the high quality of the interior finish.[36] When Harriet Otis called on Mrs. Tayloe in January 1812, she "found her in her elegantly furnished parlor with seven of her twelve children—her working materials about [and] dressed in a calico wrapper."[37]

By the 1820s the Octagon, unless redecorated and refurnished,

Mustard pot by William Simmons with spoon by Thomas Streetin, silver and cobalt blue glass, 1791 (Octagon Museum Collection). Engraved with the family crest, this small but elegant piece was ordered by John Tayloe III from London. The Tayloes were among the small number of Washington elite diners.

probably seemed a bit out-of-date, although the effect undoubtedly remained grand.[38] An 1828 manual prescribed that in drawing rooms the "stiff, high-backed, undeviating chairs, and the clumsy, unwieldy tables of our grandfathers" should be replaced by "the easy elegant curve of the Grecian chair and couch, which combined strength and lightness." The new designs had two disadvantages; they were costly and "as changeable in fashion as female dress." The "light and airy style" intended to "excite lively and interesting conversation" was not for the dining room. In "the place of rendezvous for *the important* concerns of the table," a householder was to aim for "solid simplicity" and to acquire substantial "mahogany chairs, tables, and side-boards." Curtains were to be "frequently of moreen, and sometimes of crimson and scarlet cloth," but lighter fabrics, such as chintz, were to be avoided. The same author mentioned "pictures, busts, and similar specimens of art" as ornaments. The colors of the walls, carpet, and curtains were to be chosen for their light-absorbing qualities, so that pictures would stand out in reflected light.[39]

Few Washingtonians met these literary prescriptions for elegance in their selection of furniture.[40] Although most of the tables and sideboards were mahogany, their relative values suggest that only one or two people bought fashionable ornamented pieces. Nearly everyone considered plainer designs adequate. One piece of furniture, the center table or sofa table, was new in the 1820s. Its permanent position somewhere other than against a wall was an innovation that came to have particular significance in the changing patterns of family life and public entertaining.[41]

While their furniture did not make much of a show, the elite and aspiring of the city smartened up the interiors of their public rooms with decorative elements like carpets, mantel ornaments, paintings, prints, and window hangings. The houses of the richest were the best lighted. Some of their candlesticks were fitted with chimneys and lustres or pieces of cut glass hung from the rim of the socket that held the candle. These families owned all sorts of lamps—hanging, plain mantel, plain globe, and cut glass globe.[42] This would have pleased the writer who complained that "Dinner Tables are seldom sufficiently lighted." He recommended "half as many candles as . . . guests," and their flame was to be "about eighteen inches above the table."[43] The richest inventories also itemized more looking glasses in public rooms. Like cut-glass lustres, these reflected light and enhanced its effect.

People in both the elite and aspiring categories understood the importance of visual presentation of a meal, but their possessions differed in quality and in the number of people they could serve. Robert Roberts, butler to a former Massachusetts governor and author of *The House Servant's Directory*, distinguished between dinner parties for sixteen or eighteen and smaller affairs for ten guests. In Washington the numbers were slightly higher; twenty or more attended grand dinners and aspiring hosts invited ten or twelve.[44] Essential objects that put an inventory in the elite group included several dining tables, at least one sideboard, mantel ornaments, pictures for the walls or some other evidence of room decoration, lighting devices, waiters or trays, casters or cruets, decanters, at least fourteen dishes for the serving of two courses, and table settings for twenty. To equip each diner at a large party, the household had to have at least forty plates and not less than twenty knives and forks for both dinner and dessert, tumblers, wine and champagne glasses, tea or coffee cups and saucers, and teaspoons.

Only a few people at the top of Washington society owned enough equipment to lay an elegant, fashionable table for at least twenty guests. Those in the aspiring group mostly owned fewer glass and ceramic items and the values of these were lower. Roberts called these people "small families" and noted that in their households confusion

45

Platter by Crown-Derby factory, porcelain, 1800 (Octagon Museum Collection). Only a small number of Americans were wealthy enough to afford porcelain imported directly from England. This piece was part of a set probably used by the Tayloe family at the Octagon.

often occurred "through not having a sufficiency of things for the party, without having to wash plates, spoons, &c."[45] People at the lower end of the aspiring group owned few serving dishes and no napkins and may not have had serving dishes to match their plates. At the upper end were those well supplied for family dining or for small dinner parties for at least ten guests. The decision to put an inventory in the aspiring group rather than the decent group was based first on the presence of knives and forks, second on the quantity of tableware, and third on a subjective judgment about whether the family's possessions reflected attention to the visual presentation and procedure of serving meals as well as tea, coffee, and alcoholic beverages. Both were important in the prescriptive literature about dining and in discussions of gentility.[46]

References in the prescriptive literature to careful spacing and symmetrical arrangement and in the inventories to matching sets and even numbers of objects indicate attention to the ordered appearance of the table and sideboard. Robert Roberts instructed house servants in the fine points of laying a cloth on a table so the woven patterns or ornamental work would show to good advantage. He also

Tureen, cover, and stand, porcelain with polychrome and gilded decoration, ca. 1800 (Collection of Mount Vernon). This serving piece survives from a very large set of Chinese Export porcelain purchased in England about 1804 by Washington developer Thomas Law for his wife Eliza Parke Custis.

wanted to see carefully folded napkins, concealing a roll or piece of bread, on each plate.[47] In this respect, Washington tables would have disappointed him. "A very few elegant Tablecloths" with matching napkins (one seven yards long with twenty-four napkins) were sold in the area, and the elite and aspiring inventories record tablecloths. However, fewer napkins were listed, suggesting they were not used regularly for dining. Perhaps people thought forks eliminated the need to wipe messy fingers.[48]

Roberts next had servants position the tableware. Dinner plates and serving dishes were to be "at equal distance from each other."[49] They were also to be in a straight line and to "match in size and colour."[50] Here the inventories of the elite and aspiring groups show significant differences in quality and quantity. Sets of many items were more likely to be owned at the top.[51]

Knives and forks were positioned with "the knives at the right hand, with the edge of the blade towards the plate, and the end of the handle to come even with the edge of the table." Roberts also told how to space carving knives and forks, ordinary dinner knives and forks used for the same purpose, and serving spoons. The latter were to be placed "with the bowls upwards, as they show much better to advantage."[52]

Roberts's method for correctly locating tumblers to the "right side of each plate, about three inches from the edge of the table" was even more elaborate. Wineglasses were placed in front of them toward the edge of table. Glassware of the wealthiest decedents was valued at about $50.[53] Items for individual use were plain, fluted, and cut glass tumblers; plain, fluted, and "fine Deamond Cut Glass" wineglasses; champagne, punch, lemonade, preserve, and jelly glasses. For serving, there were dishes, bowls, celery goblets, stands, and decanters, all of glass.[54] Some of these items were placed on the dinner table and others stood on the sideboard, whose array of silver, glass, and china Roberts described as carefully as the table.

In the early nineteenth century when people sat down to eat at a dinner party, they expected to find large serving dishes arranged along the center of the table. Smaller dishes, sauce containers, and items like celery goblets and pickle dishes filled the interstices. Decanters with water occupied the corners. This first course sometimes was followed by a second with an equal number of meats, vegetables, pickles, and sauces. During either course one or two of the major dishes, called "removes," might be taken away and replaced with another. Then the table was completely cleared, the cloth taken away, and a full dessert course set out. At the very end it was customary for everyone to drink a glass of wine. If any ladies were present, they departed for the parlor and a cup of tea or coffee. The gentlemen lingered at the table drinking and joined the ladies later. Variations were acceptable. For instance, the second course might be turned into dessert and the table stripped of its cloth just before the final pouring of the wine. Whatever the specific procedure, a large number of serving dishes was essential.

The most elegant dishes were those of sterling silver. The possessions of the military hero Stephen Decatur, who died in 1820, were unusual because he owned enough silver dishes to serve a meal. Louisa Catherine Adams, who attended a grand entertainment at Mrs. Decatur's house in 1822, appreciated the display of "all the beautiful Plate which was presented to her husband as tributes."[55] Most people even at this level did not receive such gifts and were likely to set their tables with more ceramic than silver dishes.[56]

Octagon dining room, 1990 (photograph by Lee Stahlsworth). One of the few surviving Octagon furnishings, this French silver plateau displays pyramids of fruit and candy in an arrangement described by a Tayloe family member.

Letters exchanged in 1806 between Rosalie Stier Calvert, who lived at Riversdale northeast of Washington, and her father in Europe reveal the way one young hostess made decisions about how to set her table. Henri J. Stier had offered to give his daughter a full dinner service of silver, "twelve to fourteen oval-shaped plates and an equal number of round ones." He recommended "intermixing them with small porcelain dishes" for a dinner of one or two courses and he asked his daughter to express her opinion.[57] She assessed her tableware and concluded that other pieces would better meet her needs. As soon as she and her husband could afford it, they planned to import a porcelain dinner set, so she very politely asked her father to give them matching porcelain serving pieces and some miscellaneous items of silver. She carefully specified those she wanted "the most first on the list," which she wrote in French:

2 pairs of candlesticks
2 pairs of candlesticks having 3 branches if possible, or else 2
6 salt cellars
1 vinegar caddy
4 butter and sauce boats
4 wine "coolers" [in English] like the ones placed at the four corners of the table with a

1 bread basket
2 small cabarets, 9 inches long, 7 inches wide, or approximately
1 large cabaret, 34 inches long 36 inches wide, or approximately
2 soup tureens

Basket attributed to Denière et Matelin, gilded bronze, ca. 1817 (White House Collection). President and Mrs. James Monroe refurnished the burned-out White House with the imported French furnishings then at the height of fashion. This ornament is the center of the original ensemble for the Monroe plateau.

The correspondence sums up the required serving pieces and acceptable alternatives laid out at elite dinner parties.[58] Serving dishes in the inventories of the aspiring group at best were made of various kinds of ceramics.

About 1800 the custom of placing large numbers of dishes down the center of the table began to give way to a new practice. In June 1789 Tobias Lear, George Washington's secretary, tried to purchase on the President's behalf "a sett of those waiters, salvers, or whatever they are called, which are set in the middle of a dining table to orna-ment it—and to occupy the place which must otherwise be filled with dishes of meat, which are seldom or never touched."[59] During an extensive correspondence, Lear's terms became more specific, moving from "mirrors for a table with neat and fashionable but not expensive ornaments for them" to "surtout" and finally to "plateau." Eventually, Washington acquired a silver-plated plateau with nine sections, five of which survive today in the collection at Mount Vernon.[60]

A plateau set up on elegant tables supplemented culinary abun-dance with new visual delight. The materials of which they were made—looking glass with rims of silver or silver gilt—surpassed people's expectations of light and glitter. John Tayloe owned a pla-teau, which is in the Octagon collection and which his granddaugh-ter remembered fondly. "We put kisses in it," she recounted, "Lights of wax candles and pyramids of fruit, candies, grapes and oranges at each end, which reflected in the glass, looked particularly pretty."[61] At least six other Washington residents set their tables with plateaux.[62]

Mary Crowninshield, a dinner guest of Secretary of State Mon-roe in 1815, described his table as wider than the one she was accus-tomed to. The serving dishes were silver and set round "a large, perhaps silver, waiter, with images like some Aunt Silsbee has, only more of them, and vases filled with flowers, which made a very showy appearance as the candles were lighted when we went to table."[63] After he became president Monroe ordered another plateau for the White House, and, although its design has been modified, it still occasionally dominates the elegant table set for state dinners.[64] Senator Louis McLane described the plateau of the British minister to his wife as "a long silver ornament, extending more than two thirds of the length, and one third of the width of the table—, its sides were elegantly [?] and its surface polished as the finest mir-ror—at each end of this or nearly at the ends were two gold urns, of the finest workmanship, and filled with artificial flowers and on the

No. III.

Bill of Fare for Six to Ten Persons.

Bomba Ice.

Biscuit.

Wafers.

Fruit.

Lemon Peel.

P L A T E A U.

Strawberry Compote.

Orange Compote.

Dry Cherries.

Fruit.

Wafers.

Biscuit.

Millefruit Water Ice.

Bill of fare for desserts, engraved plate in G.A. Jarrin, *The Italian Confectioner or Complete Economy of Desserts*, 1829 (Library of Congress). The plateau itself was decorated further with a combination of flowerpots, colored sand, candles, and figurines. Typically, assorted desserts were arranged in a ring around the centerpiece to complete the display.

outside of the corners 4 alabaster statues—In the centre a very superb—I forget the name—but a sort of candlesticks and on the outside of each end, another of the same sort."[65] Like Washington's secretary, McLane and others groped for the right vocabulary and spelling. Only Harrison Gray Otis turned the problem to humor when he wrote that at dinner with the Spanish minister he found "such a Plateau—taw—I never saw."[66] He and others knew a special object when they saw one.

The city's foremost citizens as well as their aspiring neighbors were well equipped for family dining and for entertaining a small number of guests with some show of gentility. However, only those in the top group could do so with anything approaching grandeur and with objects from their own pantries. When Margaret Bayard

Smith invited 170 guests to a large party in 1817, "Mrs. Barlowe [wife of the poet Joel Barlow] seem'd about as anxious as if it had been her own party, and wished me to make use of her servants and everything in her house which could add to the elegance of the party." Mrs. Smith wrote to her sister that she "accepted but a small portion of what she offer'd." Generosity of this sort and the probable rental of equipment made occasional entertaining possible even if one did not own all the essentials.[67]

Organizing the appraisers' lists in the five carefully defined categories of simple, old-fashioned, decent, aspiring, and elite conveys an impression of tidy distinctions from household to household. Aspiring or elite possessions seem to imply appropriate use and behavior. Simple diners' lack of equipment suggests they were oblivious to the use of knives and forks and the niceties of genteel behavior. Maybe, but perhaps not. The lifeless lists don't tell about the many uses and meanings of all these possessions in people's lives.

An illuminating case

The different experiences and attitudes of the members of Margaret Bayard Smith's McCarty family and household show the contradictions and ambiguities that could be combined under a single domestic roof. With financial prosperity, husband and wife have bought the trappings of a life about which they know nothing. In a long line of McCartys the parents are the first generation to enjoy the domestic equipment needed for the refinement they still cannot attain. They have acquired goods in which they justifiably take pride but which they don't know how to care for or use.[68] The author does not scorn material achievements, but she is concerned about behavior. The extent of the McCartys' ignorance and their need for a broad education in the ways of the genteel world unfold on page after page.

When *What is Gentility?* opens, their "large three story, handsome brick house" is new and the so-called parlor well-furnished with mahogany tables, a large mahogany sideboard, painted and gilt chairs, looking glasses, and scarlet worsted curtains. Plated candlesticks and "mould[ed] candles with cut paper round them" stand on the mantelpiece, and a tray holding "china cups and saucers, and [a] plated tea-pot, &c." show "pretensions to elegance." Accustomed "to

Detail, "Manners at the Table, 1800" by Lewis Miller, watercolor, 1865 (The Historical Society of York County). Many early nineteenth century Americans ate their meals simply, seated at a bare table set with the minimum number of plates, serving pieces, and utensils.

the scanty and coarse comforts of the poor," Mrs. McCarty wonders whether the President has a grander drawing room. Unfortunately, the newly bought finery has been spoiled. The colors of the once handsome carpet are covered with mud, and the other furniture is dirty and marked because no one in the family knows to scrape their boots or wash their hands. The cloth should have been in the wash tub and not on the table, and the fancy molded candles need dusting. In short, although the McCartys could afford to buy fashionable consumer goods, they did not appreciate that personal and domestic cleanliness were essential to gentility. Not only do they have to learn how to behave, they have to learn the refined presentation of the equipment essential for genteel manners, which, if they could master them, would mark the possibility of their entry into a new kind of life.[69]

Mr. McCarty understands the gulf of knowledge and experience that separates him and his wife from real gentility. Although he never expresses why he admires this way of life, he seems intuitively aware that his generation will never attain it. However, he provides opportunities for the children to internalize its values and to learn and practice appropriate behavior. After their years of education at Princeton and a Philadelphia boarding school, son and daughter return to Washington. Their homecoming requires a dinner celebration, a scene full of contrasting ideas about menus, room use, and serving procedure. Among the elite at that time great joints of meat and whole roast fowl were less in favor than a spicy beef soup called a "boulli" and smaller dishes prepared by carefully cutting meat and serving it with sauces in the tradition of French cookery. Mrs. McCarty's ideas for a meal appropriate for so happy an occasion differ from those of her cook. The cook, who is "as good as any French cook, seeing she had lived with the *quality*, and seen how French cooks managed," prefers a "bullion" at the head of the table and recommends that fricasseed chicken and what her employer calls "little mean scanty dishes" make up the rest of the menu. Mrs. McCarty believes that on this wonderful day "every one should have a plenty." She orders a round of beef, a roast pig, the "biggest turkey, biggest goose, biggest ham, in fine, the largest of every thing, . . ."

Before the great feast is served, mother and daughter disagree about the use of the two downstairs rooms. Both have just been redecorated. Mrs. McCarty reckoned that the drawing room would be "opened only on high days and holidays" and that for everyday living the family would use the parlor. Catherine announces it is not genteel to "eat in the room where you sit." Since the house did not boast drawing room, parlor, and dining room, she insists upon converting the parlor into a dining room and making "an every-day room of the drawing room." Mrs. McCarty, who longs to please her daughter and wishes to be genteel, orders the servant to light another fire. When the family gathers for the grand meal, Mr. McCarty picks up a "large China bowl of apple toddy" that is standing on the parlor stove and proposes, "come let us drink a happy meeting and great luck to ye all." He drinks and then hands the bowl to Mrs. McCarty, who helps herself and passes the liquor on to the eldest son. When the bowl comes to Charles, he first offers it to Catherine

55

who is disgusted and rejects it. He politely helps himself and comments that by drinking from the same bowl they are following "the ancient usage, not only of common people, but of princes, heroes, and poets." Catherine pronounces the practice "obsolete and vulgar" and declares the fashion is now to "have small, very small punch glasses; and lemonade, instead of toddy."[70] These different ideas about meals and their service, some old-fashioned, others decent and unpretentious, and still others aspiring, are all mixed up in the same household. Since Mr. McCarty was paying all the bills, differences between Mrs. McCarty, Catherine, Charles, and the cook did not derive from disparity in their income or wealth levels. Instead they reflect their different knowledge and experience with the ways of the world and a complicated variety of cultural preferences, some deeply entrenched and others, like the possessions, recently acquired.

The relationship between possession of goods and behavior is one of mutual dependency. Without the acquisition of specific things, some performances are impossible. Conversely, without lessons to establish at least a rudimentary level of use, objects can give only the satisfactions derived from ownership and display. The fine-tuning of accomplished performance is not instantaneous but requires practice, which is possible only with continued experience with certain goods. For some lucky individuals in early nineteenth century Washington, D.C., the opportunity to learn to live with a complex assortment of dining equipment was assured at birth. These children grew up with a certain set of assumptions about their own behavior based on the furnishings and tableware they had always known and the actions of others around them. The inventories taken during the eight years from 1818 to 1826 demonstrate that this experience was not widely shared; Washingtonians grew up with significantly different kinds of dining equipment. There had to be corresponding discrepancies in their dining behavior.[71]

The inventories also show the material diversification in people's lives that resulted from a century of improved production, distribution, consumer demand, and ability to buy. In 1720 many families in the Chesapeake could not pull chairs up to a table, and very few could eat with knives and forks. In the inventoried households of the nineteenth century, the basic furniture is universal and knives and forks are owned by a majority. Over the long term, goods were becoming more widely distributed throughout the population. The increasing homogeneity of objects, however, seems to have encouraged a zeal for distinguishing status by greater demands for objects of specialized design and by closer attention to the fine points of using them.

The Delphian Club of Baltimore Celebrating its First Anniversary by Abraham
Kenukkofritz, watercolor and gouache, ca. 1816 (collection of the Maryland Historical
Society). In this humorous portrait of a men's club dinner, participants follow few of the
"little rules" for manners and devour large pieces of chicken speared on their forks.

III. Customs and Manners: Rank and Fashion at Mealtimes

People in the past could size up social performance because they perceived differences in the range of behavior and recognized the social messages encoded in the actions of others. In Washington Margaret Hall observed Miss Van Ness feeding "herself with very much-melted ice-cream with a great steel knife!" She thought the young lady's beauty evaporated with the choice of utensil.[1] Today we would consider a spoon a more sensible implement, but as Lord Chesterfield observed, common sense will never explain manners. To a large extent, performance depends upon objects. The possibility of behaving in some ways but not others may be intimately bound up with the straightforward presence or absence of an item, or it may depend upon specific characteristics of design and choice of materials. Often these variations relate closely to technological capabilities, regional availability, and cost to consumers. In the early nineteenth century, Americans who were interested in gentility paid attention to the selection and use of table utensils. Social judgments focused on forks or sets of knives and forks.

Today historians find it difficult to answer simple questions about everyday life in the past: How did people eat? In company, which aspects of their table manners were ignored and which were considered noteworthy? Did successful or unsuccessful dinner table performances lead to social decisions to accept or reject the individual under scrutiny? Few historical sources throw light on Americans' social skills and attitudes toward others, especially for the eighteenth century. Although there is somewhat more evidence for the early nineteenth century, little of it is tied to any one region. Answering the questions for Washington requires looking first at a broad geographical range of evidence and then using limited Washington material to corroborate the general picture and note a few local peculiarities. The latter were mainly related to the official character of social life in the nation's capital.

Slow evolution of dining habits

In the early eighteenth century writers of prescriptive literature
had little to say about the specific use of table utensils. By today's
standards the few guidelines for acceptable dining behavior seem rudimentary. This situation is illustrated by a few of the 110 "Rules of
Civility & Decent Behaviour in Company and Conversation" that
George Washington, a teenager in the 1740s, copied from a widely
used book of maxims:

> Being set a meat, scratch not; neither spit, cough, or blow your nose, except if there is a
> necessity for it.
> Put not your meat to your mouth with your knife in your hand. . . . Keep your fingers
> clean & when foul, wipe them on a corner of your table napkin.
> Cleanse not your teeth with the table cloth napkin, fork, or knife.[2]

Such basic admonitions had been commonplace since the sixteenth
century and were still appropriate in the 1740s, when forks were not
widely owned.[3] The book Washington copied was one of many reprints that remained largely unaltered over two centuries. But major
changes were on the way.

Around the time of the Revolution etiquette books focusing on
specific rules, many about conduct at mealtimes, began to prolifer-
ate. A successor of these, published in New York in 1792, colorfully
contrasted "an awkward fellow" with one who could mind his manners. The author gives us a good look at the old world of
Washington's copybook and a glimpse of the newer behavior to
come. The vulgar diner, he wrote, "holds his knife, fork, and spoon
different from other people; eats with his knife, to the manifest danger to his mouth, picks his teeth with his fork, rakes his mouth with
his finger, and puts his spoon which has been in his throat a dozen
times into the dish again." The author does not relate the two types
of behavior to differences in the design or materials of the utensils,
nor does he say precisely how to hold a fork. But he clearly intended
to convince readers that table manners influenced social judgments.
The right way might bring acceptance; the wrong way probably
spelled rejection.[4]

Although it is not always possible to determine whether prescriptive literature established new trends or codified acceptable practice,
generally there is a correlation rather than a contradiction between
what one group of writers advocated and another observed. In 1777

one careful mother wrote to her daughter at boarding school and asked her to write telling "how you have improved in . . . holding your knife & fork."[5] An early settler in Ohio reminisced about his mealtime experiences in the early nineteenth century. His employer ate with a knife and fork skillfully, quickly, and probably deliberately. The laborers, who were not so proficient in the use of knives and forks and did not know how to continue eating politely after their master had finished his meal, left the table hungry.[6]

English travelers to America in the early nineteenth century regularly described menus and table manners. They noted the wolfish haste of American eaters, the lack of conversation at table, the scarcity of napkins, and the practice of knife-eating. Basil Hall and his wife, traveling in 1827 and 1828, separately described American utensils and behavior. While Mrs. Hall was writing for her family's entertainment, her husband's account was intended for publication.

Margaret Hall was well pleased with the proprietors of establishments in the Catskills and Albany who provided "silver forks, a luxury not to be met with at the best inns in this country." She went on to note that English persons who thought they would not miss a luxury like "a three-pronged fork (two-pronged being all that we are indulged with in this uncivilised country)" would be surprised. Like many travelers to foreign places who carefully watch native behavior, she discovered in the contrast her own cultural predispositions. She deplored the universal practice of eating with knives, "It goes rather against one's feelings to see a prettily dressed, nice-looking woman ladling rice pudding into her mouth with the point of a great knife, and yesterday to my great horror I saw a nursery maid feeding an infant of seventeen months in the same way."[7]

Basil Hall confirmed his wife's observations, concurred in her judgments, and noted that peas and rice dropped between the tines when he tried to lift them in his usual way but with a two-pronged fork. He admitted having difficulty eating with a knife, although he tried to follow the rule "when in Rome, do as the Romans." Since putting a knife in his mouth was ugly, dangerous, and "followed in England only by the lowest vulgar," Hall was torn "between reluctance to do what he [had] been taught to consider ill-bred, and the desire to please by conformity."[8]

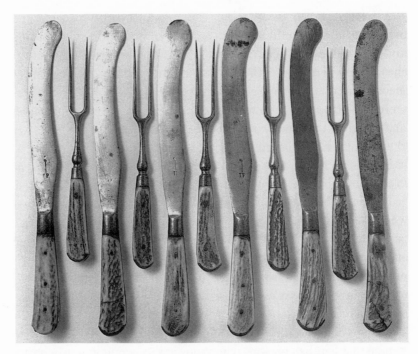

Knives and forks, steel and horn, 1750–1780 (courtesy, Winterthur). A two-tined fork held and speared food while the companion broad-edge knife was used to cut as well as to lift food to the mouth.

The Halls and most European travelers in America were likely to be affluent and well-versed in the genteel behavior of their time and place. On the road they had few opportunities for observing elite family life. The best table manners in the United States undoubtedly were not exhibited in public places. Few foreigners, especially those writing for public audiences, remembered the many parallels between the behavior of ordinary people in America and those in Britain.[9] Their widely published criticisms made Americans self-conscious about the way they ate. In 1838 Eliza Farrar, the wife of a Harvard professor, avoided the class issue and tried to turn knife-eating into a matter of national identity:

If you wish to imitate the French or English, you will put every mouthful into your mouth with your fork; but if you think, as I do that Americans have as good a right to their own fashions as the inhabitants of any other countries, you may choose the convenience of feeding yourself with your right hand, armed with a steel blade; and provided you do it neatly, and do not put in large mouthfuls, or close your lips tightly over the blade, you ought not to be considered as eating ungenteelly.[10]

Mrs. Farrar was an exception. Throughout the nineteenth century most English and American authors of etiquette books hoped to stamp out the habit.[11] Their eventual success owed less to their rhetoric than to the growing commonness of forks with closely spaced tines, a connection made by at least one post-Civil War observer. "There are a few rules which must not be violated," he wrote. "Your knife was made to cut your food with, and is never to be put to your mouth. The four or five pronged fork, now in general use, has this intention."[12] By the 1870s etiquette writers had lost interest in the topic.

Neither those who prescribed behavior for Americans nor those who observed it remarked whether the objects people used forced particular forms of behavior. Trying to skewer peas or pick up grains of rice with the widely spaced prongs of a wire-tined fork approached the impossibility of carrying water in a sieve. Since the tool could not do the job, another tool or another way of working had to be found. Some forms of social behavior, including the way a person eats, depend upon the design of crucial objects. The form and ornament of spoons, knives, and forks varied with materials, manufacturing techniques, and prevalent artistic styles. All changed over time. While nuances of ornament have their place in a discussion of the ways objects indicate status and power relationships, basic differences in shape are more important to an understanding of behavior when eating. The outlines of the utensils when viewed from above and their profiles viewed from the side reveal something of the eating habits of those who used them.[13]

Eating equipment has a history

Spoons were the most common table tool. In the early seventeenth century they looked like lollipops. The bowl was round, the handle straight, and the profile flat. By the late eighteenth century spoons of silver or less expensive metals like pewter were gracefully designed with oval bowls, narrow stems, flaring ends, and a profile that curved lengthwise and touched the table only at the lowest portion of the bowl and the tip of the handle. Users probably grabbed straight-handled spoons with their palms down but held spoons with curved handles like a pen or pencil. This change in position allowed them to rest the handle of the spoon on the sides of their fingers and precisely control its movement with the thumb.

Throughout the colonial period spoons in wood, horn, iron, latten, pewter, and silver were widely distributed throughout the population. In eighteenth and early nineteenth century probate inventories spoons were usually listed along with teaware, although they sometimes were grouped with tablespoons and dessert spoons. Appraisers rarely associated them with forks or with sets of knives and forks. The pattern of their list-making reveals that they did not think of these three basic table utensils as a single functional unit. In their minds, spoons were principally for tea-drinking and serving at table, knives and forks for dining. Spoons also differed from knives and forks in the ways they were produced and distributed. Many American silversmiths and pewterers made spoons, but very few sets of knives and forks, regardless of materials, were domestically made.[14] Manufacturers in Birmingham and Sheffield were the principal suppliers to the American market. The situation began to change in the second quarter of the nineteenth century, and thereafter importers faced increasing competition from local producers.

Until roughly 1700 knives were used exclusively for cutting and spearing meat. To accomplish these tasks the blades tapered to a sharp point. Forks made this feature unnecessary. After about 1720, when forks became more widely used, they were usually paired with knives, although merchants continued to sell knives separately and appraisers itemized households where knives but no forks were owned. Changes in the design of knives relate closely to the increasing presence of forks. They could be used to spear and hold while the diner cut with a knife. Blades grew larger, and their pointed ends were replaced with rounded ones. For functional balance and design symmetry the ballooning blade required a pistol-shaped handle. By the end of the eighteenth century the straight sides and more simply rounded end of the blade shape had more or less stabilized.

Although all knives had blades of steel, the quality and therefore the cost of this metal varied widely. The entire knife could be steel, but two manufacturing techniques that incorporated other materials were more common. If a thin rigid extension of the steel blade ran the full length of the knife, a handle made of another material could be sandwiched around it. Alternatively, a shorter steel tongue or tang could seat and secure the blade in the handle. In some cases a mount surrounded the connection. Manufacturers used many hard substances for handles—woods of all sorts, bone, horn (especially buck horn), ivory, rare stones, crystal, ceramic materials, and precious metals.[15]

Forks have a more complex history. Sucket forks, long skinny things with a spoon at one end and two spearing tines at the other, were specialized utensils intended only for eating sticky delicacies like pickled figs, ginger in syrup, or sweetmeats. Elite diners had used them since the late Middle Ages. Table forks, although introduced to England from Italy in the sixteenth century, were not much used even in court circles in northern Europe until the late seventeenth century. The few surviving European and rare American examples from that time, made of solid silver or even gold, look much like modern forks. They have three or four tines, their narrow stems flare, and bridges and tines flow in arched curves similar to the shape of spoons. For the very exceptional person who wanted and could afford these utensils, it was possible to eat more or less as we do today.[16]

By the early eighteenth century popularly priced versions of table forks had two widely spaced tines of steel wire. Their handles were constructed much like those of knives and were available in materials to match. Such forks had absolutely straight profiles. They could spear and hold, but were not ideal for lifting. Because knives had broad blades, they could lift as well as cut. Together the two-tined fork and the wide-bladed knife eliminated finger-eating. Those who owned them were equipped, and thus socially empowered, to behave in new ways although not in modern ways. These utensils turned ordinary Englishmen and their American equivalents into knife-eaters of the sort well-known in rhyme:

> I eat my peas with honey.
> I've done it all my life.
> It makes the peas taste funny.
> But it keeps them on the knife.

At the end of the eighteenth century several technological innovations affected wire tines, objects with silver handles, and objects that looked as if they were made entirely of silver. These changes improved the durability or reduced the cost of the finished utensils.[17]

Previously, because the process of hardening steel was laborious, wire tines had been merely case hardened, which made them wear down quickly. The "great lumbering, long, two-pronged" forks needed the extra length to compensate for this deficiency and increase their useful life.[18] Toward the end of the eighteenth century a new hardening process produced long-wearing tines, which were then made shorter. The profile of the fork remained straight.

After 1770 silver handles for knives or forks, which had been solid metal, could be made of thin sheets of silver, machine stamped, and filled with a resin and pumice cement. This method reduced the cost for roughly identical objects by half and became virtually standard by 1820. For solid silver spoons and forks, stamping with a drop hammer shaped and sometimes ornamented a complete object in a single operation. Operated by hand in the late eighteenth century and power-driven after the 1840s, these patent devices increased output and lowered prices for forks and spoons.

The process of covering a copper sheet with silver was invented in England in the 1740s. Although fused or Sheffield plate was used to manufacture knives and forks, the expense of finishing did not yield the cost reduction of about a fourth to a half that could be achieved for larger items. "Plated ware, consisting of Tea Pots, quart, pint, and half pint mugs, mustard bottles, candlesticks and knives and forks" were sold at public sale in Alexandria in 1801.[19] These types of articles appear in Washington inventories about twenty years later, the candlesticks and hollowware frequently, the flatware rarely. Only after the invention of electroplating in the 1840s and the consequent widespread distribution of four-tine forks of solid metal did table manners among the middle classes have a chance to change.

In the early nineteenth century Washington customers could choose from a wide assortments of goods. In 1810 one merchant advertised "table, carving and dessert knives and forks (2 and 3 prongs) with green and white ivory, bone, whale bone, horn and shambuck handles."[20] Prices and materials are important to the fine-tuning of social distinctions revealed in people's behavior and made possible by their ownership of objects. Prices in Washington stores varied; in 1823 the value of a dozen knives and forks ranged from a low of 31 cents to $2.25. Unfortunately the merchants' inventories

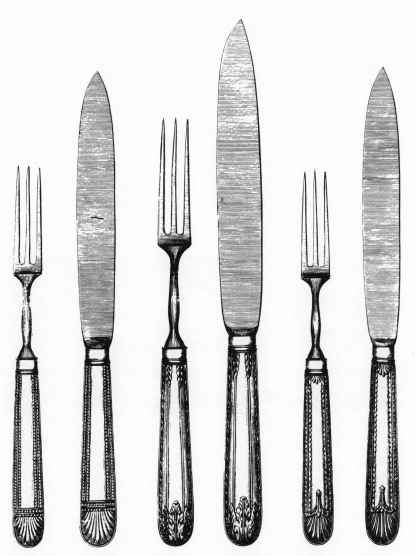

Forks and knives, engraved plate in *Metal-Work Trade Catalogue*, ca. 1815 (courtesy, Winterthur: Printed Book and Periodical Collection). By the nineteenth century the knives and forks found in America were imported from English manufacturers in a variety of materials and styles and sold in sets to the consumer.

that list prices do not describe handle materials or color.[21]

An analysis of 224 probate inventories from the city between 1818 and 1826 has shown how households were differently equipped. Even at this late date 20 percent of all decedents did not own knives, forks, or spoons. Table manners in these families must have been simple at best. Another 20 percent seem to have been old-fashioned diners. They had spoons but no other table utensils. The materials from which they were made are usually identified. Pewter, other base metals like iron, and silver plate are rare; householders preferred high quality silver for their spoons. In the 60 percent of inventories listing knives and forks their materials were infrequently mentioned, leaving low values to imply their ordinary appearance. Decedents often owned common knives and forks in small and seemingly random numbers, for example, "6 knives & 3 forks" at 30 cents and "5 [knives] & 8 forks" for one dollar. They, too, owned silver tea and table spoons, often listed by the half or full dozen.[22]

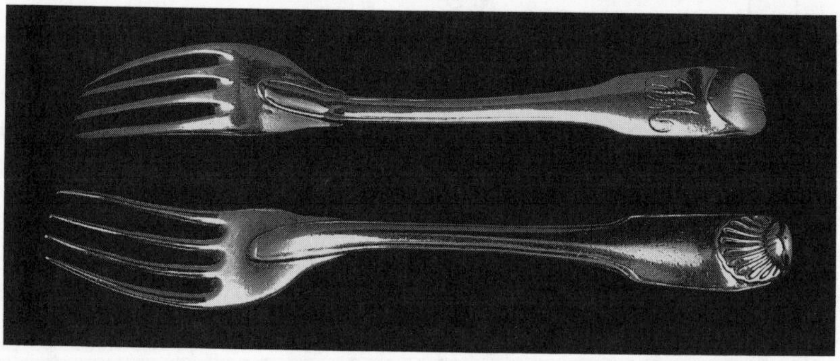

Forks, silver, 1792 (Gunston Hall Collection). Solid silver forks were used by a select few. The 1801 inventory of the White House included "18 French forks" among its solid plate. This pair was part of a set purchased by John Mason during a visit to Bordeaux, France.

The estates of elite diners in Washington show greater numbers of all utensils, but even in this circle silver forks were not the rule at this time. Franklin Wharton's inventory valued 139 knives and forks of different sorts for carving, dining, and dessert at $50, too low a sum for silver. An additional fifteen pairs of knives and forks, appraised at one dollar and found in the kitchen, were probably for servants' use. His three dozen tea, eighteen dessert, and eighteen table spoons were silver and totaled $80.[23]

Because no inventory for the Octagon has been found, the utensils on the Tayloes' Washington table remain a matter of informed guesswork. John Tayloe's 1805 payment of £100 for silver items received from a London merchant lists eighteen teaspoons, twelve tablespoons, and no knives or forks.[24] His house associated with the ironworks at Neabsco was equipped with a dozen silver tablespoons ($18), a dozen silver teaspoons ($8), and eleven knives and forks ($2).[25] The 1816 inventory of another Tayloe property, the Hopyard, lists "6 silver hand. Knives & Forks."[26] Presumably the Octagon, where the Tayloes entertained during the winter social season, was equally well furnished. Tayloe seems to have fit the general pattern of Washington elite. Of 224 inventories only four list silver forks.[27] Silver-handled ones were equally rare.[28] The Tayloes and other wealthy householders owned more common utensils as well, perhaps to set the children's or servants' table.[29]

What may seem like trivial details today were carefully observed by contemporaries. Many Americans in a generation that was learning good manners for the first time paid close attention to differences in equipment. Sometime between the revolutionary period and the decade of the 1820s silver forks became objects whose showy appearance caused comment and whose acquisition was debated. In Washington they were more likely found on ambassadorial and a few executive and high administrative tables than anywhere else. White House inventories for John Adams and Thomas Jefferson record silver-handled knives and "French forks."[30] Mary Boardman Crowninshield pronounced an event hosted by Secretary of State Monroe in 1815 as "the most stylish dinner I have been at" and added that "the forks [were] silver, and so heavy I could hardly lift them to my mouth, dessert knives silver, and spoons very heavy— you would call them clumsy things."[31] Not everyone approved of this kind of extravagance. As late as 1772 no less a man than Charles Carroll of nearby Annapolis considered spoons "the only necessary Plate Article." He argued against fashionable design, pride, and vanity, and advised his son, who was placing a large order for silver utensils, to "keep an Hospitable table. But lay out as little money as Possible in dress furniture & shew of any Sort, decency is the only

69

Point to be aimed at."[32] Their inventories show that for the next fifty years many conservative Washingtonians agreed with him.

Ordinary Americans eyed expensive utensils on politicians' and officials' tables with suspicion. To those concerned about the proper conduct of a republic their presence was an offensive contradiction to democratic simplicity and government frugality. The anonymous "editor" of *The Fudge Family in Washington* (1820) deplored government spending on luxury goods for official entertaining. He feared the "well earn'd glory" of the new nation would be "stuck to death with four-prong'd forks" or "brought to pass In knives of silver, and cut glass."[33] In the election year 1820, a guest at an elegant dinner "where he had a four pronged silver fork" amused the company by reporting that he knew of some people who would never "vote for a man as President of the United States who makes use of such forks."[34]

In the long run both admonitions and jokes fell on deaf ears. In the 1840s the discovery of new silver mines reduced the price of sterling silver objects, and the invention of electroplating made silver-plated objects correspondingly cheaper. About the same time the design of steel-pronged forks changed. Production of wide-spaced, wire-tined versions declined in favor of those with curving profiles and wide tines, which were probably stamped with a drop hammer. At last ordinary Americans could afford the equipment for genteel fork-eating. A prescriptive manual published in 1851 made the connection clear, "If silver or wide-pronged forks are used, eat with the fork in the right hand—the knife is unnecessary."[35]

An American peculiarity

The story of how Americans became fork-eaters does not explain the zig-zag manipulation of utensils that sets Americans apart from Europeans. Today most Americans hold a fork in the left hand to steady food while cutting with the knife in the right, then return the knife to the plate, and switch the fork from the left to the right hand before lifting food to the mouth. Most Europeans keep the fork in the left hand, heap food on its back, and eat with the tines turned down and without resting the knife on the plate or changing the fork from hand to hand.

Wm. H. Ladd's Eating House, Boston, by J.C. Sharp after Fitzhugh Lane, lithograph, ca. 1840 (American Antiquarian Society). Public eating houses and hotel dining rooms served a predominantly male clientele. European visitors frequently were astonished at the amount, speed, and noise with which Americans ate.

The American national consensus about how to eat with wide-pronged forks may reflect the vague but pervasive cultural influence of the French, who were the preferred arbiters of American taste in the early nineteenth century. The anonymous American author who laid down *The laws of etiquette* in 1836 did not connect the method of fork-eating with the French, but he did associate them with the object. He asked, "Where, excepting among savages, shall we find any who at present eat with other than a French fork?"[36]

Limited evidence suggests that among those Europeans who carried food to their mouths with forks the French and Germans of about 1800 ate like Americans today. The British were the odd men out. A late eighteenth century French traveler wrote, "In England the fork is always held in the left hand, the knife in the right. The fork holds the meat down, the knife cuts it and the pieces may be carried to the mouth with either. The motion is quick and precise."[37] Continentals made the change sometime in the nineteenth century. Efficiency and fashionability seem to have been their reasons. When authors in England and America were trying to stamp out knife-eating, at least some writers in Germany and France were trying to discourage hand-to-hand manipulation of forks. In 1832 a German writer called the English method of eating a "simplification" and recommended it to Continental people, "who mostly lay down the knife when they have cut with it, then take in the right hand the fork in order to convey the food to their mouths."[38] In 1853 a French manual advised, "If you wish to eat in the latest mode favored by fashionable people, you will not change your fork to your right hand after you have cut your meat, but raise it to your mouth in your left hand."[39]

Throughout the nineteenth and into the twentieth centuries social signals continued to be complex. Knife-eating lingered in a few backwaters, but outside their local settings these practitioners were immediately labeled as rustics. At the other end of the social scale, among those with international contacts, a different standard for social discrimination prevailed. In the 1920s Emily Post did not condemn zig-zag eating, she simply dismissed it as beyond the range of her experience where everyone ate European style. Her offhand remark had little impact on Americans, who by then had national self-confidence and were in an isolationist mood. At least one American writer, echoing Mrs. Farrar of the 1830s, reported that "many exceedingly well-bred people in this country . . . say they will not be influenced by imported manners."[40] To this day, most Americans eat with forks, left to right.

The national preference to eat first with a knife and fork and then to manipulate them in a specific way came about very slowly. If the focus were shifted from cutlery to any of the other categories of objects used to set Washington tables, similar stories of raw materials, technological processes, and design could be told. For objects made of glass and ceramics the details differ, of course, but the essentials of the outline—an increase in the volume of production and a widening of the range of cost for functionally similar items—are repeated. Furthermore, changes in practical use and social performance of all the tableware (cutlery, ceramic plates and serving dishes, and glassware) are interconnected in ways that are not fully understood and can only be hinted at here. Random coincidence does not fully explain the relationship between the declining popularity of pewter plates, the increasing desirability of those made of ceramic materials, and the growing use of forks. Other unanswered questions also arise. For instance, can the presence of those same forks be associated with consumers' relative lack of interest in table linen, especially napkins, at a time when the volume of textile production was increasing exponentially?

Looking at the changing table customs in early nineteenth century Washington in the context of the capital city's social order shows how the pace of change differed from class to class. "Traditional" behavior coexisted alongside fashionable innovation. The social significance of knives and forks can be glimpsed amid the jumble of individual decisions to embrace, ignore, or resist prevailing fashion. Although the distribution of objects reached ever larger numbers of people and was seemingly more egalitarian, new objects and new patterns of use indicate that hierarchical notions were not overthrown. The changes emphasize the interdependence of all people in a social order, the ongoing importance of power relationships on the social ladder, and the inventiveness with which people established these distinctions.

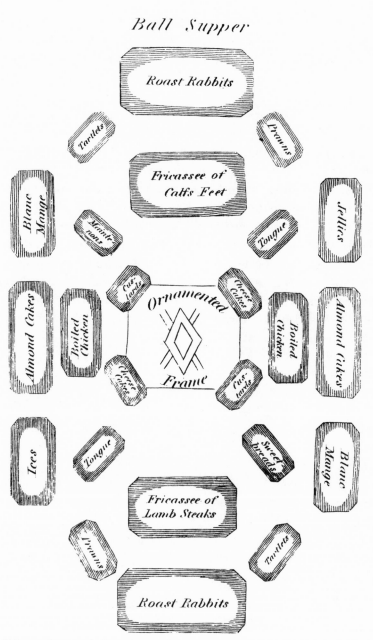

"Ball Supper," engraved plate in R. House, *The Family Cookery*, 1810 (courtesy, Winterthur: Printed Book and Periodical Collection). Cold suppers were laid out in buffet fashion during late evening entertainment. The table was laid with an emphasis on a display of abundance, leading Mrs. Trollope to call these suppers "massive meals."

IV. Ladies and Gentlemen: At Home, with Friends, in Society

The Reverend Manasseh Cutler, who served in Congress from 1801 to 1805, tantalizes modern researchers with a letter to his daughter saying the pressure of business prevents him from telling her "some history of a dining day, of the table and its furniture."[1] Unfortunately many of Washington's residents, both permanent and temporary, shared Cutler's opinion about the best use of their time. Although they described the occasional grand event, sometimes in considerable detail, and expressed pleasure or anxiety over their participation, they did not write extensively about everyday dining room furniture, table settings, schedules for meals, menus, staffing, and service procedures. Even less frequently did they compare customs elsewhere with those in Washington or comment on differences between dining in family settings and at social events. Whether they ate in their own homes, at someone else's house, or in a public place, those at the top of the social order took the presence of domestic servants for granted and expected men and women to behave very differently.

The daily schedule for serving meals probably varied from family to family and in Washington according to the hours when Congress met. The usual time for breakfast in the city seems to have been eight o'clock. Dinner, traditionally an afternoon meal, was pushed later and later during the early decades of the nineteenth century. Since Congress adjourned around three, the hour was generally four o'clock. People attending winter dinners often commented that candles were lighted before they left the table.[2] After dinner tea and coffee were offered. Nothing precluded the serving of these and other beverages to visitors at other times, but when people said they were taking tea with someone, they usually meant they were going out for the evening, about seven or eight o'clock.[3] During the Washington social season of 1827–28, Margaret Hall noted that dinner was at five and, because there was "no sitting after dinner," people were ready to go to the evening parties by half past seven.[4] "If you step[ped] in of an evening," very little food was served, only "tea and crackers or cold bread."[5] Suppers came late in the evening. They could be family snacks served before bedtime or elaborate refreshments offered at parties or balls. Dinner, tea, and supper were separate events on a day's agenda, but they also could be combined to suit specific occasions.

The records of individual encounters and points of view flesh out the history of dining in the nation's capital. If Manasseh Cutler, John Tayloe III, Ann Tayloe, and Margaret Bayard Smith ever attended the same dinner or evening party—and the last three certainly did—they undoubtedly would have had different experiences and come away with different perceptions. The significance of the events and people's individual reflections about them depends upon how widely they were shared and whether they had any effect on other aspects of life at the time. The diaries in which Anna Maria Thornton sketched her own and her husband's daily routines offer the story of one couple's dining days in early Washington.

Mrs. Thornton's social round

Anna Maria Thornton and her husband, Dr. William Thornton, were at the top of the social order, although it is not clear whether they could serve a dinner for as many as twenty. On several occasions they invited ten guests to dinner. Their country house, about two hours' ride from central Washington, was not so well equipped as their principal residence. In April 1800, when they invited about six people to a country dinner party, they had to send a servant back to town for "some Plates & knives & forks," as well as coffee, salt, and some other supplies. Back in January they had ordered more utensils, a tea set, and dinner service from England, but when they finally came in May the knives and forks were rusty, the ware from Wedgwood too expensive, and its gilt border not durable. Mrs. Thornton packed most of it off to a Georgetown store for resale. She kept only part of the dinner service, "two baskets with Stands" and four "Club Compotiers."[6]

Only modestly affluent, Dr. and Mrs. Thornton were well edu-

William Thornton (1759-1828) by Gilbert Stuart, oil on canvas, 1804; Anna Maria
Thornton (1775-1865) by Gilbert Stuart, oil on canvas, 1804 (both, The National Gallery of Art). Intimates of the John Tayloes, Dr. and Mrs. Thornton were fixtures on the
Washington social circuit, and many visitors to the capital city commented on the
couple's intellect and singular personalities.

cated and socially prominent. Dr. Thornton never practiced medi-
cine, which he had studied at Edinburgh. Instead he drew salaries
for successive civil service appointments and probably earned com-
missions for architectural projects. He drew the initial plans for the
Capitol and designed houses for several elite men, among them John
Tayloe III. Horses were Dr. Thornton's great love. In his most prosperous years he owned a farm where the couple spent summers, grew
produce for their tables in town and country, and bred and raised his
favorite animals. Dr. Thornton's professional activities and equine
interests as well as his and his wife's social know-how and qualities
of mind made them both welcome in the upper reaches of Washington society.[7]

When the Thorntons moved to Washington in 1794, the city
streets had hardly been laid out on a landscape of farms and wood-
land. Even so, the diary Mrs. Thornton kept until shortly before
she died was decidedly the record of an urban life. Her surviving
diaries begin in 1793, a few years after her marriage. Although they
continue past Dr. Thornton's death in 1828 until 1861, only a few
years before she died, there are gaps in the later years. For the analysis of dinners and evening events only selected years between 1800

and 1812 have been examined.[8] During these years Mrs. Thornton occasionally took the time to write descriptive entries, which were not her usual style. Mostly, she related the schedule and identified the characters at each occasion, but she never set events in motion or told how people behaved. Brief daily entries note the weather, cash expenditures, and social engagements. The consistency and abbreviated format of these entries make them a good source for routine aspects of social life. Mrs. Thornton emerges from the pages as an economical domestic manager, a practiced musician, a competent amateur artist, a great reader, and a careful conversationalist. One of her few personal comments hints at her private thoughts about her place in society in relation to Dr. Thornton, who was sixteen years older, and to the importance of her own daily activities: "This little Journal is rather an account of my husband's transactions than mine, but there is so little variety in our life that I have nothing worth recording."[9]

Mrs. Thornton was not housebound. Between January and June 1803 she either attended or hosted sixty-one teas, nineteen dinners, four parties, and one ball. She shopped, made friendly and ceremonial calls on other women, observed Congress, toured building projects, enjoyed the theater when a troupe came to town, attended other performances and exhibitions, watched artists paint portraits, sat for her own, went to the races, and made infrequent appearances at church. However, in the diaries for the years studied she never ate in a tavern unless a rare long trip, like the ones she made to Mount Vernon in 1801 and to North Carolina in 1805, required it.[10]

Nearly all of the social events recorded in Mrs. Thornton's diaries took place at private houses, although she mentions a few public locations. Whether she was the caller or guest and the occasion was friendly or ceremonial, casual or elaborate, Mrs. Thornton precisely recorded the names of those who visited or were present at dinner or tea. Her lists imply attention to reciprocity. People did not often impose themselves on other households for the day's main meal, but hosts and guests were more relaxed about showing up for evening tea.

For Washingtonians of the Thorntons' social class, dinner time came in the middle or late afternoon. Three was the usual hour, which left much of the day for work or other activities. Even when guests were invited, the meal ended before evening. On August 14, 1800, Mrs. Thornton noted that her company had left by six o'clock. Most of her references to time are too vague to determine whether the dinner hour was pushed later when Congress was in session. Other sources, however, show the time grew later as the years passed.

Dr. and Mrs. Thornton customarily ate their dinner together and at home. In January 1800 they were alone or with Mrs. Thornton's mother, who lived with them, on twenty-three days. Although Mrs. Thornton never says anything about table settings or menus, she distinguishes "family" dinners from more ceremonial and lavish events. Once she noted a cold dinner and twice a cold snack, and once a "small dinner" had to be covered with a tablecloth when someone called unexpectedly.[11] Dr. Thornton left his wife at home and dined out at least twice during the month, and possibly a third

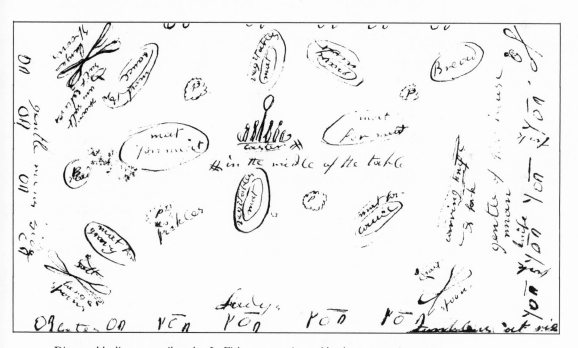

Dinner table diagram attributed to L. Fiske, manuscript cookbook, ca. 1860 (courtesy, Winterthur: Joseph Downs Collection of Manuscripts and Printed Ephemera, No. 63x56). Carefully orchestrated meals and corresponding behavior were not restricted to the elite. For this middle-class Massachusetts dinner, with the food and dish placement carefully sketched out by the hostess, gentlemen were seated at the head and foot of the table and all the women placed on the sides.

time.[12] On one of those days Mrs. Thornton dined with a male guest without her husband. Mrs. Thornton did not leave the house for dinner without her husband, but twice during the month they dined out together at other private residences. The first occasion, a party of twelve at Mr. Marbury's on January 14, was among the most elaborate she recorded in four and a half years. It was special because the afternoon dinner extended into an evening of tea and dancing, to which additional guests were invited. The second meal out was shared with only the host couple, and Mrs. Thornton labeled it a "family dinner."[13] On three days Mrs. Thornton mentions having dinner guests. Once she had invited another couple, presumably for a family meal, and twice a single extra man called and then stayed, more for convenience than prearranged sociability.[14]

On February 25, 1800, Dr. Thornton gave a large dinner for eight male guests who arrived between two and three in the afternoon. Presumably Mrs. Thornton presided at the table and felt very isolated, because she expressed her desire to have included two women, "but most of the Gentlemen having Wives, could not invite some without appearing to slight others." Within the year the Thorntons gave another large all-male dinner.[15] Mrs. Thornton fussed over these two occasions more than any to which women were invited.

The Thorntons' after-dinner activities varied from evening to evening. Sometimes they remained at home together "working" or ventured out on various errands or visits, together or separately. Evening teas ranged from casual to elaborate. Although Mrs. Thornton sometimes issued invitations to tea, on other occasions she and her friends sent or received word that they would like to come to tea that day. On October 27, 1800, she noted an exchange more precisely than most: "About noon Mrs. Barry sent wrd she wou'd drink tea with us. I sent word we shou'd be glad to see them." The casualness of most evening visits suggests that no one in Mrs. Thornton's circle considered these teas as a serious imposition on limited resources. In her January diary in 1800 tea-drinking is mentioned on six days, once as a continuation of a large dinner party, then on two occasions when Mrs. Thornton went out alone or with her mother, and finally when a couple or one or two gentlemen called on the Thorntons.[16] Married women went to casual evening teas at their pleasure with or without escorts. In June 1803 Mrs. Thornton first noted, "Dr. T. went to the farm—we [Mrs. T. and her mother] drank tea at Mr. M[adison]'s," and the next day, "After dinner Mama & I & Mrs. Forrest went to Mr. Key's to tea. Dr. T. and Mr. Forrest joined us there."

The Thorntons went to and very infrequently gave teas that differed from the usual casual sort. On April 8, 1806, Catharine Mitchill wrote to her sister, "Yesterday I was at Mrs. Thorntons rout. . . . Mrs. T as usual had a full house. She plays on the piano, and gave us some musick in the course of the evening."[17] To Mrs. Thornton the events were simply teas or parties. Her use of the phrase "Drawing Room" in the 1812 diary applied strictly to evening receptions at the White House.[18] Although Mrs. Thornton never described a menu or listed refreshments, her notes about expenses for ingredients or ready-to-serve treats like cakes and muffins, apples, oranges, lemons, raisins, and almonds roughly match the dates when guests came to planned, friendly teas, dinners, and other evening events. Sometimes refreshments were simple, at other times they were very fancy.

In the diaries in these early years Mrs. Thornton and her husband took walks to see buildings under construction, including the Octagon. By 1807 the house was long completed and the Tayloes were living there during the winter social season, usually from November to April.[19] During these six months, individually or as couples, the Tayloes and the Thorntons enjoyed each other's company about twice a week.[20] The two women visited each other a little less than once a week. They paid calls together twice. Dinners were monthly events. Dr. Thornton went to the Octagon alone on three occasions, once for an all-male dinner and twice because Mrs. Thornton was ill. She accompanied him twice, and they entertained the Tayloes to dinner once. Evening teas or other events were three times more frequent than dinners. With or without their husbands, Mrs. Tayloe and Mrs. Thornton attended many of the same teas at private houses in Washington. The Thorntons went to the Octagon for one dance and two other parties. Once Mrs. Tayloe went to the Thorntons for tea alone. On another evening her husband and three children accompanied her.

The Thorntons' dining days as Mrs. Thornton recorded them

The Peckham-Sawyer Family by Robert Peckham, oil on canvas, ca. 1817 (courtesy, Museum of Fine Arts, Boston). Four generations of a New England family are grouped around a table with fruit and refreshments. It is nearly two o'clock, and the scene may follow dinner or represent another event.

from 1800 to 1812 reveal a pattern that other elite Washingtonians experienced in the early nineteenth century. Urban activities differed from their rural counterparts in significant ways, and family life, about which Mrs. Thornton wrote so little, was strictly separated from social life. Like other men of his class, Dr. Thornton had more opportunities than his wife to participate in society. Her role, like that of most wives, was limited by social conventions, domestic duties, and family responsibilities. The contrasts established by city and country locations, family and social contexts, and male and female roles provide a backdrop for the details of paying calls, issuing invitations, giving dinners, and hosting evening teas or other parties.

Different customs in country and town

Whether private, public, or official, the patterns of stepping-out in Washington or any other city differed from what happened in the country. Although financial resources and social class meant similar distinctions in both places, relatively short distances, a higher population density, and an atmosphere—real or illusory—of fashionable display gave special glamor to urban places. Comparative evidence of urban and rural furnishings for these decades points to different standards. In the country the pursuit of fashion was ignored or lagged, although people of higher status and regular urban contact may have made more of an effort. Furthermore, when rural people entertained, they were less likely to schedule well-timed events and more likely to extend an open-ended offer to "come for the day."[21]

Maryland plantation mistress Martha Ogle Forman often used the phrase in her diary to record the visits of her friends and relatives. She noted the expansion, renovation, and refurnishing of her house, and she was as concerned as any Washington hostess about the appearance of her table. In the spring of 1819 two families "spent the day," and Mrs. Forman proudly described her artistry with dessert. In the center of the table she placed "a large silver goblet of ice cream ornamented with a half blown moss rose" and flanked with decorated floating island in silver bowls. Symmetrically positioned and chosen to be color-coordinated were glass bowls of preserved grapes and oranges and the season's first strawberries. There were also two plates with custards, two more with "Poumpin rice," and "four plates each containing three jelly glasses of ice creams." Finally, there were glass dishes containing different kinds of sweetmeats; the yellow oranges were "perfectly transparent" and the prettiest Mrs. Forman had ever done. The whole table was "ornamented with roses which gave it a very pretty effect."[22] Like this party, probably for twelve, Mrs. Forman oriented all of her entertaining around close friends and their families. Although she never wrote specifically about how they behaved, the diary conveys an impression of easy intimacy among these rural residents.

When the day's main meal was served at three or four in the afternoon, a long evening stretched between the last cup of after dinner tea or coffee and bedtime. The popular conception of eighteenth century life in which men, women, and children appear to sit or casually wander around a tea table and to take pleasure in each other's company is well documented.[23] This pattern persisted into the nineteenth century, especially in the country and within families and

"Small Desert for Winter" and "Small Desert for Summer," engraved plate in Duncan Macdonald, *The New London Family Cookbook*, 1808 (Library of Congress). Many well-to-do Americans seem to have varied the elaborate rules illustrated in nineteenth century cookbooks for the placement and serving of food. An English visitor noted in 1822, "Tarts, fruit and cheese are always put on the table at the same time in this country, except at quite dress parties, when the fruit is a separate concern."

small circles of intimates. This genial mingling of both sexes and different age groups appears to contradict the separation of the sexes and the stiffness of some social occasions only if the distinction between family life and social life is forgotten. What was acceptable in the family arena was beyond comprehension in society.

For Margaret Bayard Smith the family of Attorney General William Wirt was the "beau-ideal" of "domestic habits, style of living, and character." She modeled the fictional family in *Winter in Washington* on her experiences with the Wirts. In both the scenes in the novel and her letters to her sister, Mrs. Smith emphasized the differences between rural and urban experiences and between family life and activities in society. Her preferences were clear. A fictional heroine claimed to "love Country tea better than city tea." The former she defined as sitting "around the tea table" with "hot biscuits, and apple pies, or sweet meats and milk, or some such nice things. But in the city . . . we cannot sit round the table, and only have a little toast, or bread and butter, and cake, and it is not half as sociable."[24] From real life Mrs. Smith reported an evening visit to the Wirts. Although living in the city, the family provided "a union of comfort and elegance." Coffee and dried fruits were served, but "the best part of the entertainment was intellectual." Harp and piano music interrupted conversation about books and the examination of poetry and paintings the Wirts' daughters had created in their albums. These intimate occasions were far more to Mrs. Smith's taste than those of general society.[25]

Although the ideals of private domestic happiness and rural wholesomeness captured the imagination of members of the carriage set in Washington in the early nineteenth century, many of them filled their real lives with a hectic routine of formal and friendly visits, dinner parties, and evening events from teas to drawing rooms, routs, and balls. Participation in these various social situations and the behavior expected at them depended upon an individual's gender and private or official status. Especially during congressional sessions and their accompanying social season, people came to the city to see and be seen. Catharine Mitchill expressed the point directly, "You know, sister, I came here for the express purpose of seeing and being seen . . . I am therefore ready to receive all invitations, and visits the Ladies think proper to favour me with. . . . And altho I do not think . . . that I am calculated to shine as a star of the first magnitude, in the circles of the gay and the great; yet, I have the vanity to believe, that your Sister is not inferior to many of her new associates."[26] Paul Fudge wrote that he decided to travel to Washington partly to learn whether Virginia influence in presidential politics would persist but mostly "to try the fortune of my daughters."[27] At least one young man came "to this gay world to rub of[f] college rust and learn gentility."[28] Sometimes visitors had fewer opportunities to display themselves and look at others than they anticipated. In May 1820 Elizabeth Wirt wrote that because of Mrs. Monroe's illness and the death of Stephen Decatur "the gaieties of the season" were over "much to the disappointment of the many strangers who have lately come to Town."[29]

Cupid at a Rout at Cincinnati by Auguste Hervieu, pen and ink and watercolor over traces of pencil, 1830 (Cincinnati Art Museum). Mrs. Trollope observed that the Cincinnati social gatherings she attended were segregated by gender: "The women invariably herd together at one part of the room, and the men at the other. . .this arrangement is by no means peculiar to that city."

A man's urban world

Prescriptive literature of the period mostly sidesteps matters of family life and country practice. Rather, it addresses the concerns of urban society. This social "intercourse of persons on a footing of equality, real or apparent," once an all-male arena of activity, only gradually came to include ladies.[30] In the early eighteenth century, writers of manuals for the conduct of life perceived home as the proper place for ladies. For them the public sphere was full of treacherous places where they should not be seen. Given this restriction, ladies were not fully social beings.[31] Although by 1800 changes were under way, different gender-specific prescriptions for the behavior of husbands and wives reveal the complex customs that governed general society. Gender affected an individual's participation in or exclusion from an event, his or her demeanor, opportunities to speak, appropriate topics for conversation, and physical mobility.

Traditionally, when ladies entered general company, they were entering the sphere of men and the rules of deference that indicated inferiority, which applied to children, women, and males of low status, went into effect. Although the assumption persisted that general society was rightly male, especially in conservative circles, by the late eighteenth century the presence and participation of ladies was increasingly accepted. Among "republicans" the cause of the common man encouraged more egalitarian treatment. Ladies were no longer to behave according to the rules of deference but to be guided by the quality of modesty, the nature of which writers never fully defined. By the 1820s a new concept of deference had appeared in the prescriptive literature. Men were to defer to or help ladies. This was deference due the weak, not deference based on rank. Although ladies' behavior was certainly not to be like that of men, it was less restricted and less inhibited than formerly. By 1855 one writer had denounced separate gatherings of gentlemen and ladies and proclaimed that "the love of the sexes for each other . . . is the indispensable element of society."[32] If considered at all at the turn of the century, such a titillating sensibility would have seemed more dangerous than appealing.

Scholars interested in women's experiences in the nineteenth century have emphasized female domination of the home and family life. In urban areas men and their income-producing activities moved out of the house, creating separate physical locations for activities identified with gender.[33] However, this concept of twin spheres does not provide an adequate model for the lives of husbands and wives who were part of the very small but very visible Washington high society. A two-part scheme does not encompass the whole range of their time-consuming activities not strictly related to work or family life. The houses of these families were centers for a variety

87

of social events. Much of this entertaining was male led and ladies'
opportunities to participate were limited, although their subordinate
roles had begun to change by the early nineteenth century. Ladies'
presence increased, and sometimes men welcomed them as social
partners. Nonetheless, many activities of general society took place
outside the home, especially at taverns. This world remained almost
entirely beyond female experience.

As late as 1839 *Etiquette for Ladies*, published in Philadelphia,
offered advice that cannot be taken as avant garde. Over and over
ladies were advised "to say too little in company [rather] than too
much."[34] On the other hand, the author was unwilling to acknowl-
edge women's inferiority. He wrote, "To a mind well formed there
is more real pleasure derived from the silent consciousness of supe-
riority than the ostentatious display of it."[35] In these conservative
laws the gentleness of wit and lightness of topics other writers considered suitable for the female mind and for display in public were
not mentioned, but the author implied his idea of appropriate female
conversation with admonitions not to monopolize dinner conversation and on all occasions to raise the voice only loud enough to be
heard.[36] Other writers were more direct in their suggestions that
women develop verbal skill but avoid all serious topics, especially
politics. Some authors went so far as to tell men their character
would be improved if they talked with women. It's hard to judge
how strictly the rule of silence was applied and how far into the nineteenth century people remained aware of it. The Baron de
Montlezun, who visited Norfolk, Virginia, in 1815 and 1816, was
accustomed to European salons where ladies played a very active
role. In Virginia he found that "in company, the women do not cut
much ice. On returning from a party one will say of a woman whom
one wishes to praise: 'Madame behaved herself wonderfully: she
didn't open her mouth.'"[37]

Young, unmarried ladies were not at liberty to move freely
through cities. Men or older ladies were to escort them from one
destination to another. Older women had greater freedom of movement, but propriety kept them from venturing independently into
public places. As late as 1828 Margaret Hall did not think she
would be welcome at a lecture about transporting freed slaves to Af-
rica. The knowledge that "ladies made part of the audience" came
too late for her to profit from it.[38]

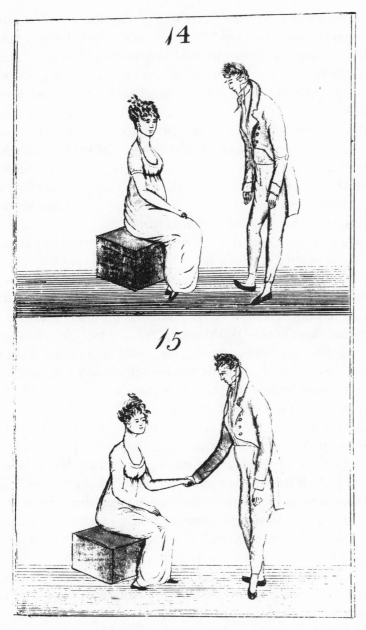

Invitation to dance, engraved plate in Francis D. Nichols, *A Guide to Politeness*, 1810 (courtesy, Winterthur: Printed Book and Periodical Collection). Etiquette manuals promised to teach genteel behavior, particularly how to perform in mixed company. Boasting of your possessions, one book admonished, would remind your audience that "you were, not long ago, somebody's washerwoman, and cannot forget to be reminding everyone that you are not so now."

Throughout the period ladies seem ambivalent about attending balls and eating food in public places. While they dined at public tables in taverns when they traveled, they rarely took meals in public places in their home cities or towns. The earliest Washington newspaper advertisements for tavern or hotel meals specify they are for gentlemen. In 1808 and 1809 a few proprietors announced special public teas for ladies and gentlemen. These were late afternoon or early evening events that included dancing.[39] By the 1820s changes were under way. Solomon Drew did not mention gender when he advertised that his "Beef Steak and Coffee House" opposite the Centre Market provided "Dinners, Suppers, or occasional Refreshments, either for the public or select parties."[40]

As late as 1864 one arbiter of social practice warned young ladies against appearing at tavern and subscription balls too frequently.[41] The gaiety of Washington's social season and the distinction between public and private occasions were stressed in an advertisement for a spring dancing school in 1831. The dancing master, who claimed ten years' experience in Washington, preferred to teach in Baltimore during the winter and to come to the capital after the height of the social season. He thought his dancing schools and balls could not compete with "the numerous private parties, levees, &c affording ample source of amusement and recreation."[42]

Even at a private social event, all ladies might be segregated from gentlemen and escorted to chairs that convention prescribed they must keep. At private balls the host was instructed first to procure seats for the ladies and then to mingle "again among the gentlemen who are standing, and who form groups or walk about the room."[43] At the end of the dance the gentlemen were to return the ladies to their places.[44] Frances Nichols illustrated the respective seated and standing postures in *A Guide to Politeness*, published in Boston in 1810. If a lady had to leave a dining room or ballroom, she was, if married, to ask a female friend to accompany her or, if unmarried, to seek her mother's assistance.

Whether the writers of prescriptive literature between roughly 1775 and 1840 were discussing women's presence in general society, their participation in conversation, or their physical mobility, they did not make consistent recommendations. In any case, it is unlikely that people everywhere followed the most modern models. Particularly among the older generation, alterations in behavior may have been so slight as to be imperceptible in the historical record. Younger aspiring gentlemen and ladies predictably were more eager to learn new ways. The improvement of general education, especially for ladies, encouraged confidence and increased knowledge. Greater ability to converse about music, literature, art, and travel eased people's social awkwardness and, regardless of gender, made them more comfortable in each other's presence.[45] Without comparative studies of behavior in other American cities it is impossible to say whether Washington practice was progressive or conservative. However, foreigners and Americans who had lived abroad seem to have taken greater pleasure in mixed company. "The British," Juliana Seaton noted in 1821, "are half a century before us in style."[46]

Some gentlemen were eager to enjoy the company of ladies and complained when they felt deprived. William Wirt told his wife, "I have but little to do with the gay world—except that I have dined out two or three times—and then not in the gay world unless you call a male party the gay world."[47] Once in a while a man talked or wrote to his wife about politics. In 1804 Senator Samuel Mitchill of New York went so far as to explain to his wife that although women could not vote, they were counted in the apportioning of representatives to Congress. He wrote that he had previously referred to their "social and conjugal relation," but he was now writing to her in her "sovereign and political capacity."[48] Even with such an enlightened husband, Catharine Mitchill accepted social conventions. In Washington with him in February 1809 she was invited to Kalorama, Joel and Ruth Barlow's house, to see Robert Fulton's demonstration of the effect of torpedoes. Although she "had a strong inclination to be present," she declined. The distance was significant, the weather ominous, and Mrs. Barlow confined to her room with an illness, but most of all Mrs. Mitchill stayed at home because "it was a gentlemens party altogether, no Lady being invited but myself."[49]

While some gentlemen viewed female roles progressively and were willing to encourage their full participation in social activities, the prevailing wisdom of the period assumed that ladies' first and foremost responsibility was at home. Women were the managers of the domestic sphere. Satisfactory arrangements—housing, furnishing, staffing, and the conduct of daily family life—required attention to details, whether the results were intended for private pleasures or the benefit of public eyes.

Servants a necessity for the elite

Although servants were essential for the conduct of family life and social activities among the elite, in the United States good ones were hard to find.[50] Margaret Hall commented on the servant problem as an explanation for the poor quality of presentation and service at American tables.[51] Advertisements expressed the irritation of those who searched for help. For instance, a family "wearied out by a succession of Female Kitchen Servants" would pay liberal wages to "a Male Cook or Kitchen Servant" who did not dread the fire, had no aversion to carrying water, and was willing to work hard.[52] The old family retainer was mostly a myth; the turnover in domestic labor was high.

Mrs. Smith appreciated the value of good servants, having experienced the good and the bad over the years. In her early married life her situation was not always satisfactory. In 1804 she was in the kitchen two or three hours every day, cooking the family's dinner. The old woman who worked "in the kitchen as a drudge" could not cook. Mrs. Smith was eager to get rid of "a miserably idle dirty girl as a waiter" as soon as possible. There were two bright spots in her staff of four. Milly, who cleaned the house, made beds, ironed, and clear starched, was her "stand bye," and a "gay, good temper'd and well behaved" five-year-old girl recently bound to Mrs. Smith played with her daughter. She was eager to hire someone else at 12*s*. 6*d*. a week, so she could resume her old employments of music, reading, and writing.[53] In 1816 her domestic arrangements were in such good order that she claimed she had nothing to do and scarcely realized she was keeping house. An "excellent woman in the kitchen" kept the key of the storeroom and went through her work "without requiring any direction." Mrs. Smith took only five or six minutes in the morning to give orders for dinner. The girl who did the chamber work and washing was "very good," and the boy who waited in the house "uncommonly good." Mr. Tracy, the only servant she named, was the *"maitre d'hotel* as well as coachman." He

Detail, *Life in Philadelphia, Sketches of Character: At Home* by H. Harrison, lithograph, ca. 1832 (The Library Company of Philadelphia). At the Octagon as well as in comparable households, all of the kitchen staff were slaves. In Washington the employment of white servants, generally immigrants, began in the 1850s.

drove the carriage, put up curtains and bedsteads, ran errands, and did the marketing and shopping.[54]

Mrs. Thornton's household staff was probably larger, and her role was always supervisory. She never wrote about cooking or doing housework herself, nor did she mention giving daily directions. Instead she recorded those occasions when she sent Joe, John, and others on specific errands. She also noted payment of wages. The farm manager and his son earned £50 per year. In 1803 and 1804 she mentioned thirteen slaves or servants by name. Although the list may not be complete, together they staffed both town and country residences. One woman is specified as white, another as mulatto. Since the gardener and farm manager are addressed as "Mr.," they were certainly white. No cooks or waiters are identified.[55] Staffs like those in the Smith and Thornton households were small compared to that required to run a house like the Octagon. Even when the servants in a smaller household were working at their best, they could not take on the elaborate tasks probably considered routine at the Octagon or the establishments of the foreign ministers.

When John Tayloe died in 1828 he left his wife the Octagon, its furnishings, $2,000 "for her current expenses of that year," and "twelve house servants." In previous years they had hired a nurse and tutor for their growing children.[56] The number of servants specified in Tayloe's will seems appropriate or even a little small for such a large establishment. Robert Roberts referred to a staff of fourteen at Gore Place, the residence of the former governor of Massachusetts for whom he worked, and Louisa Catherine Adams refers to a minimum of the same number in her undated instructions for servants.[57] An inventory of 1808 lists twenty-eight domestic slaves at Mount Airy, six adult male and five female "house" slaves, three cooks (two male and one female), two women for the dairy, two for the hen house, and one for the laundry, two male coachmen, three grooms, and four gardeners.[58] Mount Airy lists from several years later strongly suggest an unusual degree of stability among the Tayloes' domestic staff. During John Tayloe III's life the size of the Octagon staff probably varied with the social season, and until he made the Octagon the family's permanent residence, slaves undoubtedly moved back and forth from Mount Airy to Washington. In the country occasional labor was less readily available than in the city, and some domestic chores probably overlapped with plantation affairs.

Tayloe provided his male servants, porters, waiters, and grooms who were in the public eye with livery. According to one son, "The Servants wore Blue Quaker Cut Coats Turned up with Red—Red

Vests—Collers & Pockets Gold laced—Breeches, Whitest long stockings, Shoes & Buckles—The full Costume Shoulder straps or Small Epaulettes."[59] When Thomas Jefferson ordered livery for four servants, he similarly chose blue lined with red and trimmings of silver lace.[60] The appearance of these servants would have added to the grandeur of a meal, but Americans generally did not like to wear badges expressing a condition of servitude.[61] Slaves, of course, had less choice in the matter.

Whether slave or free, most servants who waited on table were probably dressed rather casually, like the men who served at a dinner Harrison Gray Otis hosted in February 1819. Otis had to give one man "elementary instructions in placing the desert *Etcetera*" because another whose wife had not washed his shirt "had *none* on his back, and was therefore degraded to the second fiddle."[62] Mrs. Seaton observed the other extreme in servants' dress on New Year's Day at the White House in 1814. She was about to leave when she saw "a rolling ball of burnished gold, carried with swiftness through the air by two gilt wings." It was the French minister "weighted with gold lace." The wings were "gorgeous footmen with *chapeaux bras*, gilt braided skirts and splendid swords."[63]

For an American citizen John Tayloe III made a fine, but not too extravagant, show. Augustus Foster, the British minister, wrote that Mount Airy and the other farms provided Tayloe with most of what his household needed. He "had to purchase nothing but clothes for himself and family, wines, furniture or other luxuries, which were however not very costly, though it must be owned that he lived, as to outward appearance, in the best style of any Americans not in office."[64] Everything known about the Octagon—its floor plan, high quality of interior finish, furnishings, and the frequency of the Tayloes' entertaining schedule—suggests a life of fashion and elegance, but there are no hints of wasteful extravagance. Writing in 1801 to the Baltimore merchant Charles Wirgman, who was on his way to England, Tayloe urged him to purchase wisely. The Tayloes' goods "must not be too Costly—for a Man with six children, & the expectancy of one annually for yrs to come,—it won't do to throw away money in Trifles."[65] Both Harrison Gray Otis and Louisa Catherine Adams, who were sometimes quick with their criticisms, visited the Octagon frequently for dinners, balls, and evening par-

Kitchen scene, engraved plate in R. House, *The Family Cookery*, 1810 (courtesy, Winterthur: Printed Book and Periodical Collection). Without our modern conveniences, housework was monotonous and exhausting. Women who could afford it employed (or owned) several servants of both sexes to cook, clean, wash, and wait on the table.

ties. They seem to have anticipated a high level of service and were neither disappointed by parsimony nor shocked by excess.[66]

When Mrs. Smith wrote that her housekeeper kept the keys to the storeroom and her coachman did the marketing, she contradicted two other sources that suggested employers generally procured supplies and kept control of them. Interestingly, the man of the house apparently did the marketing in most households. Robert Roberts told fellow servants, "Your employer will generally attend to going to market, to suit himself, but your experience, if you should be called upon to do this duty, is of the utmost consequence." He also noted that it was "not very common" for the cook to enjoy "the confidence of her employer so much as to be intrusted with the care of the store-room."[67] Carolyn Gilman indirectly confirms the practice of gentlemen going to market in *Recollections of a Housekeeper*. One of the reasons she cited to promote her "cooking establishment" was that "husbands would no longer be seen haggling with butchers at their stalls, or balancing raw meat in the open streets."[68] The evidence from Washington for these years suggests that both men and women did the marketing.[69]

A good cook may not have done the marketing, but he or she was probably as highly valued as a steward or housekeeper. Robert Roberts stressed that a steward or butler had to learn to know the cook if he was to do his job well. He implied that domestic cooks would be female.[70] The gender of a household's cook may have indicated its status or perhaps its location. Roberts's experience had been in New England. In the South cooks in elite houses were likely to be male slaves.[71] In the early nineteenth century value had an appallingly literal meaning when slaves could be purchased. In 1816 William Wirt would have been happy to spend $1,200 for a well-trained cook. The one offered was "about 18 or 20 years of age." Col. Tayloe had said "he was raised by the best cook in America," with whom he had worked for nine years. Neither William nor Elizabeth Wirt ever mention the name of the "famous Cook." They seem to have had trouble getting a good character reference for the young man, and so purchased another who was "supposed to be the best cook . . . with a few exceptions" in Richmond.[72] A few years later when Wilson Cary of Virginia was in financial trouble, he made "a very good sale" of a woman and her three children for $800. Although someone offered him $1,200 for Billy, the family cook, Cary assured his wife he would not sell Billy for the "enormous price." He wrote to his wife of the possibility only "in the way of conversation, and not with any serious idea of depriving you of your cook who is so valuable and trusty."[73]

Whether slave or free, blacks dominated food services in Washington and other urban areas. Portraits of a black waiter or butler appear in Henry Sargent's *Dinner Party* (1821) and *Tea Party* (1824), and Lewis Krimmel depicted a young black girl carrying a

Cook in Ordinary Costume by Baroness Hyde de Neuville, watercolor and pencil, before 1822 (courtesy, The New-York Historical Society, New York City). Mary Randolph advised housewives in 1824 to keep a close eye on the servants by giving daily orders each morning. "Let all the articles intended for the dinner, pass in review before her: have the butter, sugar, flour, meal, lard, given out in proper quantities; the catsup, spice, wine, whatever may be wanted for each dish, measured to the cook."

tea tray in *The Quilting Party* (1813). Until about 1830, when employment agencies began actively matching would-be workers and employers, both parties advertised in Washington area newspapers.[74] The fullest information about the appearance and personalities of slaves who waited on table shows up in advertisements for runaways. Charles Parker absconded from Washington in 1810. His owner suspected he would seek household employment as a free man since he was said to carry a "pass to that effect, with the name of William Thornton, Esq., forged thereto." About thirty years old,

Parker, who had an "African face," was described as slender, active, "talkative, smiling, insinuating, and yet something impudent in his manners."[75] John Hobe, who was thought to have fled in 1819 from Charles County, Maryland, to Washington or Baltimore on his way to safety in Philadelphia, was said to be "a good waiter, carriage driver, and carpenter" and "a very polite negro, of easy familiar speech."[76]

Roberts, himself a man of color, addressed *The House Servant's Directory* to his "young friends Joseph and David," who were about to enter gentlemen's service. He compared them to a Biblical hero who had been sold into slavery as a "domestic servant and in this capacity . . . acquitted himself with honesty and integrity."[77] Roberts wrote mainly about how a good servant was to perform his various duties. Keeping furniture polished, fires lighted, and table utensils, lamps, and clothing clean took up much of the working day. Waiting on table was clearly important. Although Roberts thought "one good servant that understands his business, can do more work in its proper order than three awkward ones," he considered waiting on eight or ten at dinner too many for one servant "to do it to perfection."[78] Carving was a duty that a house servant was "seldom called upon to perform" at the master's table, but he might "perhaps daily or frequently find use for your talents at the servant's table, or, when you quit service and have a family of your own."[79] At night the servant had to extinguish the lamps and lock the doors. Roberts stressed the importance of good interpersonal relations among the staff and told them how they should behave at the servants' table. Everyone was to be clean at mealtimes, to arrive promptly, to "be polite and help all round, before yourself," not to expect service from others, to wait for others to finish, and to avoid vulgar conversation.[80] Basically, these courtesies were the same ones stressed by etiquette guides for guests at the master's table.

Dinner parties were major events, even in a household where a large staff could provide assistance. They never happened at all in most families, and Lydia Child knew better than to mention the possibility when she published *The American Frugal Housewife* in 1827.[81] Another writer, who cared little about entertainments, expressed hope for a "cooking establishment" that would prepare food for families, thus saving the housewife from endless toil and allowing friends the luxury of dropping in "without disconcerting a family."[82] The "decent" households, which made up the largest group of Washington inventories studied, certainly cooked their own dinners, but they gave few signs of attempting an overwhelming project like a dinner party. As Robert Roberts put it, "In small families . . . a dinner is seldom given." If it had to happen, he recommended hiring a cook "to help dress the dinner" rather than a charwoman to help the cook-hostess with the dirty work.[83] In one Washington novel the narrator rails against people who lacked "the salutary restraint of prudence" and kept a carriage, paid morning visits with cards, gave evening parties, and went to assemblies. He did not add dinners to his list, presumably because even such pretentious people did not attempt to give private dinner parties.[84]

For those who did not regularly give large dinners, but now and then needed to reciprocate the generosity of others or wanted to celebrate a special moment, temporary help could be hired. In 1810 Honoria Julien advised his clientele that he would "serve any Private Family in any capacity of Cook by the day, if previous notice be given." At his F Street specialty store he sold fresh fruits and vegetables, including mushrooms and tomatoes, and prepared delicacies such as fruits in brandy, cordials, and "confectionery & cakes of all kinds."[85] In 1819 Elizabeth Wirt noted that to engage a temporary cook for a party it was "the practice either to bespeak their services for two or three days before hand at your home, or to allow them to make the desert at their own home—which they most frequently do." These cooks had skills few housewives could match. They could "bone a Turkey and dress it up with Jelly in such a style and form, as would lead you to suppose it anything else than a Turkey."[86] In the same year, when Harrison Gray Otis gave a dinner party at his boardinghouse he ordered four French dishes, which were delivered in a hack.[87]

One well-known "public servant" was Henry Orr, "the most experienced and fashionable waiter in the city." Margaret Bayard Smith hired him to advise her and to coordinate a dinner she planned to give for Harriet Martineau, the reform author, when she came to Washington in February 1835.[88] Mrs. Smith had avoided dining out or giving dinners for a number of years and considered her judgment and skills rusty. She knew that fashion declared the height of good taste one year to be vulgar the next, and since she wanted this day to be a success she needed Henry. She described him to her sister as "almost white, his manners gentle, serious and respectful, to an uncommon degree and his whole appearance quite gentlemanly." She trusted him and his knowledge of fashionable dining, but she also knew her own taste and did not want him to carry her too far beyond it. For her dinner for twelve he recommended a boulli, boiled fish, canvasback ducks, and pheasants as "absolutely necessary" for main dishes and a very small ham, a small turkey, partridges, mutton chops or sweetbreads, a macaroni pie, and an oyster pie for side dishes. He dismissed Mrs. Smith's preference for potatoes and beets, saying they would "not be genteel," and suggested stewed celery, spinach, salsify, and cauliflower. He pronounced plum pudding "out of fashion," with "all kinds of puddings and pies." Dessert should be "forms of ice-cream," jellies, custards, blancmange, cakes, sweetmeats, sugarplums, and "a pyramid of anything, grapes, oranges, or anything handsome." Mrs. Smith insisted on "only having 8 dishes of meat," some of the old-fashioned vegetables, and decidedly vulgar puddings and pies for dessert. She told Henry to order "the pies, partridges and peasants from the French cook" and said that her own Priscilla could do the rest. Henry arrived and so did Harriet Martineau. The day went off to perfection.[89]

The Smiths, like the Thorntons and the Tayloes, were experienced in running households where guests were welcome and the level of service was appropriate for the occasions and the different fortunes of the host families. The Tayloes lived elegantly. The Thorntons made less of a show. The Smiths were undoubtedly merely aspiring. These three men and three women had different roles and responsibilities in their families and in their domestic establishments. An understanding of prescribed gender roles and the extent of household staffing in a variety of elite settings sets the background for the details of visiting, extending invitations, giving dinners, and throwing parties. All make up a context for the history of dining days among the upper levels of society in early Washington.

Detail, *The Quilting Party* by John Lewis Krimmel, oil on canvas, 1813 (courtesy, Winterthur). In the corner of a parlor in this modest household, a plentiful tea or supper of slices of bread and cake is laid out. A young black servant or slave carries a tray of mismatched teaware.

V. Being Host, Being Guest

Although fashionable people pursued their rounds throughout the year, the pace of activity in Washington picked up during the winter. "The customs of society at this season differ, I presume, in some degree, from those portions of the year when congress is not sitting," wrote Henry Fearon in the winter of 1818. "Tea parties and private balls, are now very frequent."[1] Washington's social season did not precisely correspond with the dates when Congress was in session. In the early years the season began in January and lasted about six weeks, but gradually it was extended to the end of March. During these weeks permanent and seasonal residents looked forward to seeing friends from out of town and to an increased number of private and public dinners and parties. Until about 1816, when they made Washington their principal residence, the Tayloes came to town toward the end of October and stayed through April. Visitors usually did not stay so long. Husbands and fathers, who might precede their families, arranged accommodations and worried about expenses. Wives and older daughters looked forward to exchanging family routines for a month or so of gaiety.

Rules for visiting

Private citizens needed to perform several small but essential ceremonies before they could entertain each other in their homes. Individuals had to be formally introduced and exchange visits or calling cards. According to Cooley's *A Description of the Etiquette at Washington City*, published in 1829, "Nothing is of more importance than to know, and attend to the etiquette of the first order of society at Washington." Failures were considered "the next thing to a crime with the fashionable world."[2] After the proper steps of etiquette were taken, residents and strangers might look forward to extending or receiving invitations to dinners or evening parties.

In the early national years the procedures for introducing people to each other suggest a social order that had become less obviously hierarchical and less intimate. The procedures had a porous quality that allowed people to slip through social barriers. Later they may have become more rigid again. Cooley explained, "A private honest citizen, undistinguished, must in an indirect way, ask to be admitted, by being firstly introduced, and leaving his card . . . that they may know where to send his invitation, if they are disposed to send him one."[3]

The various moves of the visiting game seem better suited to satire than to social intercourse. Morning visits were made between noon and nearly three o'clock, "for in the most fashionable parts of the world, morning seems to continue until dinner-time."[4] An exception was made for congressmen, whose government responsibilities kept them in sessions from eleven to three, so they visited each other just after breakfast.[5] A lady did not need a male escort or a female companion to call on other ladies if she went in a carriage or public hack. If a lady walked anywhere, a gentleman usually attended her, although making calls on foot was permissible if two ladies went together. When Mrs. Tayloe and Mrs. Thornton accompanied each other on morning visits, they probably rode in Mrs. Tayloe's carriage. Manpower and the ability to control wealth were required to perform the ceremony, as indicated in the rule that ladies were not to knock on doors themselves but to send their outriders or footmen to ring the door bell and inquire for the lady of the house. If she were out, the would-be visitor sent in her card, a procedure that substituted "among all fashionable people for a visit."[6] Most people had cards with copperplate engraving, but blank ones could be purchased and names written on with a pen. The cards were to be carried "in a little fanciful case to keep them bright."[7] The author of *Etiquette for Ladies* told people to keep lists of all ceremonious visits. Friendly visits required less regulation because intimates knew what pleased each other.[8] Visits were also a way to express thanks. By the 1830s a specific *visit de digestion* had been instituted. A guest was to call within the week of an entertainment to converse about "the dinner, of the pleasures . . . enjoyed, and of the persons . . . met there."[9]

Visiting was time-consuming, even if one only sent in a card, "a fashionable mode of proxy" that relieved "such an arduous under-taking as a fashionable life."[10] In 1804 Margaret Bayard Smith told her sister, "It is so entirely the custom to visit of a morning here that if we keep up any intercourse with society, our mornings are most of them sacrificed." In November 1829 she noted that "from mere curiousity I have commenced an account of our visitors." In three weeks the total was 197 or about nine per day, "not all different in-dividuals but the aggregate of each days visitors, who are often the same persons."[11] When she was in Washington in 1815 and 1816, Mary Crowninshield made morning visits with Mrs. Decatur. One day they "called on fifteen—only two at home." Perhaps the ladies were out, but possibly they were avoiding company.[12] Louisa Cath-erine Adams recorded that she "paid 25 morning visits." The fol-lowing month she noted someone had called to take leave, adding, "This I suppose is fashion."[13] Her more limited ideas about the role of visits, which were shared by others in government, brought her, her husband, and the Monroe administration censure from the Washington community. That story, however, belongs to the topic of politics and official entertaining.

After introductions were made and calls paid, one waited for an invitation. An 1857 etiquette book explained, "The established cus-tom of the fashionable people at Washington, is such, that getting an invitation to their parties, depends very much on those (of a fair character) who are desirous of obtaining them."[14] In other words, one could be decently aggressive. The procedures for inviting guests to dinners, teas, or balls must be pieced together. In the early years none had a long lead time. Invitations were extended a day ahead or early in the morning of the day itself, often by word of mouth from husbands or servants on other errands about the town. Written in-vitations or notes of acceptance or regret and advance scheduling were beginning to be used, however, especially during the social sea-son. In 1801 a columnist in a New York newspaper implied that written invitations were better than verbal ones as regulators of so-cial intercourse: "He that complies with every verbal and general invitation cannot fail to be often a very unwelcome guest; while he who accepts only that kind of invitation which cannot be misunder-stood, a formal and written invitation, will rarely fail of being ac-ceptable."[15] Fifteen years later in Washington the practice was to extend verbal invitations on the day of the party during the summer and to provide more lead time and written invitations during the winter social season.[16]

Invitations to dinner were not often casually extended or accepted. In August 1800 Dr. and Mrs. Thornton went to Mount Vernon and stayed with Mrs. Washington. There they found a young man and woman who had no letter of introduction but had "sent in to ask leave to see the house." Although that was acceptable, Mrs. Thornton strenuously objected when the visitors "staid to dinner & did not seem to be conscious of the impropriety of their conduct in taking such a liberty."[17] On the other hand, Margaret Bayard Smith was pleased when her husband brought home an unexpected dinner guest, who apologized, "I have come to take my dinner with you without your knowing anything about it." She thought this preface served "as the first course for the feast of reason." They had good appetites for roast beef, cold veal, peas, porridge, and a dessert of Indian pudding. It was not up to dinner party standards, but the meal was "season'd with some wit and a great deal of mirth and good humour."[18] Mrs. Thornton may well have been more of a stickler for ceremony than Mrs. Smith. But more likely the difference lies in the distinction between formal social events and friendly, or almost family, situations.

Everyday dinners and changing times

Whether the family dined alone or entertained guests, the style of the table in the houses of the elite and affluent may have held more or less constant. Among families of the next rank the menu and display on the daily table were probably determined more by convenience and economy than fashion. One writer who knew Washington well said the number of gentlemen of fortune was small, and although they were "surrounded by great possessions" they were still relatively poor and did "not partake of the same magnificance and splendour [as those] of other cities."[19]

In the summer of 1805 Augustus Foster, then the young secretary to the British legation, and his servant were in Washington "keeping a sort of House," while the minister and his wife with whom they lived were enjoying cooler air in the countryside. For dinner one afternoon the servant prepared and served a leg of lamb and some cabbage. When Foster wrote to his mother about the meal, he expressed the hope that she was enjoying "more variety, tho I am content, I assure you."[20] Although Foster did not say whether this simple menu was customary or unusual, he certainly could have eaten differently if he so desired. His annual income totaled £7,000 pounds, £300 of salary and £6,700 from private sources.[21]

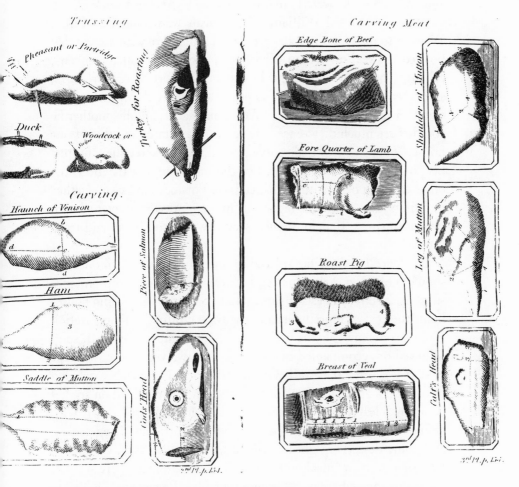

Diagrams for trussing and carving, engraved plate in R. House, *The Family Cookery,* 1810 (courtesy, Winterthur: Printed Book and Periodical Collection). Following English practice, meats and poultry usually were roasted, stewed, or fried. Mary Randolph in *The Virginia Housewife* (1824) recommended roasting meats (except beef) carefully so they did not brown as "the whiter the other meats are, the more genteel are they."

Another description of ordinary meals in a relatively prosperous household also dates from 1805. Margaret Bayard Smith wrote to her sister about her housekeeping arrangements, "I have had a close stove put up in the kitchen. . . . Our standing dinner is one dish of meat, two of vegetables, and soup, and the stove exactly holds these." The family ate hot rolls for breakfast and "biscuit or other little cakes for tea." Mrs. Smith explained that their farm near the northwest border of the District supplied vegetables and occasionally butter and added that she went to market only once or twice a week.[22]

Attorney General William Wirt's meals were somewhat fuller. Writing to his wife in 1820 he expressed pleasure with a meal that boasted "a sweet small ham of bacon," a goose, two boiled chickens, cabbage, beets, potatoes, and beans. For dessert there were tarts, sweetmeats, cheese, peaches, and pears, all washed down with a good claret. A month later his son, a West Point cadet, told his mother he couldn't see much difference between military fare "and that of our house." He recorded "good coffee, bread, butter, and either chipped beef or venison" for breakfast. His dinners were "one day beef, the other day fat pork" with cabbage, Irish potatoes, and rice or other puddings. For supper he regarded "nice coppras tea sweetened with brown sugar" as delicious when served with good bread and fresh butter.[23]

Evidence for daily fare placed on the tables of the rich does not show up often in early nineteenth century records. Common sense suggests that in these establishments and certainly in aspiring households the cost of ingredients and the time required for preparation limited some meals to the two courses Mrs. Smith mentioned, soup followed or accompanied by one meat and two vegetables. Perhaps dessert was offered as well. On the other hand, the richly detailed information about food and service at dinner parties and on special occasions clearly indicates these tables were weighted down with abundance. Thirty dishes of meat, a large assortment of vegetables, and many desserts might be offered to fewer than twenty guests.[24] Whether everyday meals among the elite and aspiring were simple, lavish, or somewhere in between is a matter of guesswork.[25]

Although wealth provided well-furnished and well-staffed houses, fine dinners, and fancy entertainments, the general standard of living in America at the time was such that fashionable people kept bumping into other ways of living. Some did so to obtain information to encourage charitable giving, others because they were traveling and had to accept whatever room and board was available.[26] Sailing from England to America in the winter of 1796, the architect Benjamin Latrobe carefully sketched and described the "Breakfast Equipage set out for the Passengers of the Eliza." Salt beef, maggoty biscuits, butter, tea, coffee, and sugar were on the table. Since there were more people than equipment, passengers breakfasted as the utensils became vacant. Items were assigned multiple functions as needed, "The Slop basin also feeds the Goat, and serves to wash Mrs. Taylor's baby." Neither appetizing nor sanitary, the conditions were undoubtedly widespread on land as well as at sea.[27] Furthermore, those who traveled with servants found, often to their surprise, that they were expected to eat the same fare at the same table.

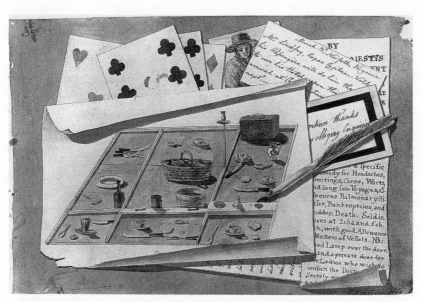

Breakfast Equipage set out for the Passengers of the "Eliza" by Benjamin Henry Latrobe, pencil, pen and ink, and watercolor, March 4, 1796 (collection of the Maryland Historical Society). In recreating his rudimentary shipboard table, Latrobe noted that the utensils were shared by his fellow passengers and the accoutrements fulfilled more than one function. The mustard pot "serves the Captain in the double capacity of a Coffee cup and tea cup."

The experience could also be reversed. Those whose upbringings had been meager or isolated might suddenly find themselves better equipped or exposed to completely new environments. Anne Royall, who later became a writer and journalist in Washington, wrote in 1818 that she was "never better pleased, than when seated alone by a bright fire, a clean swept hearth, a lighted candle, and a pair of snuffers. I have a snuffer-tray too, but one who was raised in the woods, you know, can easily dispense with a snuffer-tray."[28] Two senators who came to drink tea with Margaret Smith in 1808 were astonished to hear piano music. "I believe," she wrote, "it was the first time they had seen or heard such a thing." They examined the keyboard and the "internal machinery" and seemed to suppose that the "sweet melody was drawn by chance or random from this strange thing." Their curiosity and lack of comprehension fascinated Mrs. Smith, who admonished her sister not to think these good men fools, "far from it, they are sensible men and useful citizens, but they have lived in the backwoods, that's all."[29] It's no wonder that many who came to Washington were forced to adapt quickly to city manners and were amazed when served strange dishes. The French minister Hyde de Neuville, according to John Quincy Adams, enjoyed having fun with food and puzzling his American guests, who were accustomed to simpler fare. He served "turkeys without bones, and puddings in the form of fowls, fresh cod disguised like a salad, and celery like oysters."[30]

Menus and methods of service at dinner parties

Many guests described the dinners they were served at the White House and the residences of public officials or foreign ministers. These meals are probably also representative of the range offered on special occasions at the best private houses in the city. Whether they were private or official, dinner menus and methods of service were undergoing changes in the early years of the nineteenth century. In her memoirs of the years 1804 and 1805, Louisa Catherine Adams maintained that in Washington "luxury was unknown except in the Houses of the Foreign Ministers and there were very few who aimed at great and ostentatious display." She implies that times had changed from those when "there were no Confectioners &c or

French Cooks and the Ladies prepared there own entertainments at the expence of much labour and anxiety but generally with success."[31] To the old concept of a table laid abundantly with many unadorned meats and a few plain vegetables cooked in traditional English style was added a new interest in sauces and other complexities borrowed from French cooking. Although the two types of

Fruit coolers attributed to La Courtille factory and believed decorated by Stone, Coquerel and Legros d'Anisy, porcelain, ca. 1810–1825 (collection of the Maryland Historical Society). Also called a glacier, this porcelain pail was used to serve iced fruit for dessert. This pair is one of two sets of coolers in a large group of French porcelain originally owned by Elizabeth Patterson Bonaparte.

cookery can be distinguished, neither one seems to have gained an edge. Throughout the early decades of the nineteenth century, hosts and hostesses served their guests both, sometimes mixing them indiscriminately. The national labels marked differences of class and service procedures as well as cuisine. Preparation of French food re-

Desserts, engraved plate in M.A. Careme, *Cuisinier Parisien*, 1828 (Library of Congress). The table at one of French Minister Hyde de Neuville's balls in 1818 was decorated with "cloud cap'd towers and gorgeous palaces of White Sugar." Such confections were made by a professional pastry chef called a confectioner.

quired special know-how and was associated with luxury and refinement. English country cooking was practiced by those who were certainly not penurious but preferred economy.[32]

The Fudge Family in Washington, an epistolary novel in verse published in 1820, contrasts the culinary taste of Dolly with that of her father, Paul Fudge. Dolly has recently left a fine Philadelphia boarding school. Visiting Washington with the rest of her family, she longs for fashionable French fare.

> Ah! when shall I see 'stead of ham, always ham
> As it always is here too, dress'd *en epigramme*— . . .
> Ah when shall I see *tete de veau en surprise*
> And *cremes a la glace* which will make one's breath freeze, . . .
> And *souffles* and *pates*, both *gros* and *petits*
>   with *gateau* and *gelees*, and *citrons confis*,
> And "*temple de Solomon*," built up "*en* flummery"
> And all the *et cet'ras* of eatable mummery?

Such nonsense with food did not impress her father, who found more than enough French food in Washington. Although his for-

Ad for George Kneller in the *Daily National Intelligencer*, July 6, 1815 (Lloyd House, Alexandria Library). Confectioners sold ready-made foods that ordinary people purchased for their meals. In 1798 an Alexandria shop advertised that beef steaks, mutton, veal, and chicken pies were available "for the accommodation of families."

tunes had risen (the Fudges were once Drudges), he was not an awkward member of the newly rich but a prosperous citizen without pretense in his preference for the familiar.

> The table also little pleas'd me,
> The names of dishes they so teaz'd me, . . .
> I did not see a dish I knew,—
> Though those I know are not a few:—
> There were *fricasses*, *ragouts*,
> Serv'd up in all shades and hues,
> Of sav'ry scent and handsome sight,
> Though somewhat in their substance light.

At parties in Washington he finds it humorous to see folks he last saw fighting over bear meat and possum "disputing about wine, . . . As if they had been us'd to dine" with such gentility.[33]

Congressman Manasseh Cutler sometimes wrote out menus and described unfamiliar dishes. When he ate an "excellent dinner" at Secretary of State Madison's in February 1804, he described the popular soup "called Bouilli," made of a much boiled round of beef and seasoned with spices and "something of the sweet herb and Garlic kind" with a rich gravy. He also mentioned a large ham with a vegetable that "appeared to be Cabbage, much boiled, then cut in long strings and somewhat mashed." He was just as uncertain about two of the desserts, which looked like apple pie but were "in the form of the half of a Musk-melon, the flat side down, top creased deep, and the color a dark brown."[34] Two years earlier he had been baffled at Jefferson's presidential dinner table by a "pie called macaroni, which appeared to be a rich crust filled with the strillions of onions, or shallots." Another guest told him he was eating an Italian dish made of flour and butter. Cutler did not like the strong flavor. Among the dishes served at this same dinner, he mentioned rice soup, eight meat dishes, no vegetables, ice cream, a pudding with a cream sauce, and "many other jimcracks" with "a great variety of fruit, plenty of wines, and good."[35]

Juliana Seaton observed that in Washington the style at dinner was extravagant, even though she did not like to see "pastry and puddings going out of date and wine and ice-creams coming in."[36] She was pleased with a dinner served at the Madison White House in 1812. "There were many French dishes, and exquisite wines," but she admitted being "so little accustomed to drink" that she could not distinguish sherry from "rare old Burgundy Madeira." For dessert, instead of pastry she noted "ice creams, maccaroons, preserves and various cakes," followed by "almonds, raisins, pecan-nuts, apples, pears, etc."[37] A year later the Scottish barrister Lord Francis Jeffrey judged the Madison table differently. "The dinner was bad . . . a meagre soup and a whole array of fowls and little dishes. . . . The second course consisted of an infinite number of little plates ranged in two long rows down the table with a couple of apples in one and a handfull of raisins in another, six or seven walnuts in a third and so on, like a feast in a nursery."[38]

Food was presented and served in two principal ways in Washington high society during the early nineteenth century. Because individuals seem to have varied the methods to suit the occasion and their personal situation and preferences, differences are not precise. In traditional *service à l'anglais* all the dishes were placed on the table at once, and the hostess and perhaps the host served guests from the array. There might have been several courses, each with the same number of dishes. Meats and vegetables were served together, perhaps with puddings and pies. Generally the trend was to differentiate the main meal from dessert. A course might include a dish called a "remove," usually a substantial platter of meat that was taken away during the course and replaced with something else. After the courses of the main meal were finished, the table was stripped of its cloth and wine was served with fruits and nuts.[39]

According to the format for *service à la français*, servants played a prominent role and dishes were more likely to be on a sideboard than lined down the center of the table. Rosalie Calvert expressed her preference for three courses rather than "the American mode of serving all the meats and vegetables together," and she thought she would introduce her own ideas about their sequence because "in this country everyone does as one likes."[40]

Margaret and Basil Hall did not agree about "the comparative merits of the etiquette of English and French dinners." Basil, who ate only one dish at a meal, was bored by the offer of twenty or thirty no matter how they were presented or who served them. Margaret found it "easier to refuse the offers of the servant than to resist the solicitations of the master and mistress of the house." She liked to see them enjoy their company rather than wear themselves out "doing

Champagne glass and wine-glass, 1765–1780 (White House Collection). Champagne was enjoyed at Washington dinners and evening parties. One diplomat claimed "a dinner or supper is prized and talked of exactly in proportion to the quantity of champagne given and the noise it makes in uncorking." These glasses were probably used by both John Adams and John Quincy Adams.

the honours and carving large joints." However, the French style required a large fortune because "many more servants are requisite." An alternative was for guests to help themselves from the nearest dishes. When they wanted something out of reach, they asked others not to pass the serving dish but to transfer some to their plates. Margaret Hall did not like the method, which obliged guests "to go through the labor of cutting up," but because of the servant problem in America it was common practice.[41] The Halls' comments imply little regard for excessive abundance and diversity. They did appreciate well-appointed tables and good service. Their expectations, based on so-called English and French practices, varied from the ways Americans adapted both procedures to suit local circumstances.

When the butler announced that dinner was served, the dining room and its furniture and tableware became a stage set. In the "great business" of putting everyone "entirely at his ease," host and hostess aimed to strike a middle course between exerting themselves too much or too little. "To perform faultlessly the honours of the table, is one of the most difficult things in society," wrote one arbiter of etiquette.[42] Commenting on the stiffness of the British minister's parties and particularly on the way his wife, Mary Bagot, labored "too much in the exercise of her function as entertainer," Louisa Catherine Adams generalized about social skill. "To entertain well you must forget that you are so engaged and your company will feel perfectly at their ease and forget they are visiting. . . . This like most things is easier in theory than in practice."[43] Ten years later, when John Quincy Adams was president, Margaret Hall considered Mrs. Adams "a very ladylike person" and her dinner party "very showy." However, British standards came to the surface when she concluded that "no American ever understands doing those things really well."[44]

Although the fashion in dinner parties was changing, the anxiety did not abate. In the 1840s one writer observed that "even at the best tables" what was considered "the height of good taste one year" was declared "vulgar the next." Furthermore, individual households or social sets practiced "customs peculiar to their own clique, and all who do not conform *exactly* to their methods are looked upon as vulgar persons, ignorant of good-breeding."[45] Whatever the table etiquette at a tidewater Virginia plantation in the 1770s, Philip Fithian, a Princeton-educated tutor to the children of one of the great families, alluded to his former discomfort with "the Ceremonies of the Table." After he and one of his charges unexpectedly had to do the honors, Fithian wrote, "happily for me I have them at last all by heart."[46] Half a century later Eliza Farrar told her readers not to overstay their welcome. "A dinner, well performed by all the actors in it, is very fatiguing and, as it generally occupies three hours or more, most persons are glad to go away when it is fairly done."[47]

Women's attitudes toward elaborate dinners were not overwhelmingly positive. After Louisa Catherine Adams served twenty-two guests a "tolerable pleasant" dinner in March 1819, she noted it was "the 12th we have had this winter and I hope the last."[48] In 1829 when Margaret Bayard Smith had to give a dinner for one of her husband's business associates, she wrote to her sister, "I would rather give a dozen evening parties."[49] Even Margaret Hall commented

The Dinner Party by Henry Sargent, oil on canvas, ca. 1820–21 (courtesy, Museum of Fine Arts, Boston). At this all-male dinner party, believed to be a meeting of Boston's Wednesday Club at the house of the artist, two servants stand in attendance. The cloth has been removed and the final course of wine, cake, nuts, and fruits is underway. Under the table is a crumb cloth, a baize carpet that protected the rug during meals.

she "should dislike much to be obliged to give such huge dinners."[50] Perhaps women's opinion about formal dinners can be explained by their worry over criticism of their preparations and performances.

Dinner parties for gentlemen only

Dinners that were considered social events rather than family or friendly gatherings had a decidedly masculine emphasis. By the early nineteenth century the segregation by gender associated with them was no simple matter. In addition to occasions that were all male, there were times when the hostess was the only lady present. When women were more numerous, arrangements varied. Men and women may have been seated alternately around the table. They also may have eaten sequentially from the same table, first the women and then the men, or, if the party was small enough, simultaneously at different ends. The English practice of women leaving the table before men was yet another form of gender distinction at dinners. All of the possible arrangements show up in descriptions of private events in Washington, but they are read to best advantage against a background of fuller references from other cities.[51]

Caroline Howard King, who grew up in Salem, Massachusetts, remembered that "once or twice a year my father gave a dinner party to his gentlemen friends, and then all the resource of our house (and sometimes of the houses of our friends) were called into action." She does not say whether her mother sat at the table.[52] Social pressures and cultural predispositions established the primacy of the male guest list. A few women might be added, but the possibility of reducing the number of male guests and inviting all wives never occurred to many couples. "No lady but Mrs. Washington dined with us," wrote one guest about his dinner with the President and nearly twenty members of Congress in Philadelphia in 1795.[53] The practice was recognized in prescriptive literature and not limited to political working dinners. In some cases men were instructed to issue their own invitations, "even if it is intended that the mistress of the house shall be at the table."[54] Margaret Hall brought a foreigner's insight to her observation that men were likely to outnumber women at American dinner parties because often only women belonging to the family were present. "There is at all times a separation between the ladies and the gentlemen in society," she reported. Someone told her that "many of the ladies of the first families in New York have never dined out."[55]

Men could do the honors of the table as well as women, but sometimes, especially in the eighteenth century, when women performed the role they did so silently. In 1780 the Marquis de Chastellux observed one of his hostesses, who "from her countenance, her dress, and her deportment, perfectly resembles a painting by Vandyck." Furthermore, he said, "She punctiliously does the honors of her

119

house, presides over her table without saying a word, and the rest of the time she is merely there, like a family portrait."[56] In Philadelphia a few months later at the house of Samuel Huntington, a member of the Continental Congress from Connecticut, Chastellux met "Mrs. Huntington, a stout, rather good-looking woman, but no longer young," who "did the honors of the table, that is to say, she helped everybody without saying a word."[57] Chastellux, whose previous experience was with French ladies who had been educated in the fine art of social conversation for over a century, clearly found this silence remarkable. The American ladies were of the old school, and their behavior indicates they adhered to the rule of deference for women in society.

Sequential service seems to have prevailed only when there were large numbers of guests. In Baltimore in the 1820s a splendid supper followed a meeting of a concert society at Barnum's Hotel. A visitor "counted one hundred and two ladies seated at one table." After they finished their meal, the gentlemen took their places.[58] The practice of women leaving the table before men seems to have persisted until today as a remnant of the largely male character of dinners. Most writers took it for granted. When Robert Roberts instructed servants to light the candles and lamps in the drawing room after dinner and prepare to serve coffee or tea, he commented that "the ladies never stop long in the dining room after the dessert is over."[59] In *The laws of etiquette*, after the ladies retired the gentlemen dispensed with "the service of the decanters" and sent the bottles that had "been standing in a wine cooler since the commencement of the dinner," down the table.[60] The European-educated South Carolinian Thomas Pinckney had no use for the practice, which he thought spoiled good company. He sounded very much like an etiquette manual when he wrote to his wife about the "abominable Custom," which required "the whole Company rising from Table immediately upon the Cloths being withdrawn after Meals, and the Ladies retiring to Their Apartments." He claimed the practice prevented "that intercourse of the Sexes which serves to polish and improve both, and in short reduces a Man to the disagreeable necessity of losing his Dinner or the agreeable Conversation of the Ladies."[61]

The full range of gender distinctions at events was noted in Washington. "Last night William had a supper," reported Juliana Seaton without further comment.[62] On the other hand, on February 1, 1801, Harrison Gray Otis dined with a "party of both sexes & select."[63] Mary Bagot, wife of the British minister, described wedding festivities and noted going to visit the bride and finding her dining with the gentlemen: "No women were present [she probably meant, at the table] but herself & the dinner consisted of above 20 gentlemen—Her bridesmaids stood behind her chair & waited upon her at dinner."[64]

Behavioral practices associated with dinners seem to have changed slowly. The traditional American experiences of Mrs. Smith, the Thorntons, and others contrast markedly with the attitudes of Louisa Catherine Adams. Brought up in Europe and experienced in the social ways of European courts, she was not inhibited in male company, even when she was the only woman. She also was capable of taking a calculating look at all-male dinners. She wrote that she "adopted the plan of not inviting ladies to dinner because my rooms were small and it was impossible to entertain all the Ladies who came to Washington without an expense which could be utterly unsupportable."[65] On one occasion Mrs. Adams and sixteen men ate "an odd sort of mixed dinner I sat between Mr. Law and Mr. Vaughan and never was more amused in my life—Mr. L.—entreated me to read a work of his entitled instinctive impulses . . . I told him I would if he would not insist upon my conversation."[66]

Although Mrs. Thornton had a modest house and plenty of cause to economize, the wistful tone of her desire for women's company at an all-male dinner suggests a more conservative frame of mind and a generational difference. In 1800 the probability was greater that host and guests thought of general society as exclusively male. Later they could more readily accept women's presence. Mrs. Adams made a deliberate decision; Mrs. Thornton did not think it her right to do so. A further bald statement by Mrs. Thornton about one of Dr. Thornton's dinners exposes another dimension of women's participation: "After dinner at Dr T's request I played two or three Songs the piano forte being in the dining room, and then withdrew."[67] Mrs. Thornton does not say how she passed the time during dinner and whether she conversed freely or was silent. She may have been little more than a functionary overseeing meal service and a performer displaying musical skill. Margaret Hall reached this

121

conclusion in the late 1820s: "Women are just looked upon as house-keepers in this country, and as such are allowed to preside at the head of their own table, that they may see that all goes right."[68]

Dining out-of-doors

Dining alfresco seems to have been comparatively informal and much enjoyed in Washington in the early nineteenth century. People took picnics, although they probably did not use that term, to the falls of the Potomac and elsewhere. They also carried meals with them when they traveled. In October 1817 the British minister and his wife were riding through the Virginia piedmont. While their servants ate at the tavern where the horses were baited, Charles and Mary Bagot took "some cold partridges, wine &c." to "a sunny spot by a stream in the wood."[69] Some occasions, like the Tayloe party described by Louisa Catherine Adams, were very elaborate. Elbridge Gerry, Jr. suggests the fare and the entertainment at break-fast and tea "in the garden under the trees" required little planning and preparation. He and his friends amused themselves "with walk-ing, running and leaping." He was sorry he missed a barbecue "on the other side of long bridge." As a New Yorker the outing may have been strange to him, because he wrote, "This term is applied to a festival for young people, and at it, they had a dinner, which always is of roast meat, and in the eve they danced &c."[70]

Margaret Bayard Smith and a party of twenty, about half of them children, had scheduled a *fête champêtre* in the summer of 1811. Planned as an outing "at the old Cottage" to be hosted by another couple, it took place at Mrs. Smith's summer house because of the showery morning. When the guests gathered, they "amused them-selves rifling my flower borders, and making wreaths." Then they ate dinner and moved out to "a table with benches round it in the front Piazza" for dessert. This course consisted of "pine apples, or-anges, cakes, sugar plumbs nuts figs &c &c adorn'd with the gayest flowers and lilies in abundance; to which elegant repast (for such it really was) I added nothing but ice-creams."[71]

In May 1816 Thomas Law hosted the Bagots and about twelve others to a party at the falls. Taking guns and fishing rods, "everyone went their own way after their different amusement untill three

The Tea Party by Henry Sargent, oil on canvas, 1821–25 (courtesy, Museum of Fine Arts, Boston). Although respectable women participated in evening routs and parties, they were expected to behave decorously as "ornaments of society." Washington may have been different. In 1814 Margaret Bayard Smith observed that "women here are taking a station in society which is not known elsewhere." She found at evening parties women mingled among men with "more ease, freedom and equality" and walked around the room rather than remaining seated in one place.

o'clock when . . . we dined on boards laid upon the rocks & seated upon the rocks." The menu was "fish broiled upon hot stones . . . cold meat, bread & cheese & oceans of wine, punch & brandy." Although the military band present played poorly, their appearance among the rocks reminded Mrs. Bagot of several literary scenes. She found the landscape wild and romantic. Especially memorable were vignettes of "the black women cooking our dinner" and "a group of

123

fishermen [who] collected to see us." They headed for home about six and finished the long day with a ten o'clock supper at the Bagots' house.[72]

Nighttime entertainments

Evening social events sum up the contradictions and complexities of the early national period. Requiring several hours of attention from all participants and substantial financial outlay for the hosting couple, they must have served an important purpose. The newness of the occasions, the displays of consumer goods, the abundance of refreshments, the private urban settings, the presence of large numbers of people, the participation of both ladies and gentlemen, and the formal behavior of all embody aspects of both older traditional and more modern ways of associating with others.

Balls or any party in high society where there was dancing depended upon the presence of women, and to some extent evening tea parties seem to have been deliberately organized to provide them with further opportunities for outings. However, even in the 1820s, many elite women were reserved about participating in conversations, accepted restrictions on their physical mobility even at private parties, and hesitated to attend functions in public places. Because early etiquette books did not describe the different kinds of tea parties, their distinguishing features have to be worked out from the chance comments of guests. On the other hand, later books did describe etiquette associated with two other kinds of evening parties, the rout and the conversazione.

Distinctions centered first on the types of entertainment—conversation, music, cards, and dancing—which ranged from the casual to the fully organized. The number of guests, the number of rooms opened to accommodate them, and the quality of refreshments further separated simple from elaborate events. Because the picture of elite social events in Washington is complicated by the combination of private and official events, the features of government entertaining will be highlighted in a separate discussion. Here, the characteristics of private functions in the capital city will be set against a backdrop of definitions and instructions for parties as well as descriptions from other urban areas.

George Channing, who reminisced about his childhood and teen-age years in Newport, Rhode Island, between 1793 and 1811, satirized his experiences with tea parties "formal enough to satisfy the most rigid asceticism":

When the company had assembled, the reception-room being ready, with high-back chairs placed in close order round the room, near to the wall, every one took the seat most agreeable to himself. No one stood: it was not thought genteel. . . . All, then present being starched to the wall, and perfect silence reigning, a side door would be set ajar, and gradually opened for the entree of tea on one waiter, and sugar and cream upon another. . . .the supplying of each with two or three cups was a work of time. . . . With the addition of eatables of all sorts . . . the whole constituted a feast fit for the gods, provided the gods lived, breathed, and drank sub silentio. . . . At the proper time, nuts, raisins, figs, and apples were distributed; . . . When, at about the close of such *festivities*, things were growing hopeless, someone, having no respect for good manners, would propose the singing of a song.[73]

Newport parents were introducing their offspring to proper behavior at events that others from Richmond to Cincinnati, Albany, and Salem described as events for adults. As they grew older the inhibited and silent behavior of the boys changed more than that of the girls. The dozen or so contemporary descriptions indicate that handed teas had general but not necessarily uniform features. A traveler in New York in 1807 observed "when there is only two or three [guests] they make tea in the room," but when "there was above 30 the tea was made in another room & brought in on trays and handed about on it by a black man."[74] Sophie du Pont explained that their family was so large, they never had "tea on table, but it is handed round."[75]

Several characteristics dominated conservative versions of handed teas in urban society early in the nineteenth century. First, female guests were permitted little or no movement through space but had to sit stiffly on chairs or benches around the perimeter of the room. Men moved more freely. Second, all waited for servants to pass refreshments in sequence. Guests held plates and cups in their laps or hands. Conversation was subdued. There is some indication that following refreshments the behavior of the company eased somewhat and that occasionally guests retreated from the circle to card tables, music, and maybe even to dancing. Differences in later years and among the avant-garde seem largely to have affected women's behavior, allowing them to talk and move more freely.[76]

Johnny Q, Introducing the Haytien Ambassador to the Ladies of Lynn, Mass. by John
Childs, lithograph, 1839 (courtesy, Essex Institute, Salem, Massachusetts). At handed
teas women usually remained seated and servants, here at the doorway, carried separate
trays of refreshments and cakes to serve each guest individually. This peculiar print cru-
elly lampoons the anti-slavery sentiments of John Quincy Adams who supported the
black republic of Haiti.

In 1828 Frances Parkes made it clear that "the preparations for a
rout, with the exception of removing the carpet, chalking the floor,
and providing music and a supper," were similar to those for a ball.
Refreshments were to be handed round, but otherwise guests were
"left to amuse themselves, if amusement can be found in a crowd
resembling that which fills the lobbies of a theatre on the first night
of a new performance." Routs were sometimes called "drawing
rooms" or less formally "squeezes" or "jams" because of the large
numbers of people crowded into the rooms opened for the occasions.
Conversaziones were more select. They were for "persons of rank
and fortune" who wished to patronize literature. Guests of varied
background were preferred because they gave "variety and interest
to the conversation," which was "the object of the assembly." The
hostess was to spread tables with magazines, prints, drawings,
shells, fossils, and other natural productions "to excite attention and
promote remark." Conversaziones were said to be relatively unpop-

ular because they did not include music, "without which no species of entertainment" was regarded as worthy of attention.[77]

Sometime before 1820 Washingtonians began to use the term "squeeze" to refer to large evening parties, public or private. Harrison Gray Otis asked his wife whether he had told her he went to a private house "where we had a squeeze and I staid only a few minutes—The Stowage was too close—."[78] Margaret Bayard Smith preferred a small select party for about thirty over "the usual squeezes and crowds."[79] Margaret Hall added another dimension to the problem of large numbers when she expressed delight with the beauty of New Year's Day 1828, "otherwise the smell of wet coats and boots would not have added to the pleasures of the squeeze."[80]

When they built the Octagon and moved to Washington, John and Ann Tayloe signaled their desire to enjoy urban social life. Throughout the years, in spite of her frequent pregnancies and his

Sliding door between the dining and drawing rooms of Com. Decatur by Benjamin Henry Latrobe, ink and washes, April 2, 1818 (Library of Congress). City residences were designed with special features suited for grand parties. Sliding doors between adjacent public rooms created the effect, in the words of one guest, of "two rooms thrown into one." Louisa Catherine Adams attended a "very brillant and very crowded" ball at Decatur House in 1820 for which six hundred invitations were issued.

ill health, they seem to have done so consistently. Although some observers resented the family's wealth, deplored their ignorance of current issues, or disagreed with their conservative politics, the Tayloes' acquaintances seem to have valued their company and accepted their frequent hospitality. Their social circle included William and Anna Maria Thornton, Harrison Gray Otis and his wife Sally, John Quincy and Louisa Catherine Adams, William and Elizabeth Wirt, and Charles and Mary Bagot.[81] All of them attended dinners, evening parties, and balls at the Octagon. These couples reciprocated, but they entertained the Tayloes less often than they went to the Octagon.[82] The Tayloes seem always to have behaved with propriety. "Mrs. Tayloe was pleased to say that there was one general sentiment of regret at your absence," wrote Otis to his wife.[83] Anticipating a long ride "with Mrs Tayloe in her coach and four," Otis reassured her, "Dont be jealous of Mrs T—her husband & daughter go with me, & She is passee and always *secek*, but a very amiable and courteous lady."[84] In two rather long comments about the Tayloe family, Louisa Catherine Adams focuses positively on their wealth, house, respectability, and service to friends.[85] For their many courtesies and all their private entertaining at dinners and evening parties, the Tayloes were well regarded, but they did not seem to create excitement or inspire affection.

In 1803 the Thorntons attended "a party at Mrs. Law's a dance and supper—In high stile." And again, "went in the evening to a party at Mr. Tayloe's . . . large company—handsome supper."[86] Guests entertained themselves principally with conversation and music and occasionally with chess, cards, or dancing.[87] In January 1819 Margaret Bayard Smith invited 170 to a grand party. About 120 accepted and moved through four rooms, "two down-stairs, for dancing, one parlour and one supper room up stairs." In the latter, "the table was so arranged that 25 or 30 could sit down at a time and a side board of dishes supplied those that were consumed at table." She thought "4 musicians from the *Marine Band*" increased the pleasure of her guests, and she was grateful for Mrs. Barlow's offer of extra party equipment and help from servants.[88]

When Lafayette visited Washington in 1824 Juliana and William Seaton considered themselves fortunate to receive him at a party, "being the only private individuals so honored." Three hundred and sixty guests, "within a score of those invited" attended, and Mrs. Seaton admitted the party was very crowded but, she hoped, not unpleasant. She and her servants had worked hard. "My chamber and the large nursery were *deranged* and *arranged* for the occasion, serving as card and supper rooms." The Marine band played for dancing in the dining and drawing rooms, "the latter opened for the first time, and thus pleasantly inaugurated."[89]

Two classes of people were clearly affected by parties like these—the acquaintances, whose large numbers filled as many rooms as the host couple could open for the purpose, and the servants. Servants were vital to the progress of such an occasion. They had to be well trained and to have a manner and demeanor appropriate for the event and the host's status. Very wealthy hosts might have used only their own permanent staff. Others may have hired waiters for the evening.[90]

Servants were obviously involved in the extensive preparations required to accommodate and feed thirty, sixty, or even several hundred people. They rearranged furniture and may have transported benches and chairs that were borrowed or rented. Sometimes doors were removed and baize hangings put in their place. During the party the servants' visible task was to serve refreshments. First, they handed round tea and coffee on trays. A frugal hostess might offer only pound or sponge cake and milk biscuits. More generous offerings included jellies, sweetmeats, preserves, fruits of different kinds, ice cream, cakes, and wine.[91] At these events the preference for individualized service was carried to extremes. An almost endless sequence of little containers with all sorts of delectables replaced the old notion of displaying everything at the same time.

Refreshment service at some balls resembled that at both handed teas and dinners. The difference was a matter not of the occasion but, at least sometimes, of the gender of the guest. In 1801 Harrison Gray Otis attended a private ball in Washington at which the "entertainment consisted first of tea served out about 8 oclock—Then the dancing continued without interruption untill *twelve. After that* chocolate in cups with dry toast was handed round among the ladies, and *after that*, the gentlemen were regaled in a back parlour with a cold ham, mutton & tongue."[92] An illustration by Auguste Hervieu for the 1832 edition of *Domestic Manners of the Americans* shows similar treatment of men and women at a ball supper at a hotel in Cincinnati. Frances Trollope commented that this differentiation "constantly recurs." She carried her generalization further, "In America, with the exception of dancing, all the enjoyments of the men are found in the absence of the women." She then put into words what Hervieu sketched:

> The gentlemen had a splendid entertainment spread for them in another large room of the hotel, while the poor ladies had each a plate put into their hands, . . . servants appeared, bearing trays of sweetmeats, cakes, and creams. The fair creatures then sat down on a row of chairs placed round the walls, and each making a table of her knees, began eating.

Several people explained that neither economy nor room size determined the procedure. Simply, "the gentlemen liked it better."[93]

Correct deportment at parties

The laws of etiquette instructed a male guest on the proper entrance to a party. His first obligation was to "salute the lady of the house before speaking to any one else." If she had stood by the entrance he could have done so easily, but a fashionable hostess sat or sometimes stood at the far end of the second room the guest entered. He thus had to bypass Circes and Calypsos on every side and "traverse the length of two rooms in order to reach her."[94] Margaret Hall described the arrival from a lady's perspective:

> We were invited to tea [at Governor Clinton's in Albany] and went at eight o'clock. On entering the first drawing room both Basil and I started back, for we saw none but gentlemen, not a single lady, and we thought there must be some mistake in asking us there, but in a moment the Governor came forward and giving me his arm hurried me into the adjoining room at the top of which sat Mrs. Clinton who placed me on the seat next to herself.[95]

Later in her letters to her family Mrs. Hall refers back at least six times to the "formidable ordeal" or the "Albany sin of a circle," which she described most fully after the evening at the Clintons'.[96] She mentions the chairs crammed round the room with "a lady upon each" and her introduction to "at least a dozen of those who were nearest me." "In the course of the evening," she wrote,

> the gentlemen did venture into the room and stood for a short time talking to one or other of the ladies . . . and altho' occasionally the ladies had courage to cross the room and change places with each other I never saw any lady standing during the whole evening, and the

Cincinnati Ball Room by August Hervieu, engraved plate in Mrs. Frances M. Trollope, *Domestic Manners of the Americans*, vol. 1, 1832 (Library of Congress). With some horror, Mrs. Trollope described a Cincinnati ball she attended where all the gentlemen enjoyed a seated supper together while the women in the adjacent ballroom ate off plates balanced on their knees.

Mistress of the House alone seemed to enjoy the privilege of moving at her ease about the rooms.[97]

Used to greater physical mobility, Mrs. Hall was not pleased to be rooted to her seat but, like her husband, had been taught when faced with "unforeseen cases, [to] follow the example of company."[98] Careful observation and private correspondence were her only ways to ease frustration.

By the 1820s behavior at some of these events had grown more relaxed. A few days after the party at the Clintons' Mrs. Hall attended another at the Van Rensselaers' house, which was better

because the inner room, a library, contained several tables covered with books of prints and it was a relief to get leave to stretch one's limbs a little whilst looking over drawings of scenery. . . . The outer room was, as usual, bare of furniture except for the awful range of seats next to the walls.[99]

On several more of her evenings out, the small size of the group mitigated the Albany circle or she found informality around a center table.[100] A dinner and evening she and her husband spent with twelve Bostonians was notable for its comfort, cheerfulness, and conversazione format. After a fine meal the company was seated informally in the dining room, where "there was a table in the middle of the room covered with books and prints, and it was the centre of attraction, but both gentlemen and ladies moved about like free agents, and did not appear to be glued to their chairs."[101]

In *Recollections of a Housekeeper*, published in 1834, Mrs. Gilman recounts the evening party or conversazione she and her husband gave shortly after their marriage. Because they "were somewhat ambitious of intellectual display, and the time [was] beginning to pass away when ladies did not feel themselves pinned to the same seat for three hours," they bought and borrowed some prints and a magnifying glass, which they arranged on the sofa table and lit with a newly purchased astral lamp. In their house and at the Van Rensselaers' a center table (which A. J. Downing later called the "emblem of the family circle") was a ticket to female mobility in the social sphere. The table played an active role in changing men and women's social behavior, their movements in space, their conversational opportunities, and their social relationships.[102]

While Margaret Bayard Smith did not call her January 1817 party for about forty guests a conversazione, she did say it was "small, but very select and agreeable." Guests played chess or sat by the table and "conversed in groups." There was enough room for men and women to "sit, as well as stand." She reported receiving "many compliments on the greater rationality, as well as pleasure of such a small select party, than the usual squeezes and crowds."[103] In *Winter in Washington* she created a dialogue between a Washington hostess and a "titled foreign gentleman" in which both criticized grand entertainments for their "rich variety and perpetual succession of refreshments" and expressed a preference for "little besides a cup of tea." Not only did the simple way spare "trouble and vexation and expense," but there was "more intellectual feasting" because the company was not interrupted by "constantly eating and drinking, servants pressing through the crowded rooms, the tinkling of glasses, spoons, forks, &c."[104]

Two paintings by Henry Sargent, one of an all-male dinner party and the other of a mixed gender tea party in Boston in the 1820s, epitomize the urban social experience. The interiors conform to the best evidence about public rooms in elite private residences. *The Dinner Party* depicts a conservative, traditional event. Two servants, one black and one white, wait on the table where twenty gentlemen are about to enjoy dessert and wine. In *The Tea Party* the stiffness of handed teas is nearly a thing of the past. In the room in the foreground most of the chairs are arranged around the perimeter. A few are studiously disarranged, one close to a sofa or center table. At first glance the guests appear to be in easy informal relationships with each other, but closer reading of the parlor identifies groups of seated women and a few gentlemen who talk with them. In the room to the rear of the painting both men and women stand and talk with each other. On the far left a black waiter carrying a tray is about to circulate among the company.[105]

Some men and women enjoyed the changes in social events of the early national period. They expressed personal preferences for large parties where everyone squeezed together or for smaller gatherings where conversation was the chief attraction. At the same time, others adhered to traditional habits. For example, Molly and Dolly, the two daughters of the Fudge family, had received different educations. Molly remained at home in the country where a maiden aunt brought her up to be the equal of her husband. Dolly went to boarding school in Philadelphia. United with their family in Washington, the girls exhibit behavior particular to their separate upbringings. Dolly is progressive, while Molly expresses more conservative attitudes. When they debate whether to attend public or private balls, Molly argues that Episcopal clergymen favor private parties,

> At "public balls" only their *canon* they level,—
> As its only *that kind* which sends one to the devil.

Although the "poet" explains in a footnote that the Anglican Convention at Winchester had determined there was no scriptural distinction between private and public balls, still the one was considered "a *patrician* assembly, the other promiscuous." Molly agrees to attend a private one, but she sticks to her old-fashioned ways and censures Dolly for her looser behavior—talking freely to men, eating when hungry, and waltzing—

> Then you can't think how silent amidst all the buz.
> Before, at, and after the supper I was;
> Though at home as you know, I have no lack of tongue,
> Yet I vow, as I live, I'd agree to be hung,
> Before I'd, as Dol does, unbridle it so,
> As to say, at a ball more than just *yes* and *no*.[106]

Although fictional, the two sisters and their different social behavior probably represent an accurate range of acceptable practice about 1820.

All of these parties presupposed "a fortune and good *ton*."[107] Whether others from lower socioeconomic levels organized and attended similar parties remains an open question. However, one of the Washington novels claimed that subordinate officials lacked "the salutary restraint of prudence" and indulged in ruinous spending. They gave evening parties, paid "morning visits, with cards, in their own carriages" or any they could procure, gave routs, went to assemblies, and, in short, exhibited "every folly their superiors think proper to practice because it is said to be *haut ton*, and they cannot think of being unfashionable, whatever may be the result."[108]

Even among the fashionable these occasions did not always create happiness. After describing a party she gave for 170 guests, an exhausted Margaret Bayard Smith wrote that it gave her "no pleasure, but I hope it did others."[109] Once when Mrs. Thornton had a headache and the rest of the company seemed dull, she concluded, "Tea drinking is very stupid."[110] William Wirt's daughter was more specific about her displeasure with an evening party at the Decaturs' in 1819: "Upon the whole it was rather a dull party—Very little that could be called conversation & no music! Mrs. Burnford & some others were at cards in another room."[111] In *Domestic Duties* Francis Parkes noted the seemingly inexplicable popularity and fashionable character of these parties or routs. She then explained the secret of their success, "Few expect any gratification from the rout itself; but the whole pleasure consists in the anticipation of the following day's gossip."[112]

When the ladies and gentlemen of Washington's high society dressed up and stepped out, they frequently moved beyond the intimacy of family and friendly gatherings and entered the general social arena. The formal procedures and the relatively large scale of morning visits and party-giving were a peculiar feature of the urban scene. Although by no means cloistered, ladies did not enjoy equal status with men. Some of the gender distinctions seem to have been similar at private parties throughout the United States, but perhaps conversational openings for ladies were more limited in Washington because it was preeminently a political city. Although most social

activity was set in people's houses, much of it combined or even confused private functions with political and official events.

Congressional boardinghouses, photograph, 1861 (Library of Congress). Visible beyond the crowds gathering for Lincoln's inauguration in March 1861 are a row of boardinghouses built circa 1800 along A Street to accommodate members of Congress.

VI. Base and Superstructure: From Boardinghouses to Official Parties

In the fall of 1802 a "monument of human weakness and folly" as large as a millstone and weighing over 1,200 pounds traveled over the roads and waterways from Cheshire, Massachusetts, to the nation's capital.[1] A gift to Thomas Jefferson from some politically minded country women and their Baptist minister, the great cheese attracted enormous attention. In Baltimore "the taverns were deserted; the gravy soup cooled on the table, and the cats unrebuked revelled on the custards and cream. Even grey-bearded shopkeepers neglected their counters, and participated in the Mammoth infatuation."[2] Presented to President Jefferson on the twenty-ninth of December, the cheese was installed in the White House on a specially built frame, and visitors were invited to "go into the mammoth room to see the mammoth cheese."[3] For at least three years guests nibbled on it. In December 1804 a senator noted on Jefferson's table "two bottles of water brought from the river Mississippi, and a quantity of the Mammoth cheese." The latter, he said, was "far from being good."[4]

The same guest thought better of Jefferson's "elegant and rich" dinner and even more highly of the "very good" wines. "There were eight different kinds," he reported, "of which there were rich Hungary, and still richer *Tokay*—for this last he informed me that he gave a *guinea a bottle*." The elegant French dinners, prepared by the French chef or those he trained and presided over by a French maitre d'hotel, contrasted markedly with the domestic taste and folksy promotion of the great cheese.[5] A good picture of the strange new capital city society and the importance of public events and official party-giving emerges from a look at the places and conditions in which congressmen and others lived. These mostly modest and definitely makeshift accommodations formed the base from which these individuals sallied forth to much grander official events.

The Washington boardinghouse

Throughout the first three decades of the nineteenth century many congressmen and transient officials in Washington became familiar with boardinghouse life. The other types of rental accommodations, hotels and taverns, were either not available or were less suitable for their needs. The financial failure of the Union Public Hotel promised by Samuel Blodgett in the 1790s meant that for many years Washington lacked a modern public facility of the sort that elsewhere expressed civic development and pride. Taverns, where at a moment's notice several people might be accommodated in the same room or even in the same bed, were inappropriate for legislators and others in government who expected privacy and needed work space.[6] Through the 1820s most members of Congress and their visiting wives and families lodged in the famous Washington boardinghouses.

Like other aspects of material life, boardinghouse accommodations improved over the first three decades of the nineteenth century. As the years passed, lodgers were less likely to share rooms and the number of suites or combinations of bedrooms and parlors increased. Furnishings improved as proprietors purchased washstands, bowls, looking glasses, carpets, and chamber pots for private rooms.[7] Owners of these establishments knew they had a captive market. During congressional sessions they charged high season rates, one third more than the rest of the year.[8]

Several chronologically arranged examples illustrate the variety of features and cost of life in a Washington boardinghouse. Manasseh Cutler, a Federalist from Connecticut and member of the first Congress to sit in the new capital in 1801, described his lodgings in detail. The house was one in a row of six brick buildings. It had a basement with a kitchen and three full stories with two rooms on a floor and a garret above. Eight renters occupied the second and third floors, two to a room, where they slept on "narrow field beds" with curtains. By Cutler's standards, they had every "necessary convenience." On the ground floor a single parlor met their needs for receiving company and dining. The proprietor, Mr. King, and his wife and teenage daughter, Anna, lived in the rear room.[9]

During the same winter Albert Gallatin also shared a room,

which he considered "a great inconvenience" and for which he paid "Conrad & M'Munn" fifteen dollars a week "including attendance, wood, candles, & liquors." The Munns' establishment was larger than the Kings'. Gallatin estimated between twenty-four and thirty sat at table, "and had two wives not been part of our mess" it would have looked "like a refectory of Monks." He confirmed the scarcity of vegetables, "the people[?] being obliged to resort[?] to Alexandria for supplies." He wrote, perhaps preparing his family to economize when they came to Washington, that "upon the whole, living must be somewhat dearer than either at Phila or New York."[10]

When the poet Joel Barlow and his wife first moved to Washing-

BASE AND SUPER-STRUCTURE

ALPHABETICAL LIST OF BOARDING HOUSES, WITH THE MEMBERS IN EACH.

MR. BURCH, (Capitol Hill.)	MR. BROWN, (Near General Post-Office.)	MR. DOWSON, No. 2, (Capitol Hill.)	MR. GAITHER, (Pennsylvania Avenue,)	MR. HUDDLESTON, (Near G. Post-Office.)	MRS. MATHERS, [Capitol Hill]	MRS. SUTER, [Pennsylvania Avenue,]
ason Archer, P. Barbour, a H. Bryan, Caldwell, W. Clarke, s Hawes, es Hooks Pickens, d Smith, tt Yancey.	Oliver C. Comstock, Thomas Fletcher, Richard M. Johnson.	James Barbour, (S) John C. Calhoun, Weldon N. Edwards, Daniel M. Forney, William C. Love, Nathaniel Macon, (S) Charles Tait, (S) John Taylor, Thomas Telfair.	Thomas Newton, James Pleasants, junr. William H. Roane.	Daniel Avery, Ephraim Bateman, Henry Crocheron, Henry Southard, George W. Townsend.	Ezra Baker, Victory Birdseye, Peter H. Wendover.	James Johnson, John Kerr, Peter Little, William M'Coy.
	MR. CLAXTON, (Capitol Hill.)		MISS HEYER, (Capitol Hill.)	MRS. HAMILTON, [Near Treasury Office.]	MRS. MEYER, [Pennsylvania Avenue.]	MRS. STANNARD, [Georgetown.]
LEY'S HOTEL, (Capitol Hill.)	Burwell Bassett, James Carr, Samuel S. Conner, William Lattimore, Albion K. Parris, Abraham H. Schenck, Micah Taul, John Tyler, Jonathan Ward.	DAVIS'S HOTEL, (Pennsylvania Avenue.)	William Baylies, John L. Boss, George Bradbury, Daniel Cady, Thomas Clayton, Outerbridge Horsey, Joseph H. Hopkinson, James B. Mason, William Milnor, Thomas Smith.	Jeremiah B. Howell, (S) John W. Taylor.	Dudley Chase, (S) William Darlington, Joseph Desha, Joseph Heister, Thomas Moore, James M. Wallace, John Whiteside, James I. Wilson. (S)	Benjamin Huger, Thomas M. Nelson.
. Ashmun, (S) e M. Troup, (S) t Wright, 1s Tate.				MRS. LINDSAY, [Pennsylvania Avenue.]		SEMMES'S HOTEL, [Georgetown.]
		John Condict, (S) Peterson Goodwyn, William Hendricks, John Lovett, Aaron Lyle, Jeremiah Morrow, (S) Samuel M'Kee, William Piper, Nathaniel Pope, James B. Reynolds, Erastus Root, Benjamin Ruggles, (S) John Scott, Solomon P. Sharp, Isham Talbot, (S) Thomas Ward.		David Clendennin, Isaac Griffin, John Hahn, Samuel D. Ingham, Abner Lacock, (S) William Maclay, Thomas Wilson, William Wilson.		John Randolph.
. BAILEY'S RDING HOUSE, (Capitol Hill.)	MR. COYLE, (Capitol Hill.)		MR. HERRONIMUS'S, (Pennsylvania Avenue.)		MR. O'NEALE, [Near 6 Buildings.]	MRS. THOMPSON, [Six Buildings.]
1 R. Betts, niel Ruggles, Stearns, B. Sturges, nin Tallmadge, as Ward.	David Daggett, (S) John Davenport, jun. Cyrus King, Charles Marsh, Timothy Pitkin, Th. W. Thompson. (S)		William G. Blount, Geo. W. Campbell, (S) Newton Cannon, Bennet H. Henderson, Jared Irwin, Hugh Nelson, Samuel Powell, Montfort Stokes, (S) Isaac Thomas, Lewis Williams, John Williams, (S)		Rob.H.Goldsborough,(S) Charles Goldsborough, Benjamin Hardin, Alney M'Lean.	James Breckenridge.
IR. BRUSH, nnsylvania Avenue.)	MRS. CLARKE, (F Street.)	MRS. DOYNE, (Pennsylvania Avenue.)		MRS. M'CARDELL, [Capitol Hill.]	MRS. ODLIN, [Pennsylvania Avenue.	MR. VARNUM. [Seven Buildings.]
lgate, Alexander, nin Bennett, Brooks, m Crawford, ald S. Clarke, Glasgow, . Taylor, (S) W. Will in.	William A. Burwell, William H. Harrison, James Noble, (S) Stephen Ormsby.	Thomas Rice, Solomon Strong.		Charles H. Atherton, Samuel Dickens, Luther Jewett, Chauncey Langdon, Asa Lyon, Hosea Moffit, Jeremiah Nelson, Timothy Pickering, Isaac Tichenor.	Daniel Sheffey.	Joseph B. Varnum, (S)
	MR. CRAWFORD, (Georgetown.)		MR. HYATT, (Pennsylvania Avenue)		QUEEN'S HOTEL, [Capitol Hill.]	MRS. WILSON, [Seven Buildings.]
	Thomas P. Grosvenor, John C. Herbert, Joseph Lewis, junr.		Benjamin Adams, Epaphroditus Champion, William Hale, Lyman Law, Jonathan O. Moseley, John Noyes, John Reed, Roger Vose, Jeduthun Wilcox.		George Bear, Thomas Cooper, William Hunter, (S) John W. Hulbert, Elijah H. Mills, William H. Wells, (S)	John J. Chappell, William Creighton, Martin D. Hardin, (S) William Irving.
R. BESTOR. Near the Theatre.)	MR. DOWSON, No. 1. (Capitol Hill.)	MR. FROST,. (Capitol Hill.)		MR. M'LEOD, [Capitol Hill.]		DR. WORTHINGTON, [Georgetown.]
ulpeper, n Woodward.	James Brown, (S) John Gaillard, (.) A. T. Mason, (S) Thomas B. Robertson, Nathan Sanford, (S) Samuel Smith, Henry St.George Tucker.	Jeremiah Mason, Daniel Webster.		James Birdsall, Lewis Condict, William Findley, Jabez D. Hammond, John P. Hungerford, John Ross, John Savage, Westel Willoughby, jun.	MRS. QUEEN, [F Street]	William Gaston.
		MRS. FITZGERALD, (New Jersey Avenue.)			John Forsythe, Richard H. Wilde.	PENN. AVENUE.
		Jonathan Roberts, (S)				Henry Clay, (Speaker)
					MR. SCOTT, [Capitol Hill.]	CAPITOL HILL, [New Centre Market.]
					Benjamin Brown, Samuel Taggart, Laban Wheaton.	William Lowndes.
						GEORGETOWN. George Peter, Henry Middleton.
						NEAR THE NAVY YARD.
						Philip Stuart.

Those marked thus (S) are Senators.

"Alphabetical List of Boarding Houses, with the Members in Each," fold-out plate in *Congressional Directory*, 1816 (Library of Congress). Washington's early boarding-houses were located in the several developed areas of the city, in addition to Georgetown. Capitol Hill was an obvious choice for a congressman, although many complained of the area's isolation. Some chose to live along lower Pennsylvania Avenue or on the parallel F Street corridor, while still others selected upper Pennsylvania Avenue between the President's House and Georgetown, perhaps for its proximity to social activities.

139

ton in 1805, they and their two servants roomed with Mrs. Doyne at the recommendation of Margaret Bayard Smith. They paid forty dollars a week for board, a neatly furnished parlor and bedroom, and stabling for an unspecified number of horses. Mrs. Smith was interested in Mrs. Doyne's financial success and noted that in addition to the Barlows she had "10 gentlemen at 10 dollars a week only for board and lodging, as they find fuel, candles, etc. and so I think she will do very well."[11]

By the twentieth of June 1807, Congress was out of session so Alexander Dick "could get very good accomod. in the Metropolis on moderate terms." He and his companions boarded at Mrs. Thomson's, "one of the best boarding houses in the place." It was "quite in the Country" on Pennsylvania Avenue near "a few Straggly houses in front & on each Side . . . an exterior Field [and] a large park with Some pretty peeps of the Potomac." Dick identified his house as part "of the *Six buildings*" that were "nearly in the Style of the London Houses." Two rooms and "an airy lobby" occupied the ground floor. They rented "a very respectable parlour with bedroom" on the second and one of the "two bedrooms & a bed Closet" on the third as a "business room." The establishment also boasted a garret, coach house, and stable. With board each member of the party paid eight dollars a week, half the charge for their New York lodgings. They did not eat at the public table but more agreeably at a separate one.[12]

Following the common practice for congressmen to roost by region if not by state, in 1810 Abijah Bigelow reported that New Englanders were lodging together at the same boardinghouse as himself. For a single room with meals, firewood, and candles he paid twelve dollars a week. Had he shared a room but slept in a separate bed, he could have saved two dollars. He must have known his wife would not understand the military term "mess" because he explained, "so the boarders at a particular house, are denominated."[13]

When Attorney General William Wirt was preparing to move his family from Richmond to Washington in the late fall of 1817, he and his wife wrote back and forth about the accommodations they needed for their large household and whether they should buy, build, or buy and renovate. They also discussed temporary housing, which seems to have been a rental unit associated with a boarding operation. For $270 per month the proprietor would furnish the table "morning noon & night in first style—we finding all our furniture, fuel, candles, & every thing." He would also supply "two first rate male servants & a first rate chamber maid," but the Wirts were to bring their own cook and four more servants.[14]

Several newspaper advertisements sum up the range of boardinghouse accommodations and the quality of their food service. One stressed a private, retired, child-free environment for two or three single gentlemen. A second, with seventeen rooms, had a larger "mess" for which food was prepared in "a commodious kitchen" with two fireplaces. Another advertisement called the attention of six or eight lodgers to a gravel walk to the Capitol, a proprietor who "knows how to live," and a "fine vegetable garden" that supplied the table and added to the comfort of guests.[15] Although congressmen preferred to "mess by themselves," landlords served all guests with the same "style and fare." One of the family always sat at the head and did the honors of the table.[16]

By habit or assignment lodgers occupied the same places for all meals. According to Margaret Bayard Smith's reminiscences, when Jefferson was vice president and living at Conrad's boardinghouse he had a separate drawing room for the reception of his visitors, but "in all other respects he lived on a perfect equality with his fellow boarders." These "democratic friends" rejected the suggestion made by a senator's wife that Jefferson's age and office entitled him to a seat near the warm end of the dining room, so "he occupied during the whole winter the lowest and coldest seat at a long table at which a company of more than thirty sat down."[17]

Edward Hooker listed menus for three dinners served at Mr. O'Neal's boardinghouse in December 1808. The first—ham, turkey, chicken, roast beef, chicken pie, pudding, crackers, and apples—he labeled "a good one but not splendid." The second consisted of goose, fowl, ham, sausages, eggs, and other items he did not name. He was more specific about the vegetables offered at the third: "goose, duck, chicken pye, Boiled cornd beef, Roast fresh beef, hominy made of dry corn and beans boiled whole, sweet and Irish potatoes, custards, roast apples, crackers and butter with cheese preserves and cyder." Although Hooker does not say how many sat down for the meals, he notes with some surprise that the "several Southern members of wealth" who boarded at O'Neal's were "very temperate drinking no wine and very little or no spirits and sitting at table only about an hour." He observed that General Thomas Sumter had "genteel military manners, making now and then a very sensible remark." On the other hand, Governor John Milledge of Georgia was "plain in dress and rude in manners." Hooker went on to give a rare specific description of someone's table manners:

If a poor man and [of] low station he might be thought ill mannerly. He took a piece of bread in his fingers, sopped in the gravy of the Roast Beef and ate it all at one mouthful though large enough for three. Afterwards there being a pretty large piece of quince on the plate of preserves and some sauce, he hauled the saucer near, took the quince in his thumb and finger and gormandized the whole at a bite.[18]

His behavior supports the widespread opinion that not all who were elected to national office had the manners people of fashion expected.

Hooker also noted that the landlord did not automatically provide liquor with the meals, but it was available upon request. Furthermore, one could "call for a cold cut of victuals any time of day if wanted."[19] Others noted that the landlords did not provide drink with their weekly rates. In 1810 the Rhode Island congressmen transported several barrels of their local cider to Washington. Abijah Bigelow and other New Englanders at his boardinghouse bought some to economize on their bills for wine and spirits.[20]

Guests who stayed in smaller boardinghouses and those who shared rooms appreciated the common parlor, which the landlord heated. In larger establishments, where at least some guests had the luxury of private parlors, the common spaces were still well used. In 1801 Manasseh Cutler was surprised that he enjoyed the company of his fellow boarders at their small house. If they happened to be in their parlor-dining room "in the first of the evening" when Mrs. King made "tea in her own room," she sent a servant to them with tea, coffee, and toast. They never ate any supper. On two or three evenings a week Cutler took so much pleasure in the entertainment of his landlord's seventeen-year-old daughter that during the following session when he stayed at another boardinghouse, he wrote that he missed "the amusement Miss Anna King used to afford us with her Forte-Piano and excellent voice."[21] In 1813 all the residents at Elbridge Gerry, Jr.'s boardinghouse seem to have had "separate rooms and parlours." They had "to visit as if in a different house, except more sociably." He noted a difference in people's preferences for private or public parlors. Some of the ladies staying at his boardinghouse sat in the general parlor, "others always stay upstairs, and only come down to dinner."[22]

Congressmen and other officials who made up a "mess" generally ate together as the name implied. The practice bored Albert Gallatin who, unless with his own family, preferred "rather now & then [to] see some other persons."[23] Occasionally, people were invited to other messes, but the only boardinghouse resident who is known to have entertained extensively and privately was that social animal Harrison Gray Otis. He had experience hosting his own dinner at his Boston home while his wife was in New York. In May 1815 he wrote to her that he was to "give a dinner this day to about 20. Nobody invited yet but Lyman who is to act Mrs O—I could be very impatient for your return, if I indulged my feelings but I do not." He added some more news and then ended the letter, "I wish you could get here by dinner time." Then he enclosed a sketch of the dinner table set with "Soup Lamb Salmon Pye Mutton Ham Soup Chickens." He labeled his own place and opposite him marked "Mr Lyman for one day only."[24] Clearly, Otis relied on his wife's domestic management, but his affectionate regard and tone of respect for her efforts mitigate the impression that he considered her merely a housekeeper.

The Boston dinner was good practice for those Otis hosted at his boardinghouses in Washington in December 1818 and February 1819. On the first occasion he and his suite-mate entertained six men, including the British and French ministers. Eight guests, including John Tayloe III, attended the second. Preparation of the rooms created "a great uproar":

My trunks are to go under my bed with the Exectuar [probably the chamber pot] which have been overturn'd more than once—And my white counterpane which has not yet been washed, is to be *turn'd*—Colo Gibsons wooden chairs are to be brot up & then my chamber becomes a drawing room—Pour la table—The Castors are broken, and the Wine glasses diminished in number, and every thing pinches a little as it did last year at Baileys you know—and I *Spose* you think the tables dont Shine, and that the Spoons are dull, and that you with Betty Webber at your heels could find out a good many Slutholes.

Two days later he reported that the "dinner went off as you say very smartly."[25]

Otis's third, last, and largest party of the season took place at the end of February, and "all the heads of departments were invited and all the public ministers." Only after he had issued invitations did he discover two other parties were scheduled the same day, "large ones and from our kitchen." He considered this "discouraging as plates etcetera are distributed by certain principles of apportionment, and breakage never being repaird, symptoms of security increase towards the close of the Session—But we borrowed two dozen plates of a lady in F street, and two dishclouts in the Sideboard drawer to wipe knives and forks and Spoons." Even after scrubbing, the table would not pass his inspection. With the loan of two tablecloths "that matter was covered." He further reported resisting "the effort to use my Chamber again for a drawing room, but made Ogden [his suitemate, Congressman David A. Ogden from New York] take down his bed." For the twelve who sat down Otis had ordered "four French dishes brot in a *hack*, about a mile and an half." This event "went off *famously*."[26] When throwing a party in a boardinghouse, even someone with Otis's high standards did not let the necessity of washing dirty utensils or using catch-can furniture and tableware inhibit the effort to keep the social engines turning. The grandest of guests seem to have accepted these expedients and enjoyed themselves.

In the winter of 1818 Otis's wife joined him in his boardinghouse lodgings in Washington. Like many others, the couple sallied forth from their unpretentious home away from home to participate in the diverse and sometimes grand social life of the national city. In January 1818 Otis wrote to his daughter about the start of the season, "What they call gaiety is begun—The Drawing room, the diplomatic feeds, the Teaparties and dances, and the dangers which shade the pleasures, in Sitting Down and taking up, among the horses and carriages, which like Congress itself, looks in all manner of directions, without any calculation about managing or arranging the ins and outs." He looked over their social calendar, "Mother and I went to Alexandria to a ball and come back at midnight—today we dine at the French Ministers—On Monday evg Musical Party at

Bagots [British minister]—Wednesday dine with President & several other things on hand[?] of less magnitude."[27]

Fashionable foreigners

Most Washingtonians looked up to the foreign ministers as leaders of fashion. They admired diplomatic dinner parties, teas, and routs. Commenting on a ball given by the British minister in 1821 Louisa Catherine Adams compared the styles of the two countries: "There is an ensemble of Elegance and Comfort which usually pervades an English house and every thing looked orderly and regular a thing scarcely comprehensible in our free Country."[28] Admiration was fine; imitation was not. Politicians and other citizens sensed that foreign practice should not become the American way. Somehow American protocol had to work a balancing act between straightforward rules setting precedence and rank order and messier, ever-shifting social practices that allowed public servants to perform the duties of their offices and did not completely contradict the philosophical ideal of the equality of all men.

The foreign ministers did not labor under these constraints. With their high salaries and allowances for furnishing and living, they surpassed nearly all Americans in matters of domestic furnishings, carriages, entertainments, and menus for meals and refreshments. They provided livery for their servants, and when they attended official functions they dressed as they would in a European court. Their parties were expensive and appropriate to their station. According to Louisa Catherine Adams, in the early years in Washington luxury and ostentatious display were "unknown except in the Houses of the Foreign Ministers."[29] The shows must have been impressive, but in American descriptions of these men, their families, and their style of entertaining one detects an edge of irritation. The foreign ministers, who were accustomed to the traditional vision of the rightness of a hierarchical order, knew their place was close to the top. They were better educated than most Americans, and they bore themselves with social assurance derived from European experience and long practice with the *je ne sais quois* of gentility. Sometimes their attitude seemed like arrogance. Harriet Otis tells of the afternoon in 1811 when her half brother Harrison Gray Otis

BASE AND SUPER-STRUCTURE

brought "his excellency Mr Foster," the British minister, into their lodgings. He "threw us into a terrible dilemma by hoping he should have the pleasure of seeing us next Monday—No said papa—extremely sorry we are engaged—Ah! I'm very sorry—a party on that night! I did not know there was any other than mine pray where is there a party?!!! Ye powers of effrontery support me! Never will I tell a lie to a man's face. Papa scrambled off as well as he could."[30]

Knowing that few Americans understood and fewer could match their displays of luxury, members of the diplomatic corps competed among themselves. For instance, when Charles Bagot wrote out suggestions for the goods his successor should send to Washington, he noted that he "had no ornamental furniture and the French Minister swaggered over" him in that respect.[31] The daily routine of elite French ladies and gentlemen bore little resemblance to that of leading Americans. According to the bachelor minister Augustus Foster, New York residents considered the wife of exiled French General Jean Victor Moreau "a wife merely for show." She practiced music and dancing four hours every day. Before her guests arrived she had eaten dinner "so as not to be seen at so ungraceful an operation." During the meal she followed "the fashion for French ladies" and "carved every dish in spite of all one's endeavours to take that trouble off her hands."[32] Back in Washington Vice President Elbridge Gerry and his son went to dine with Louis Sérurier, the French minister. Two liveried footmen received them. Dinner was in the "French style," by which the younger Gerry meant there were "5 or 6 courses, and as many wines, champagne, &c." and the "dishes were so disguised by the French manner of cookery, that . . . it would have been impossible to name them." After dinner the steward placed coffee without cream "on a round table in the middle of the [drawing] room." Guests helped themselves.[33]

Sérurier's successor was Jean Guillaume Hyde de Neuville. He and his wife, Anne-Marguerite, were royalists who lived in exile in the United States from 1807 to 1814. The couple had known hardship and danger as well as the luxury and style of the French grand manner. When Hyde de Neuville was appointed minister to the United States in 1816 he expressed concern about the social demands he knew were contrary to his wife's simple tastes and retiring nature. The subjects of her many American sketches confirm his opinion of her preferences; none depicts their frequent and lavish entertainments.

Harrison Gray Otis attended a grand ball given by the Hyde de Neuvilles in December 1818. After describing the compression of the crowd, the small space left for dancing, the sparkle of "lace and other diplomatic and military accoutrements," and the lack of ease of guests "from all the cultivated and wilderness quarters of this extensive country," who took their stations and kept "them like posts," he turned his attention to the food:

The supper was very brilliant—All the rooms in the second Story were dismantled (I dont mean the mantle pieces broken down) to make room for the tables . . . Whatever wore the old and familiar appeal of "beef mutton veal venison partridge & plum pudding or custard' was hurried down redelance without remorse—But the cloud cap'd towers and gorgeous palaces of white Sugar, and concatanate (good) oranges, and all the paper columns and castles in the air, escaped without being attempted by sap or assault—Our revered Signiors avoided them as if they were mousetraps; out of which something might pass to do them harm—Most of the grand ornaments I had Seen before, so that the Table had an air of familiarity. . . .[34]

Baron Hyde de Neuville (1776–1857) by Baroness Hyde de Neuville, watercolor, undated; self-portrait by Baroness Hyde de Neuville (ca. 1779–1849), watercolor, ca. 1807 (both courtesy, The New-York Historical Society, New York City). Gregarious and hospitable, the French minister and his wife gave many of the city's most lavish and memorable parties during their Washington residence (1817–1822). One guest impressed by the Baroness's hospitality and charm observed that she "with an ease and grace peculiar to her. . .devoted herself to her company, which I assure you required no little character."

Mary Bagot, wife of the British minister, attended a party at the Hyde de Neuvilles where she found "the rooms full & dancing to vile music. Came away about 1/3 after eleven & left the most disgraceful scene I ever saw going on—the men most of them drunk & running at the champaine & Madiera which they drank like savages."[35] No wonder John Quincy Adams considered parties at the French minister's "more gay" than the "very elegant" entertainments given by the British minister.[36]

Since the French minister had a chef who could produce such wonders and managed to outdo Bagot with clocks and other ornaments, presumably the table at his residence was as well set as that of the British minister. These residences were settings for parades of silver, gilt, and possibly even gold. In 1805 the Rev. Manasseh Cutler complied with a card "received eight or ten days" earlier and dined at Mr. Merry's with a company of twenty-eight. He was impressed, writing, "Table superb, the plate in the center, and in the last service, the knives, forks, and spoons were gold. Six double-branched, silver candlesticks, with candles lighted." Before the session was over he dined there twice again with smaller parties.[37] Within those same weeks he and at least 150 others received invitations to "Tea and Cards," which Cutler found also included a "band of music, and a variety of entertainment."[38]

If the schedules of the British ministers are a reliable indicator, the volume of entertaining in Washington increased between 1812 and 1818. Augustus Foster noted that he generally gave "dinners to 14 or 16 once a week and a smaller party every Saturday or Sunday." He anticipated giving a ball for about 300 people on the Queen's birthday.[39] Charles and Mary Bagot often entertained about twenty guests at dinner and frequently gave large parties. Their efforts earned them the affection of Washingtonians, and in the years following the War of 1812 undoubtedly helped restore American goodwill toward Great Britain. In one month during the winter season of 1818 they hosted three dinners for men and three large dinners for both sexes. An evening party followed each. They gave numerous balls. On the thirteenth and fourteenth of January 1817 Mrs. Bagot wrote out "cards of invitation for a ball." On the eighteenth she was busy "all morning in chalking the floor for the ball." The next two days she and the servants worked "hard in decorating the passage with pink Calico & bunches of Rose thistle & Sham-rock [?] & evergreen to turn it into supper room." To help the staff "the gentlemen dined at Baker's," but Mary Bagot reported eating "a mouthful in my bedroom to be in the way." The guests began to arrive about seven "& Kept it up until between 12 & one—All went off beautifully & the ball was a very handsome one." The following week she reported giving her second ball.[40] Months later, in spite of the heat of early September, "all hands [were] at work decorating the housekeepers room with leaves &c where the supper was to be." This time everyone "dined at Bakers & came home to dress." The guests "danced & kept it up as if it had been Christmas." The hostess was "tired to death."[41]

The following fall Harrison Gray Otis described yet another "brilliant and well conducted" ball hosted by the Bagots. He made no explicit derogatory comments about his fellow guests except to tell his wife that in addition to all her acquaintances were some "that you never saw and never Shall." Two downstairs rooms in the main house were set aside for dancing: "The floor of one . . . was handsomely ornamented by a circle chalkd with white crayons, in the centre whereof was the armorial shield of Great Britain with the motto of Honi Soit, and on different parts of the circumference were drawn the Prince Regents crest & other ornaments which were scuffled over before my entrance. The floor of the other dancing room was chalked with a corresponding circle, containing the arms of the US, and similar decorations." For those who did not dance "the back buildings were occupied by cards." Supper was in the main house on the second floor. Otis had the pleasure of taking Mrs. Bagot to supper. "She expressed a fear in going up stairs lest they should give way," but the house supported the large crowd. Otis told his hostess he was "collecting material for a description" for his wife. He wrote,

On coming to the Top of the stairs, the eye was met by a display of showy ornaments at the extremity of the great entry placed on tables forming a sort of triple sideboard, the upper platform of which was decorated with plate and flowers and the lower one contained some very richly embellished dishes—The whole producing something like the effect of a handsome Roman Catholic altar—From this altar to the head of the stairs was laid one table protected from the wind and cold air by a curtain let down from the wall—Passing this table on each side you diverged into the two great chambers in which also tables were laid and covered with a most Splendid variety of entremets, confectionary, porcelain and plate or plated ware—Probably some of both.[42]

Some months later the Bagots' "accomplished Cook," who was responsible for these elegant refreshments, got into trouble. He "had become the dormant partner of a Restaurateur." Bagot, "believing that the stock of the firm was furnished from his kitchen dismissed him" and sent to Philadelphia for a replacement. When two showed up by mistake, he organized a competition. Otis, who attended the first dinner thought it "tolerably well got up. . . . But Bagot being official censor, has damned the whole play, says it was a tavern dinner, and the other candidate goes upon the gridiron, this day." In later letters Otis failed to report the outcome.[43]

Privately, Mary Bagot found most American entertainments boring, but she could also turn critical opinion on herself. One of her own affairs she pronounced "very dull."[44] However, she limited expression of her critical judgments to her private correspondence. There is no question that she took her role as hostess very seriously and worked hard to provide frequent, glittering events for Washington society. She and her husband were well rewarded.

Shortly after Bagot announced he would be leaving the capital, the couple received an invitation from "the managers in behalf of the citizens of Washington and its vicinity and others," who wished to offer them "some testimony of their personal respect and regard." The occasion went down in the lore of the city as "the great Bagot ball." Although the managers carefully avoided any official connotations and organized the event only as a public expression of personal respect, Bagot considered a political message lurked in the "alteration in the feelings of this country towards that black sheep, the English Minister." Louisa Catherine Adams drew similar conclusions from the "many good observations and good wishes" inspired by the table decorations, "small Frigates bearing the American and English Flag united." The ballroom was decorated with the Bagots' names "written in transparency." When it was all over, Mrs. Bagot, who opened the ball with "Yankee Doodle" and would only dance with Americans, exclaimed in her diary, "Our Ball! & never did any thing go off as well. Never were individuals so feted. Never were there such a flattering testimony from a whole nation."[45] A foreign minister's generosity and style of entertaining certainly could help win the regard of a nation's leading citizens and officials.

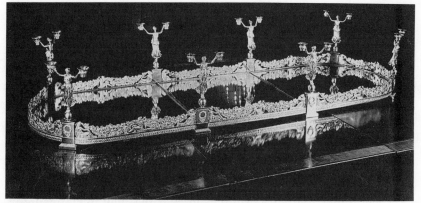

Plateau attributed to Deniére et Matelin, gilded bronze and mirror glass, ca. 1817 (White House Collection). Made either of solid precious metals or plated materials to convey wealth and mirrored to enhance their display purposes, plateaux were showy table centerpieces owned only by the very rich.

The American way

The particular flavor of fashionable Washington society derived from differences in styles of entertaining and dining—from boardinghouse "decent" to the grand displays of foreign ministers—and from a general awareness that Americans were inventing traditions for a new city, a new nation, and a new kind of social order. Both the presidents and the secretaries of state entertained in an official capacity, and their actions were much commented upon by visitors to the new capital.

The functions hosted by the secretaries of state and their wives carried some of the messages of the new government, but they were essentially private affairs, always preceded by the prescribed etiquette for visiting and formal invitations. The secretary of state took principal responsibility for entertaining foreign ministers, at both dinners and evening parties.

At dinners the composition of guest lists and menus varied widely according to the personal tastes, entertaining spaces, and pocketbooks of successive secretaries. James and especially Dolley Madison were warm and generous; James and Elizabeth Monroe and John Quincy and Louisa Catherine Adams were stiffer but perhaps more elegant or more closely attuned to foreign style. As might be expected Europeans and Americans, depending upon their previous

151

experiences, had different opinions about these official dinners. For example, in April 1816, shortly after their arrival in the capital, British Minister Charles Bagot and his wife, Mary, dined at Secretary of State Monroe's house. Mrs. Bagot called it "the dullest dinner I ever was at," saying, "Mrs. Monroe gives herself the airs of a fine lady without succeeding in being one & he was so reserved, shy & silent that he never spoke a sentence to any one." She seemed surprised, because she knew her hosts had social experience in France.[46] On the other hand, Mary Crowninshield, from Salem, Massachusetts, wrote that at the Monroes' she and her husband had "the most stylish dinner I have been at. The table wider than we have, and in the middle a large, perhaps silver, waiter, with images like some Aunt Silsbee has, only more of them, and vases filled with flowers, which made a very showy appearance as the candles were lighted when we went to table. The dishes were silver and set round this waiter. The plates were handsome china, the forks silver, and so heavy I could hardly lift them to my mouth, dessert knives silver, and spoons very heavy—you would call them clumsy things."[47]

Tureen by Jacques Henri Fauconnier, silver, ca. 1817; wine cooler by Jean Baptiste Claude Odiot, silver, 1798–1809 (both, White House Collection). The French furnishings with which the Monroes furnished the President's House in 1817 dazzled visitors. When Congressman Louis McLane attended a drawing room in 1818, he was much impressed and wrote his wife that the "taste & splendour of Europe have contributed to decorate and enrich these rooms: and have given them a splendour which is really astonishing."

According to the author of *A Description of the Etiquette at Washington City*, "The parties of the secretary of state, differ from the president's levees, in three particulars, viz: that he invites his guest[s], and dancing, and card playing, make the principal part of the amusement, at his parties: neither of which is usually done, at the president's levees."[48] When Catharine Mitchill, newly arrived in Washington in 1806, wrote about her first party at Secretary of State Madison's, she saw "nothing very different . . . from our evening parties in N. York." The ladies "were seated round the room gayly attired & making a brilliant appearance" and presumably not saying very much. The gentlemen "were standing up walking about, chatting, and amusing themselves." After tea some began to play "that studious and scientific game," chess. Others played cards, "picking each others pockets in this genteel manner." Those who didn't play games walked around, chatted, and ate "the good things handed around such as ice cream, Cordials, Punch, jelly, Cake, and fruit of all kinds." Carried around in small baskets with raisins and almonds was something so novel that Mrs. Mitchill took one and mailed it with her letter. "Small pieces of candied sugar" were wrapped up in white paper printed with verses. Before the guests departed "a dish of chocolate came in last."[49]

Other heads of departments also hosted grand parties. Juliana Seaton attended a brilliant ball given by Albert Gallatin, secretary of the treasury, and his wife in December 1812. She was sure "not ten minutes elapsed without refreshments being handed. 1st, coffee, tea, all kinds of toasts and warm cakes; 2n, ice-creams; 3d, lemonade, punch, burgundy, claret, curacoa, champagne; 4th, bonbons, cakes of all sorts and sizes; 5th, apples, oranges; 6th, confectionery, denomination *divers*; 7th, nuts, almonds, raisins; 8th, set supper, composed of tempting solid dishes, meats, savory pasties garnished with lemon; 9th, drinkables of every species; 10th, boiling chocolate." No wonder she added, "The most profuse ball ever given in Washington."[50]

When John Quincy Adams was secretary of state, he and Louisa Catherine Adams gave many successful parties. They also had some significant failures. Harrison Gray Otis pronounced one in 1818 as not worth three dollars hack fare.[51] The following year, he was only a little more sympathetic about a dismal evening tea attended by "*few*

The President of the United States, &
requests the Pleasure of Mr & Mrs Bailys
Company to Dine, on Thursday next,
at 4 o'Clock.
Jan 1. 1801
An answer is requested.

President's House invitation, printed document completed in manuscript, 1 January
1801 (White House Collection). This invitation records the first dinner given by the
Adamses in the unfinished President's House on New Year's Day, 1801. Some months
later, Margaret Bayard Smith reported that the President entertained regularly and had
"company every day, but his table is seldom laid for more than twelve."

ladies."[52] Generally, however, people were pleased to attend parties
given by the secretary of state. Wrote Cooley, the Washington social
arbiter, "As it requires an invitation to be at the secretary of state's
party, it is thought by many to be more honourable to be one of his
guests, than to be at the president's levee. . . ."[53]

Perhaps the social honor was greater at the secretary of state's, but
the openness of presidential receptions clarified the distinction between high society and official society. No matter what criteria applied to the former, the president had an obligation to the American
people to extend official hospitality more broadly. By 1829 manners
associated with two types of presidential events—New Year's Day
receptions and levees—were sufficiently important to enough people
to be detailed in *A Description of the Etiquette at Washington City.*
Successive presidents sometimes fumbled as they experimented with
George Washington's carefully considered model for entertaining in
a democratic republic. Bureaucrats and elected representatives of the
American public brought to the capital diverse ideas of who should
rule politically and who should mix socially, and they did not always

agree about matters of protocol or levels of luxury. However, they understood that immediate political gains could follow from social encounters and that citizens and representatives of foreign powers attached symbolic significance to the style of parties hosted by officials. Samuel Mitchill contrasted James Madison's chances for election to the presidency with those of his opponent, George Clinton: "The former gives dinners and makes generous displays to the members. The latter lives snug at his lodgings, and keeps aloof from such captivating exhibitions. The Secretary of State has a wife to aid his pretensions. The Vice-President has nothing of female succor on his side."[54]

Changes that occurred in the first three decades of official entertaining in Washington to some extent resulted from the varied personal circumstances and preferences of the presidents. Their entertaining styles also expressed the different political positions of these men. Federalists tended toward greater formality than Jeffersonian republicans or Jacksonian democrats, whose ascendancy marks the end of the period. As the city grew and the number of people involved in the government expanded, highly personalized procedures simply took too much time and some alterations in social practice were inevitable.

The custom of paying the compliments of the season to the president and his family between noon and three o'clock on New Year's Day was an exception that changed very little during these years. The squeeze became tighter and women more mobile, but otherwise the tradition was maintained. In 1802 Samuel Mitchill arrived late for the "great parade" of members of Congress, heads of departments, foreign ministers, and the distinguished citizens and strangers of the city. Thomas Jefferson stood in the withdrawing room "to salute and converse with visitors. The male part of them walked about or made groups for conversation, while the ladies received the bows and adorations of the gentlemen." Mitchill went on to note that "several belles from Virginia and elsewhere were brought out on this gala day."[55] When Manasseh Cutler went to the 1804 reception he observed that wine, punch in silver urns, and cake were served. The next year he added the terse note "mammoth cheese" to the refreshment list.[56]

In 1809 Catharine Mitchill expanded at length on her husband's earlier description. After commenting on the crowd ("Very few attempted to sit down, for if they had they could not have found room") and the formal exchange of "congratulations of the day" with the President, she expressed pleasure with the liberal refreshments—wine, punch, cake, and ice cream—that were set out on sideboards and handed around. She and her husband amused themselves "by walking about from room to room," listening to a band that "played at intervals martial, patriotic, & enlivening airs which reverberated through the spacious dome," and "chatting with our old acquaintances and forming new ones." They also looked at the "Indian natives," mainly men and women of the Delaware and Cherokee tribes: "The faces of these Savages were painted a bright vermillion colour, their heads ornamented with feathers, and their ears & noses adorned with rings."[57] In later years nothing changed except the man in office. Each year "at three it was all over and done."[58] Similar receptions were held on the Fourth of July, but they were not so heavily attended. In summer Congress was not in session, and many of the "fashionables" had fled to cooler places.

These two annual receptions were not entertaining burdens, but other demands on the president's hospitality were more frequent and troublesome. When he served in the position, George Washington reasoned through the problems and set the precedent for presdential entertaining. Difficulties arose from the fact that "gentlemen, consulting their own convenience rather than mine, were calling from the time I rose from breakfast—often before—until I sat down to dinner. . . . To please everybody was impossible—I therefore adopted that line of conduct which combined public advantage with private convenience. . . ."[59] Washington decided to decline all personal invitations and to receive visitors on three different weekly occasions. At his residences in New York and later in Philadelphia he invited guests, mostly members of Congress and their families, to dinner. On Tuesday afternoons between three and four o'clock he held formal levees for men only. No refreshments were served.

On Friday evenings Mrs. Washington gave less formal public levees. Abigail Adams described Mrs. Washington's introduction of a "Levey day" in New York in August 1789. The general public was informed that no special invitation was necessary. The only criteria for admission were adequate clothing and the rudiments of polite behavior. At the time both were sufficiently exacting to assure self-selection of the company. The time was eight o'clock every Friday evening. Servants announced each arrival. Ladies were received by Col. Humphries or Mr. Lear, who escorted them to Mrs. Washington to whom they made "a most Respectfull courtsey and then [were] seated without noticeing any of the rest of the company."[60] For these events Lear had ordered "plated waiters, suitable for carrying tea round to company."[61] There was conversation and music, but no card-playing or dancing. John and Abigail Adams followed these procedures.[62]

When the capital moved to Washington the practice of presidents' ladies giving "levees or drawing rooms" briefly dropped from the official calendar. Jefferson may have eliminated evening receptions because he disliked them, but possibly he did so because he was a widower and these evening events were so clearly associated with the wife of the president. Instead, Jefferson gave many more dinner parties, for which he personally wrote cards of invitation. For what he intended to be relaxed occasions, he did not think rules of precedence were necessary. Only after Mrs. Merry, wife of the British minis-

The White House by unknown artist, engraving, ca. 1840 (Library of Congress). The Washington social season revolved around the residence of Congress, which usually began in the late fall or early winter and ended in the spring. The President's House, as it was known, was the center of social life. Before the Madison administration, public attendance at presidential events was limited to New Year's and Fourth of July receptions. Visiting Jefferson on January 1, 1804, Louisa Catherine Adams was displeased to find her fellow guests "an unruly crowd of indiscriminate persons from every Class."

ter, took offense when treated like everyone else did he issue a statement describing "pell-mell" or "pele-mele" etiquette. Guests then were forewarned that notions of hierarchy did not apply at the President's table.[63]

Without doubt, of all the presidents Thomas Jefferson provided the best fare and the finest wine. Samuel Mitchill noted that Jefferson did not restrict his dinners to a single evening a week. He generally had "a company of eight or ten persons to dine with him every day." The meals were "neat and plentiful." No healths were drunk, instead "you drink as you please, and converse at your ease."[64] But even someone with Jefferson's skill could find rough traveling on the social road. Because he had ignored some friends of several Federalists he had invited to dinner, they refused his invitation and Jefferson had to ask some gentlemen from Georgetown as substitutes. Conversation at this dinner was difficult until Manasseh Cutler opened the subjects of French travel and food, which he "well knew the President always delighted to talk about." Only after the ice cream was served and "the wine began to pass round the table a little more freely" did the others relax and converse pleasantly.[65]

When Catharine Mitchill went to a White House dinner in April 1806, she was one of five women in the company of about fifteen men. The food was plentiful, well cooked, and elegantly served without "a profusion of Dishes on the table." Vegetables were presented in covered silver basons or dishes; the rest of the food was on china dishes. Like many of Jefferson's guests, she marveled at the baked ice cream "inclosed in a cover of warm paste, which gave it the appearance of having been just taken from the oven." She was disappointed that she could only manage to taste half the "many nick nacks on the table." She observed that after the second course the cloth was removed, and "the third course consisted of dried fruit of all kinds, Oranges and Olives." There was no awkwardness on this occasion. Everyone "appear'd perfectly at their ease, and conversed with as much freedom as they would have done at their own houses."[66] After Jefferson left office, his daily dinner parties became a thing of the past, and evening receptions were resumed.

The Madisons scheduled evening parties semi-weekly. The procedures that governed the levees of Washington and Adams were relaxed somewhat, and the name of the event changed. The "drawing

Dolley Madison (1768–1849) by Bass Otis, oil on canvas, ca. 1817 (courtesy, The New-York Historical Society, New York City). First Lady Dolley Madison opened her White House drawing rooms to politicians, Washington residents, and the visiting public, and the weekly events always drew great crowds. Often a tough critic of social behavior, Louisa Catherine Adams admired Mrs. Madison for pulling off "a most difficult performance" and proclaimed the First Lady "universally popular for the amenity of her manners and the suavity of her temper."

room" replaced the "levee." Announcements appeared in the news-paper, and as in earlier administrations anyone who was decently dressed was welcome. Someone well acquainted with Washington society must have explained the history and significance of these evenings to Alexander Dick, a newly arrived minor British official, who attended a levee in 1809:

Mr Jefferson had no Wife & had no Ladies parties, nor indeed public Levees except on the 1st of Jany & 4 July—Mrs. Madison the Lady of the present president announced last

159

Wedy for the first time that She wd See her friends in the Evg & she is to have a public day Weekly of this kind—We went this Evening & found a Crowd of Ladies & Gentlemen Walking thro the Apartments which were all thrown open & a band of Military Music playing—Dancing & Cards have never been permitted in the Presidents Palace, but tea Coffee, Ice Cream Cakes & refreshments were handed round which was all the entertainment, but in a place like Washington where there are Scarcely any public places at all, Such a Meeting Seems to be much relished, & then there is the honor of Seeing the President & his Lady—[and] other public characters.[67]

A substantial number of descriptions confirm Dick's general outline and amplify the details of procedures. Mary Bagot, wife of the British ambassador, described one of Mrs. Madison's evening parties, "here called her *Levee*," in detail: "The women usually sit stuck

Cup and saucer by Etienne Jean Louis Blancheron, porcelain with gilt decoration, late eighteenth century (White House Collection). France set the standards for fashionable taste in early nineteenth century America. The Madisons owned French furniture, silver, and porcelains, including this set manufactured by the famous company of Sèvres which they purchased in 1803 from James Monroe (in Paris to negotiate the Louisiana Purchase) for family use.

round the room close to the wall. The men—many of whom come in boots & perfectly undone & with dirty hands & dirty linen—stand mostly talking with each other in the middle of the rooms. Tea & coffee & afterwards cold punch with glasses of Madiera & cakes are handed round & by ten o'clock everyone is dispersed."[68]

A few years earlier, in 1811, Catharine Mitchill recorded meeting Washington Irving, "one of the literati and wits of New York," at a presidential drawing room. The setting and entertainment impressed him, but mostly he was aware of the contrast between the elegant reception rooms and the dirty stagecoach and muddy roads he had just left. Even though he knew previous introductions and visits were not essential for attendance at the levee, he was worried about how he would be received and relieved when he was made to feel welcome.[69]

Those in the know seem to have accepted responsibility for new arrivals willingly. One New York couple dredged up a memory of old acquaintance with Samuel Mitchill, and although they had never met Mrs. Mitchill, they appealed to her for social assistance. Politeness forbade her refusing to accompany them to the drawing room, and they went together. The pair "came away well pleased with the entertainment, and particularly so with Mrs. Madison."[70] Catharine Mitchill's generosity confirms the wisdom of the advice Cooley gave in *A Description of the Etiquette at Washington City*—it was acceptable to be decently aggressive about seeking social opportunities.

In 1816 Margaret Bayard Smith initiated an inexperienced guest in the ways of a presidential drawing room or levee. First, she insisted that he replace his boots with newly purchased shoes. After their arrival at the White House, she showed him "how to take my hand and lead me in &c." She admitted feeling awkward when led across the room to "the place where sat Mrs. Madison, Mrs. Monroe, Mrs. Decatur and a dozen other ladies in a formidable row." Because there was no room for her to sit, she was grateful when some of the ladies graciously "rose to talk with us."[71] William Wirt, in Washington in 1815 two years before he became attorney general, wrote to his wife that he would attend one of Mrs. Madison's drawing rooms, "it is a show and I get it without paying for it. . . ." He must have forgotten that he was a taxpayer and the show of a presidential drawing room was his very own.[72]

The timing had been good for a woman of Dolley Madison's social skill. Official and fashionable society in Washington was still small enough for her personal touch to work its magic, and her era was long remembered for its warmth and hospitality. After James Monroe was elected, another word went out, "People seem to think we shall have great changes in social intercourse and customs."[73]

They were right. Mrs. Monroe, pleading poor health, did not follow in Mrs. Madison's social steps and confer honor on new arrivals by paying the first visit. In fact, she refused to visit at all. Her daughter returned visits paid to her mother and assured the ladies of Washington that Mrs. Monroe would be happy to see her friends morning or evening. Juliana Seaton thought because all were treated alike the new procedure would "eventually go down." However, she commented, the "alteration in the old *regime* was bitter to the palates of all our citizens, especially so to foreign ministers and strangers."[74]

Goblet, 1790–1810 (courtesy, Winterthur). This glass originally belonged to the members of the Lee family of Virginia. Support for the new federal government was expressed through objects that displayed such symbols of national identity as the shield of the United States.

162

Secretary of State John Quincy Adams was forced to turn his attention to the matter in a letter dated 25 December 1819. It was addressed to the President and was widely published at the time. He followed Washington's lead and stated that to visit some would be offensive, to visit all would be impossible. "These visits of ceremony would not only be a very useless waste of time," he explained, "but incompatible with the discharge of the real and important duties of the departments." Furthermore, they were not "congenial to the Republican simplicity of our institutions."[75] Mrs. Seaton's prediction of public acceptance of the policy eventually proved correct, but two years passed before irritated citizens, especially the ladies of high society, were mollified.

Personally the Monroes and the Adamses may have preferred to reduce their contacts with the general citizenry. Their actions also reflect a practical response to the expansion of government and the growth of Washington's population. By 1829 the two antechambers and three large reception rooms might become so full at presidential receptions that Cooley in *A Description of the Etiquette at Washington City* advised guests to take food and drink "when an opportunity offers, which, at some of the fullest levees, may not happen very often; not because there is any scarcity of refreshment, but [because of] the difficulty the waiters find in making their way through the crowd with their large trays." Cooley's tone and choice of words suggest he had reservations about the entertainment value but not about the importance of attending a levee. Because there was "commonly no other amusement but conversation," strangers to the city were spectators whose only inducement for going to a levee was "the novelty, or the presumed honour of being one of a party, of the highest order in the United States."[76]

"I think it is highly important," wrote Cooley, "for all citizens of the United States, who possess the means, to visit the capital of their country at least once in their life time."[77] Not only citizens, but foreigners and fictional characters, took his advice and made their pilgrimages to the nation's new city of contrasts, where urban areas alternated with open country and development with wilderness. From many perspectives these visitors took pleasure in the public buildings, political displays, and social scenes. Their visions were colored by their different origins—inherited gentility, new boarding school sophistication, or backwoods naiveté. Some voiced concern that overspending on architecture, furnishings, table settings, and food was the road to ruin. Others expressed pride in place and in the personal achievements through which they had earned the opportunity to see the sights. Some wrote letters home, others published travel accounts, guidebooks, etiquette manuals, and novels. The excitement of the new city rippled far beyond the shores of the Potomac.

The Octagon was a place of "high society" in the new national capital. The house was planned to accommodate a large family and staff and an active urban social life. The family circle expanded when intimates came for friendly visits, acquaintances paid formal calls, and invited guests attended special events. Apparently John and Ann Tayloe selected their company along traditional lines and did not confuse members of their social circle with those bearing only political credentials. Although details about dinners, teas, balls with suppers, and picnics are lacking, the Tayloes are known to have entertained frequently and in fine style.

If the Tayloes chose to notice, they could have encountered the diverse peoples of the city within the immediate environs of the Octagon—slaves downstairs and in the outbuildings, workers in their hovels or modest houses, friends in lodgings or fashionable townhouses, and the president in the people's palace. They knew they were wealthy and privileged. Probably they were only half conscious of the efforts and skills of the growers, vendors, cooks, confectioners, scullery servants, and waiters who supplied their table with meals and refreshments.

Large squeezy parties and elegant dinners were the fashion, but those with discrimination and experience recognized that routs and drawing rooms alone could not provide long-lasting personal satisfaction. Although Margaret Bayard Smith believed that "we are social beings, and the strongest mind and warmest heart need the stimulus of society," she did not mean "the society of the gay world." In her opinion, such society "chills the affections, checks the aspirations of the soul, and dissipates the mind."[78] Harrison Gray Otis agreed. "At the Same time that my interest in what is called Company is almost amulated," he wrote to his wife, "I find the excitement of the Society of those I dearly love becomes more essential to the comfort of my existance."[79] Otis felt the amulet of family and friends protected him against fashionable and false attractions.

Ever perceptive about people and their relationships, Otis was a welcome guest and a good host. Although in Washington on and off over many years, he seems not to have noticed changes. "There is a Sameness in these scenes after awhile that is insufferably flat," he observed. "The same folks doing the Same things."[80] From other points of view the picture hardly appears static. Material life and social behavior developed dramatically in a number of directions in the course of thirty years. Traditional and innovative patterns of furnishings, styles of living, and customs of meal-taking mingled in complex ways. They embodied people's indifference or ambition and their opportunity or inability to alter their circumstances. The transformations in women's behavior stand out most sharply.

In Washington ladies played new roles in general society. While their domestic responsibilities and demeanor at dinner parties may have remained traditional, active participation in rounds of visiting and party-going expanded their lives beyond the family circle and gave them new opportunities to display musical talent, compete at games, and engage in conversation. Mrs. Smith, who restricted her comments to evening parties, was convinced that manners in Washington were "different from those in other places." With so many people crowded into entertaining rooms, women as well as men stood. As a consequence they enjoyed "more ease, freedom and equality" than was possible where "ladies sit and wait for gentlemen to approach to converse."[81] Perhaps she was well-informed, and her assertion is accurate. Mrs. Smith expressed considerable pleasure with the social power women wielded in the case of Peggy Eaton. By and large, though, ladies did not often dent the barriers around the male world of Washington politics.

Whether gender relationships were slowly changing in similar ways among other classes of the Washington social order is not known. There is little information about lower class life, whether male or female, free or slave. Changes affecting most classes, including those just above the bottom, can only be inferred from information about the ownership of goods and descriptions of the ways ordinary people used them. Over the long term in Washington and throughout the Chesapeake region a widespread and growing inter-

BASE AND SUPER-STRUCTURE

est in tableware made genteel practice at mealtimes possible for family members at many levels of society. As late as the 1820s, however, dinners and large tea parties for invited guests remained beyond the reach of all but a privileged few.

Etiquette manuals and novels of social realism set in Washington specifically described fashionable furnishings and discussed their use. Their authors dictated the do's and don'ts of genteel behavior at home, boardinghouses, private parties, and presidential drawing rooms, or they told stories about the predicaments and mistakes of the uninitiated. Several writers expressly stated a desire to help social climbers learn the rudiments of polite behavior and master the nuances of gentility. Those in "the first circle" no doubt sometimes read these humorous accounts to laugh at others. For the larger audiences for whom the lessons were intended, these important books opened doors on the worlds to which they aspired.

The American political experiment held irresistible promise of social reform, and the capital city seemed to be a place where these changes were already coming to pass. New possessions and new social skills encouraged ordinary men and women to hope for early and easy success. The knowledge and ability to use little things like forks and champagne glasses boosted their confidence and spurred on their ambitions to climb another rung or two up the social ladder. People on the make could always be decently aggressive in Washington society. Perhaps the same forwardness was possible elsewhere, but no other city offered residents or visitors such easy access to official "drawing rooms." Washington was the one and only city where any properly dressed man or woman could enter the grandest and most famous house in the nation, walk through its elegantly furnished reception rooms, and sip lemonade and eat cake and ice cream with distinguished personages. Fashionable hobnobbing made people feel good about themselves and optimistic about their country. A place where the president's house was the people's house and where political circles shaded into social circles was a place of dreams for a people who were happy to believe that "true republicanism" ensured "that every man shall have an equal chance—that every man shall be free to become as unequal as he can."[82]

166

Notes

Spelling and punctuation used in all quotations follow the source cited, whether it is manuscript or printed material.

To simplify the text of the notes, primary source collections that appear frequently have been abbreviated as follows:

Adams Papers—Adams Family Papers, Massachusetts Historical Society, Boston; microfilm edition, Manuscript Division, Library of Congress.

Dick Papers—Papers of Alexander Dick, Alderman Library, University of Virginia, Charlottesville.

Inventory—Record group 21, U.S. District Court for the District of Columbia, Entry 119, Inventories and Sales, Suitland Reference Branch, National Archives and Records Administration, Washington, D.C. The volumes are J.H.B./H.C.N. 1 (7/1/1818–4/20/1821), H.C.N. 1 (7/27/1805–11/2/1823), and H.C.N. 2 (11/23/1823–5/30/1826).

Jefferson Papers—Thomas Jefferson Papers, Henry Huntington Library, San Marino, California; microfilm edition and photostat copies, Manuscript Division, Library of Congress.

Latrobe Papers—Latrobe Papers, Maryland Historical Society, Baltimore; microfilm edition.

McLane Papers—Papers of Louis McLane, 1795–1894, Manuscript Division, Library of Congress.

Mitchill Papers—Catharine Mitchill Papers, Manuscript Division, Library of Congress.

Otis Papers—Harrison Gray Otis Papers, Massachusetts Historical Society, Boston; microfilm edition, Manuscript Division, Library of Congress.

Tayloe Papers—Tayloe Family Papers, Virginia Historical Society, Richmond.

Thornton Papers—Anna Maria Thornton Papers, Manuscript Division, Library of Congress.

Wirt Papers—William Wirt Papers, Maryland Historical Society, Baltimore; microfilm edition, Manuscript Division, Library of Congress.

Introduction

1. *Letters of Mary Boardman Crowninshield, 1815–1816*, ed. Francis Boardman Crowninshield (Cambridge: Riverside Press, 1905), p. 20.

2. Diary of Mrs. Anna Maria Thornton, entries for 23 February and 24 March 1803, once between January and April 1804, January 1807, Thornton Papers.

3. Harrison Gray Otis to Sally Foster Otis, 1 February 1801, Otis Papers.

4. Margaret Bayard Smith, *The First Forty Years of Washington Society, portrayed by the family letters of Mrs. Samuel Harrison Smith*, ed. Gaillard Hunt (New York: Charles Scribner's Sons, 1906), p. 275.

5. Others are beginning to work in this time period. I am grateful to Lorena S. Walsh for sharing with me her unpublished survey of current literature, "Consumer Behavior, Diet, and the Standard of Living in Late Colonial and Early Antebellum America, 1770–1840" (1990). The following works, which are not cited elsewhere in the notes, have helped shape the discussion of food, objects, mealtimes, and behavior: Mary Douglas, "Deciphering a Meal," *Daedalus* 101 (Winter 1972), pp. 61–81; Robert Forster and Orest Ranum, eds., *Food and Drink in History, Selections from the Annales* (Baltimore: The Johns Hopkins University Press, 1979); Peter Farb and George Armelagos, *Consuming Passions: The Anthropology of Eating* (Boston: Houghton Mifflin, 1987); and Joseph R. Gusfield, "Passage & play: rituals of drinking time in American society," in Mary Douglas, ed., *Constructive Drinking: Perspectives on Drink from Anthropology* (Cambridge: Cambridge University Press, 1987).

Chapter I

1. Diary of Louisa Catherine Adams, 11 May 1820, Adams Papers. At a picnic at the falls in 1816 Mary Bagot and her party "dined on boards laid upon the rocks." David Hosford, "Exile in Yankeeland: The Journal of Mary Bagot, 1816–1819," *Records of the Columbia Historical Society* 51 (1984), p. 37.

2. Diary of Gouverneur Morris, vol. 2, pp. 394–95, quoted in James Sterling Young, *The Washington Community, 1800–1828* (New York: Harcourt Brace Jovanovich, 1966), p. 260.

3. Abigail Adams, *Letters of Mrs. Adams, the Wife of John Adams*, vol. 2 (Boston: Charles C. Little and James Brown, 1840), p. 240.

4. Louisa Catherine Adams, miscellany, 15 February 1819, Adams Papers. On January 24, 1801, Harrison Gray Otis wrote to Sally Foster Otis (Otis Papers) about two evenings out. On the first he left his horse in a clay pit, and on the second his carriage broke down. Margaret Bayard Smith and many others commented on transportation difficulties.

5. Young, pp. 1–10.

6. Kenneth R. Bowling, *Creating the Federal City, 1774–1800: Potomac Fever* (Washington: The AIA Press, 1988). See also Frederick Gutheim and Wilcomb E. Washburn, *The Federal City: Plans and Realities* (Washington: Smithsonian Institution Press, 1976), pp. 2–18 and 75–80; Constance McLaughlin Green, *Washington: A History of the Capital, 1800–1950*, vol. 1 (Princeton, N.J.: Princeton University Press, 1962), pp. 3–20; and Young, *Washington Community*.

7. Henry Bradshaw Fearon, *Sketches of America* (1818; reprint, New York: Benjamin Blom, Inc., 1969), p. 286.

8. *Look Before You Leap: or, a few hints to such Artizans, Mechanics, Labourers, Farmers and Husbandmen, as are desirous of emigrating to America, being a genuine Collection of Letters, from persons who have emigrated; . . . particularly to The federal city of Washington* (London: 1796), p. xiii.

9. Ibid., p. xx.

10. Kathryn Allamong Jacob, *High Society in Washington During the Gilded Age: Three Distinct Aristocracies* (Ph.D. dissertation, The Johns Hopkins University, 1986), p. 8.

11. Young, p. 26.

12. "The Sessford Annals," *Records of the Columbia Historical Society* 11 (1908), p. 273.

13. Jacob, p. 8.

14. *Look Before You Leap*, p. 91.

15. For a discussion of modest housing, see Orlando Ridout V, *Building the Octagon* (Washington: The AIA Press, 1989), pp. 31–33. In 1803 British Minister Anthony Merry "secured two small houses on the Common" that were mere shells "with bare walls and with fixtures of no kind, even without a pump or well, all of which I must provide at my own cost." One of his successors in the early years of the Madison administration lived in the same house and reported it consisted of "two common three-windowed houses, built together, and with communications opened between them." Beckles Willson, *Friendly Relations: A Narrative of Britain's Ministers and Ambassadors to America, 1791–1830* (1934; reprint, Freeport, N.Y.: Books for Libraries Press, 1969), pp. 49 and 67.

16. "Sessford Annals," p. 273.

17. James Fenimore Cooper, *Notions of the Americans*, vol. 2 (Philadelphia: Carey, Lea & Carey, 1828), p. 20, quoted in Young, p. 71.

18. Young, fig. 3.

19. Harrison Gray Otis to Sally Foster Otis, 25 November 1818, Otis Papers.

20. Samuel Eliot Morison, "Charles Bagot's Notes on Housekeeping and Entertaining at Washington, 1819," *Publications of the Colonial Society of Massachusetts* XXVI (1927), p. 441. Louisa Catherine Adams worried about the small size of her rooms until she opened her new room at a large party, "It opens from the Drawing room . . . , and is twenty eight by 29 feet in size. . . . the addition to my house contains two of these halls two back rooms and six chambers with Kitchen &c—It is so planned as to make a separate house whenever we are inclined to rent it." Diary of Louisa Catherine Adams, 7 and 23 January 1821, Adams Papers.

21. James Kirke Paulding to Henry Breevoort, Jr., New York, 1 December 1815, Paulding Letters, The New-York Historical Society. President Madison appointed Paul-

ding secretary of the newly created Board of Navy Commissioners, and he lived in Washington from 1815 to 1823.

22. Of a total population of 33,039, 4,214 lived in the "residue" of Washington and Alexandria counties in 1820. "Sessford Annals," p. 273. Existing farmhouses were integrated into the Washington urban landscape. See Christian Hines, *Early Recollections of Washington City* (1866; reprint, Washington: Junior League of Washington, 1981), pp. 31–32.

23. Hines, p. 75; and Wilhelmus Bogart Bryan, *A History of the National Capital*, vol. 1 (New York: The Macmillan Co., 1914), pp. 486–89.

24. Fearon, p. 287.

25. Harrison Gray Otis to Sally Foster Otis, 5 January 1819, Otis Papers.

26. Inventory of John Krause, 3 October 1820, vol. J.H.B./H.C.N. 1, pp. 412–14.

27. Margaret Bayard Smith, *A Winter in Washington, or Memoirs of the Seymour Family*, vol. 1 (New York: E. Bliss and E. White, 1824), p. 278.

28. Household account book kept by Etienne Lemaire, 12 December 1806–1809, Jefferson Papers.

29. [Charles William Day], *Etiquette: or, a guide to the usages of society with a glance at bad habits . . . by Count Alfred D'Orsay* (New York: Wilson & Co., 1843), p. 26.

30. E. Cooley, M.D., *A Description of the Etiquette at Washington City, Exhibiting the Habits and Customs that prevail in the intercourse of the most distinguished and fashionable Society at that place, during the session of Congress* (Philadelphia: L. B. Clarke, 1829), p. 14.

31. Cooley, pp. 56–57 and 71–72. See also William Parker Cutler and Julia Perkins Cutler, *Life Journals and Correspondence of Rev. Manasseh Cutler, LL.D.* (Reprint, Athens, Ohio: Ohio University Press, 1987), pp. 50 and 60.

32. *Letters of Mary Boardman Crowninshield, 1815–1816*, ed. Francis Boardman Crowninshield (Cambridge: Riverside Press, 1905), p. 45.

33. Jacob, p. 21.

34. See, for example, the correspondence between Harrison Gray Otis and his wife, Sally, Otis Papers, and Albert and Hannah Gallatin, Albert Gallatin Papers, The New-York Historical Society.

35. James Kirke Paulding to Henry Breevoort, Jr., 25 September 1815, Paulding Letters.

36. Louisa Catherine Adams, "The Adventures of Nobody," 1805 [memoirs begun 1840], Adams Papers.

37. Frances Trollope, *Domestic Manners of the Americans* (London: Whittaker, Treacher & Co., 1832), p. 192.

38. Margaret Bayard Smith, *The First Forty Years of Washington Society, portrayed by the family letters of Mrs. Samuel Harrison Smith*, ed. Gaillard Hunt (New York: Charles Scribner's Sons, 1906), p. 312. This is supported by Harrison Gray Otis, "The country ladies who are present for the first time Squeezed into their new dresses." Otis to Sophia Otis, 15 December 1818, Otis Papers.

39. Judith Martin, *Common Courtesy in which Miss Manners solves the problem that baffled Mr. Jefferson* (New York: Atheneum, 1985), p. 4.

40. Cooley, p. 42.

41. Margaret Bayard Smith, *What is Gentility?* (Washington: Pishey Thompson, 1828), p. 140.

42. Adams, "Adventures of Nobody," 1803, p. 156, Adams Papers.

43. Smith, *What is Gentility?*, p. 140.

44. [Josephine Seaton], *William Winston Seaton of the "National Intelligencer"* (Boston: James R. Osgood and Co., 1871), p. 132.

45. Cooley, pp. 42–43. British Minister Augustus Foster was told that of the 105 members of the Pennsylvania legislature "there was not one last winter fit to be received into good Company." Foster to his mother, 30 August 1806, in Marilyn Kay Parr, *Augustus John Foster and the "Washington Wilderness": Personal Letters of a British Diplomat* (Ph.D. dissertation, The George Washington University, 1987), p. 226. Harrison Gray Otis commented on the same topic in 1815: "If all the houses were concentrated, the place would wear the semblance of a city and possess its comforts. If all the genteel people who live here permanently or temporarily were invited into a social mass, there would be enough of them to give some colouring of taste and fashion and decorum to the motley throng which now fill drawing rooms and levees, or at least sufficient to hide the glossiness[?] of the vulgarity which now predominated over all these assemblages—But all things are in groupes, and no party of decent people is sufficiently numerous in any of them, to conceal the Squalor and coarseness of the rest." Otis to Sally Foster Otis, 20 February 1815, Otis Papers.

46. Cooley, p. 18.

47. Diary of Harriet Otis, 21 December 1811, Otis Papers.

48. Mary Lee Mann, ed., *A Yankee Jeffersonian: Selections from the Diary and Letters of William Lee of Massachusetts* (Cambridge, Mass.: Harvard University Press, 1958).

49. Smith, *First Forty Years*, p. 288.

50. Ibid., p. 305.

51. Ibid., pp. 288–89.

52. *The Diary of John Quincy Adams, 1794–1845*, ed. Allan Nevins (New York: Charles Scribner's Sons, 1951), pp. 398–401.

53. Smith, *First Forty Years*, p. 311.

54. "Letters of William T. Barry," *William and Mary College Quarterly* 13, ser. 1 (April 1905), p. 239.

55. *The Habits of Good Society: A Handbook for ladies and gentlemen . . .* (New York: Carleton, 1864), p. 33.

56. *The laws of etiquette; or, Short rules and reflections for conduct in society. By a gentleman* (Philadelphia: Carey, Lea, and Blanchard, 1839), p. 19.

57. Cooley, pp. 15 and 61.

58. *Laws of etiquette*, pp. 9–11.

59. Cooley, p. 70.

60. Day, p. 52.

61. *Laws of etiquette*, pp. 12–13.

62. Ibid., p. 12.

63. Day, pp. 3–4.

64. Smith, *What is Gentility?*, p. 207.

65. *Laws of etiquette*, pp. 22 and 38. Studies of the consumer revolution interpret fashion differently. They see tradition as closed-mindedness and fashion as an indicator of mental restlessness that encouraged acceptance of innovation. See Fernand Braudel, *The Structures of Everyday Life* (New York: Harper & Row, 1981), pp. 321–24; Neil McKendrick, John Brewer, and J. H. Plumb, *The Birth of a Consumer Society: The Commercialization of Eighteenth-Century England* (Bloomington and Indianapolis: Indiana University Press, 1982); and Colin Campbell, *The Romantic Ethic and the Spirit of Modern Consumerism* (Oxford: Basil Blackwell, 1987).

66. Smith, *What is Gentility?*, p. 77.

67. Ibid., p. 222.

68. Cooley, pp. 23–24.

69. The best study of published advice on face-to-face behavior is Christina D. Hemphill, "Manners for Americans: Interaction, Ritual and the Social Order, 1620–1860" (Ph.D. dissertation, Brandeis University, 1988). Although several good bibliographies list books published or available in the United States, for the early nineteenth century there is no comprehensive study of specific or "little" rules of etiquette and how they changed during the early nineteenth century. For the broad significance of these changes, see Norbert Elias, *The History of Manners: The Civilizing Process*, vol. 1 (New York: Urizen Books, 1978); Roger Chartier, ed., *Passions of the Renaissance*, vol. 3 of *A History of Private Life* (Cambridge: Harvard University Press, 1989), pp. 167–205; and Arthur M. Schlesinger, *Learning How to Behave: A historical study of American etiquette books* (New York: The Macmillan Co., 1946). Works focused after 1830 that offer insights into the earlier years are Karen Halttunen, *Confidence Men and Painted Women* (New Haven: Yale University Press, 1982); John F. Kasson, "Rudeness & Civility: Manners in Nineteenth Century Urban America" (New York: Hill and Wang, 1990); and Stow Persons, *The Decline of American Gentility* (New York: Columbia University Press, 1973).

70. Day, pp. 3–4.

71. Ibid., p. 52.

72. *Laws of etiquette*, p. 132.

73. Ibid., p. 13.

74. *Etiquette at Washington: together with the Customs adopted by Polite Society in the other cities of the United States. . .by a citizen of Washington*, 3rd ed. (Baltimore: Murphy & Co., 1857), p. 1.

75. Margaret Hall, *The Aristocratic Journey: Being the Outspoken Letters of Mrs. Basil Hall Written during a Fourteen Months' Sojourn in America, 1827–1828*, ed. Una Pope-Hennessy (New York: G. P. Putnam's Sons, 1931), p. 27. Elsewhere Mrs. Hall noted that "in America every thing is genteel or ungenteel" (p. 89).

76. 22 September 1752, in Phillip Dormer Stanhope, 4th Earl of Chesterfield, *Lord Chesterfield's Letters to his Son*, vol. 2 (London: M. Walter Dunne, 1901), pp. 119–20.

77. Smith, *Winter in Washington*, introduction.

78. Five novels have been identified, two by Margaret Bayard Smith. The others are [George Watterston], *Wanderer in Washington* (Washington: J. Elliot, jr., 1827) and *The L. . .Family at Washington; or, A winter in the metropolis* (Washington: Davis and Force,

1822); and Harry Nimrod, "editor," *The Fudge Family in Washington* (Baltimore: Joseph Robinson, 1820).

79. Smith, *What is Gentility?*, introduction.

80. Ibid., p. 39.

81. Ibid., p. 93.

82. Ibid., p. 116.

83. Ibid., pp. 256–57.

84. Ibid., p. 240.

85. Ibid., pp. 130–31.

86. Ibid., p. 133.

87. Ibid., p. 214.

88. Ibid., pp. 270 and 272.

89. *Etiquette at Washington*, p. 89.

Chapter II

1. *Harper's New Monthly Magazine* 37 (September 1868), p. 434, quoted in Susan Williams, *Savory Suppers and Fashionable Feasts: Dining in Victorian America* (New York: Pantheon Books in association with the Strong Museum, 1985), p. 21.

2. Louis McLane to his wife, Kitty McLane, Washington, 24 January 1818, McLane Papers, quoted in Diane L. Berger, " 'Pray Let Them Be Neat and Fashionable or Send None': Dining in Eighteenth and Early Nineteenth-Century America, An Exploration of Ritual and Equipage with a Case Study of Virginia Probate Inventories" (M.A. thesis, The George Washington University, 1990), p. 58.

3. Margaret Bayard Smith, *A Winter in Washington, or Memoirs of the Seymour Family* (New York: E. Bliss and E. White, 1824), p. 265.

4. Norbert Elias, *The History of Manners: The Civilizing Process*, vol. 1 (New York: Urizen Books, 1978), pp. 60–129; and Esther B. Aresty, *The Best Behavior: the course of good manners from antiquity to the present—as seen through courtesy and etiquette books* (New York: Simon and Schuster, 1970), pp. 174–75 and 189–205.

5. Carl Bridenbaugh, ed., *Gentleman's Progress: The Itinerarium of Dr. Alexander Hamilton, 1744* (Chapel Hill: University of North Carolina Press for The Institute of Early American History and Culture, 1948), p. 8.

6. Ibid., p. 55.

7. Rodris Roth, "Tea-Drinking in 18th-Century America: Its Etiquette and Equipage," *Contributions from the Museum of History and Technology*, United States National Museum Bulletin 225, paper no. 14 (Washington: Smithsonian Institution, 1961), pp. 61–91.

8. City and country teas are distinguished on p. 7 of Smith, *Winter in Washington*. A rural visitor to Norfolk, Virginia, offers a satirical description of the city way of serving tea in which full cups are carried around on a tray and guests must balance the hot cups and their bread and butter. *Norfolk Gazette & Publick Ledger*, 21 June 1815. I am grateful to Ann Smart Martin for this reference.

9. Sidney W. Mintz, *Sweetness and Power: The Place of Sugar in Modern History* (New York: Viking Penguin Inc., 1985), p. 115. A domestic "help" in frontier Michigan in the 1830s drank strong green tea three times a day "and between . . . drank the remains of the tea from the spout of the tea-pot." See Caroline Kirkland, *A New Home Who'll Follow* (1839; reprint, New Haven: College and University Press, 1965), p. 82.

10. Carole Shammas, "The Domestic Environment in Early Modern England and America," *Journal of Social History* 14 (Fall 1980), pp. 12–16; and Lois Green Carr and Lorena S. Walsh, "Consumer Behavior in the Colonial Chesapeake," in C. Carson, R. Hoffman, and T. J. Albert, eds., *Of Consuming Interest: The Style of Life in the Eighteenth Century* (Charlottesville: University Press of Virginia, forthcoming), tables a–f in series 1.

11. Tea led the way because the whole performance was less expensive and more easily learned than that of fine dining. The menu was simpler, the behavior less complicated, and the essential accoutrements fewer in number and thus less expensive than the equipment required for dining. Teaware in most households from 1780 to 1850 cost more and was more highly decorated than tableware. Ann Smart Martin, " 'Fashionable Sugar Dishes, Latest Fashion Ware': Consumer Demand for Eighteenth-Century Tea and Tablewares," in *The Historic Chesapeake: Archaeological Contributions*, ed. Paul Shackel and Barbra J. Little (Washington: Smithsonian Institution Press, forthcoming 1992); and George L. Miller, "The 'Market Basket' of Ceramics Available in Country Stores from 1780 to 1880," paper presented at the Society for Historical Archaeology meeting, Tucson, Arizona, 1990.

12. The years 1818–1826 were selected for this inventory project because by 1818 Washington had been settled long enough to have a sizable population and established procedures for record-taking. The documents for these nine years are continuous, while the volume covering the years immediately following is missing from the series. John Tayloe III died in Washington in 1828. Unfortunately, if there was a probate inventory for the Octagon, it would most likely be in the missing volume.

Because the objective was to examine how decedents and their families presented themselves at mealtime, it was important to study only functioning households. Any inventory that did not list basic objects related to both sleeping and cooking—for instance, a pot and an old bed—was eliminated. Of 295 documents, 73 were rejected, leaving 224. The inventories were then grouped according to the kinds of dining equipment the decedent owned. Limits on time and money and the loss of a crucial volume that would contain corresponding accounts for many of the inventories encouraged this approach. Although we made no attempt to determine whether the decedent could afford his or her selection of tableware, not surprisingly cursory examination suggests a close correlation between wealth and dining practice. For an excellent example of the wealth approach, see Carr and Walsh, "Consumer Behavior."

The study in this book assumes that dining furniture and tableware are proxies for people's desires for particular expressions or presentation of self and for their decisions to allocate resources accordingly. This analysis is built on two concepts, that of performance and that of a "kit" or a collection of closely related articles that serve as essential props for the action. To stage a show for fashionable society one needed a complete "kit," the standards for which are clearly specified in the prescriptive literature, both historical and fictional descriptions, and the upper level inventories. People farther down the social ladder may have owned parts of the ensemble. If they wished to use them in the prescribed manner, they had to borrow or rent additional supplies. It is likely, however, that satisfaction for these individuals came from possession and display rather than use or performance.

Whenever inventories are used to discuss living standards or behavior, several questions are raised about biases in reporting. The inventories that met the criteria of this study represent fewer than 1 percent of the 33,000 people who made up Washington's total population in 1820. Biases of wealth are discussed in the text. For a relatively untechnical discussion of biases see Ann Smart Martin, "The Role of Pewter as Missing Artifact: Consumer Attitudes Toward Tablewares in Late 18th Century Virginia," *Historical Archaeology* 23, no. 2 (1989), pp. 2–6. For other biases of age, gender, and the like, see Alice Hanson Jones, "Wealth Estimates for the American Middle Colonies, 1774," *Economic Development and Cultural Change* 18 (July 1970), pp. 109–21; Gloria L. Main, "The Correction of Biases in Colonial American Probate Records," *Historical Methods Newsletter* 8 (1984), pp. 10–28; and Daniel Scott Smith, "Under-registration and Bias in Probate Records: An Analysis of Data from Eighteenth-Century Hingham, Massachusetts," *William and Mary Quarterly* 32, 3rd ser. (1975), pp. 100–110. For a good general introduction to inventory studies, see Ross W. Beales, Jr., Peter Benes, and Kevin M. Sweeney, "Selected Bibliography on Inventory-Based Studies," in Peter Benes et al., ed., *Early American Probate Inventories*, Annual Proceedings of The Dublin Seminar for New England Folklife, vol. 12 (Boston: Boston University, 1989), pp. 196–80.

There are also questions about whether the inventories should be taken at face value. Do they list everything a decedent owned? In instances where inventories can be correlated with relevant wills, archaeological collections, or vendue or sales accounts, discrepancies can be identified. While we will never know for certain about the point-by-point accuracy of most documents, inventories are the best evidence we have to look from the top toward, but not to, the bottom of society. The pictures they offer present a consistent pattern within groups. These patterns conform to descriptions and augment them with rough proportions of how many lived in what ways. For Washington, the records seem remarkably accurate and detailed.

Ellen Donald has compared items in selected inventories with lists of items from the same estate that were sold at auction. She discovered an almost exact correlation. The analysis is not comprehensive. Only sales lists matching inventories quoted in the text have been examined: Stephen Decatur and Franklin Wharton in the elite group and Jeremiah Hunt, Abner Ritchie, and Ann T. Woods in lower groups. A sales list for John Krause was also found, but correlating the two documents is difficult as his inventory is more extensive than his sales list.

13. Inventory of Ignatius Wheeler, 17 October 1823, vol. H.C.N. 1, pp. 539–40. See also Pamela J. Cressey, "The Alexandria, Virginia, City-Site: Archaeology in An Afro-American Neighborhood, 1830–1910" (Ph.D. dissertation, University of Iowa, 1985).

14. In Smith, *Winter in Washington*, pp. 64–80, the houses of several poor families are described. The first, once "a large and good one," was in ruins: "The fence round the yard had been pulled to pieces to supply the poor tenants with fuel; the entry door, having lost

its fastenings, was slamming backwards and forwards, and the broken windows were stuffed full of old clothes of every colour, and the shutters swinging in the wind." The second was a mere "shed" that did not deserve "the name of a hovel." It had no door, floor, or chimney, only broad flat stones laid to support the burning pieces of the bedstead. The last was a "little log dwelling, not much bigger than a pig-pen."

15. Inventory of Jeremiah Hunt, 31 October 1823, vol. H.C.N. 2, pp. 14–17. The five rooms listed in the inventory are "Large back chamber," "Front chamber," "Back Parlour," "Kitchen," and "Smiths Shop."

16. Margaret Bayard Smith, *What is Gentility?* (Washington: Pishey Thompson, 1828), pp. 7–8.

17. Smith, *Winter in Washington*, pp. 274–75. Fuel was expensive in Washington. The wife of Attorney General William Wirt reported that she was advised to install at least two or three grates and ship coal to the city before the rivers froze, "as wood sells in Washington in the depth of winter at 16$ pr cord, in place of 4$ as it is here [Richmond, Virginia]." The following winter, after the family had moved to Washington, she wrote that she had bought "15 cords of wood at 7$75 cents delivered eight cords of it cut up." Elizabeth Wirt to William Wirt, 25 November 1817 and 25 November 1818, Wirt Papers.

18. Smith, *What is Gentility?*, pp. 6–7. Charles Willson Peale's etching *Accident in Lombard-Street, Philadelphia* (1787) shows a little girl in distress because she has dropped a pie and dogs are eating it. Onlookers laugh at her misfortune.

19. John Stavely, *The Columbian Mirror and Alexandria Gazette*, 19 May 1798; and William Friend, *Virginia Journal and Alexandria Advertiser*, 21 May 1789 and 9 February 1799.

20. *Look before you leap* (London: W. Row, Walker, and J. Barker, 1796), pp. 44–45, 64–65, 83, 85, and 100. Beginning December 2, 1830, William Gamble advertised in the *Daily National Intelligencer* that his Capitol Hill boardinghouse had "the advantage of a fine vegetable Garden for the supply of his table, adding much to the comfort of his guests." Reference courtesy of Alicia Delahunty.

21. Jack Larkin, *The Reshaping of Everyday Life, 1790–1840* (New York: Harper & Row, 1988), pp. 170–71; and Richard Osborn Cummings, *The American and His Food* (1940; revised ed., New York: Arno Press, 1970), pp. 25–42. For European comparisons analyzed in the manner of Norbert Elias, see Stephen Mennell, *All Manners of Food: Eating and Taste in England and France from the Middle Ages to the Present* (Oxford: Blackwell, 1985), pp. 214–25.

22. *Daily National Intelligencer*, 31 December 1822, p. 3; Wilhelmus Bogert Bryan, *History of the National Capital*, vol. 1 (New York: The Macmillan Company, 1914), p. 541; and Constance McLaughlin Green, *Washington: Village and Capital, 1800–1878* (Princeton, N.J.: Princeton University Press, 1962), pp. 40–43 and 90–93.

23. Inventory of George Hadfield, 7 February 1826, vol. H.C.N. 2, pp. 441–44. For more details about renting, see note 38.

24. *The Washington Directory* (1822; reprint, Silver Spring, Md.: Family Line Publications, 1987).

25. Inventory of John Poor, 10 November 1825, vol. H.C.N. 2, pp. 421–23. Blue shell-edge plates were the cheapest decorated tableware available in the 1820s. See George

L. Miller and Robert R. Hunter, "Shell Edge: Alias Leeds Ware, Alias Feather Edge," paper presented at the Wedgwood International Seminar, Birmingham, Alabama, May 1990.

26. Inventory of John Krause, 3 October 1820, vol. J.H.B./H.C.N. 1, pp. 412–14.

27. Inventory of Abner Ritchie, 23 October 1819, vol. J.H.B./H.C.N. 1, pp. 242–43.

28. Inventory of Henry M. Steiner, 24 June 1825, vol. H.C.N. 2, pp. 341–43. The term "Liverpool ware" was used interchangeably with printed ware in Maryland probate inventories as late as the 1840s. See George L. Miller, "A Tenant Farmer's Tableware: Nineteenth-Century Ceramics from Tabb's Purchase," *Maryland Historical Magazine* 69 (Summer 1974), p. 209.

29. Inventory of Ann T. Woods, 19 October 1819, vol. J.H.B./H.C.N. 1, pp. 322–24.

30. Unless otherwise stated, the description of architecture and furnishings is based on evidence from twenty-six probate inventories. Eight make up the top or elite group; eighteen are "aspirers" to that status. The twelve inventories of the twenty-six that have a room-by-room list of goods are indicated with asterisks in the following lists. The lists are alphabetical. The dates cited, which may refer to either the day the inventory was taken or the day it was recorded in court, are in each case the earliest given in the document. All the inventories were found at the Suitland Reference Branch of the National Archives and Records Administration in Record group 21, U.S. District Court for the District of Columbia, Entry 119, Inventories and Sales.

Elite inventories

*Ruth Barlow, 8 June 1818, vol. J.H.B./H.C.N. 1, pp. 331–37.

*Walter S. Chandler, 16 June 1825, vol. H.C.N. 2, pp. 354–62.

Henry H. Chapman, 18 December 1821, vol. H.C.N. 1, pp. 242–48.

*Stephen Decatur, 5 April 1820, J.H.B./H.C.N. 1, pp. 339–42.

Henry Foxall, 1 April 1824, vol. H.C.N. 2, pp. 147–55.

John Graham, 8 March 1821, vol. J.H.B./H.C.N. 1, pp. 455–59.

*Benjamin J. Orr, 3 August 1822, vol. H.C.N. 1, pp. 412–16.

*Franklin Wharton, 26 March 1819, vol. J.H.B./H.C.N. 1, pp. 115–26.

Aspiring inventories

Dr. James H. Blake, 23 October 1819, vol. J.H.B./H.C.N. 1, pp. 234–37.

John Bridge, 8 April 1819, vol. J.H.B./H.C.N. 1, pp. 144–47.

Mary Brumley, 27 April 1826, vol. H.C.N. 2, pp. 475–77.

George Clarke, 1 March 1823, vol. H.C.N. 1, pp. 524–30.

*Thomas Daugherty, 18 October 1822, vol. H.C.N. 1, pp. 421–25.

*Constant Freeman, 24 March 1824, vol. H.C.N. 2, pp. 203–09.

Thomas Tasker Garett, 1 June 1818, vol. H.C.N. 1, pp. 270–77.

John Law, 15 September 1822, vol. H.C.N. 1, pp. 491–503.

*Josiah Meigs, 27 September 1822, vol. H.C.N. 1, pp. 326–30.

John Moore, 9 July 1824, vol. H.C.N. 2, pp. 167–70.

John Ott, 25 November 1818, vol. J.H.B./H.C.N. 1, pp. 32–88.

William Prout, 28 October 1823, vol. H.C.N. 2, pp. 61–74.

*Edmond Rice, 4 August 1821, vol. H.C.N. 1, pp. 98–104.

Eliza Robertson, 8 October 1825, vol. H.C.N. 2, pp. 384–86.

Andrew Ross, 1 February 1822, vol. H.C.N. 2, pp. 105–107.

*John Wiley, 29 March 1819, vol. J.H.B/H.C.N. 1, pp. 131–43.

*James R. Wilson, 4 August 1820, vol. J.H.B./H.C.N. 1, pp. 384–88.

*Moses Young, 18 December 1822, vol. H.C.N. 1, pp. 458–60.

An example of the difficulties involved in creating these categories is the case of Col. Samuel Archer, U.S. Army (9 December 1825, vol. H.C.N. 2, pp. 437–38). Archer owned $300 in plate and many other items that would have put him in the aspiring group. Because no knives, forks, or spoons are specified in his inventory, for consistency he had to be placed in the simple group.

31. The rooms were not always clearly labeled in the inventories. In four of them the appraisers numbered rather than named them. In two cases names indicated a front-to-back spatial relationship, but which room faced the street is not clear. One etiquette manual instructed guests arriving at a party to walk through the back room to greet the hostess who was to stand at the head of the front room. Either the room on the street was called the back room or guests traveled the length of a passage, entered the second room, and paraded toward the front of the house. Most of the room names in the inventories suggest function, drawing and dining in four cases, dining and office once. *The laws of etiquette; or, Short rules and reflections for conduct in society. By a gentleman* (Philadelphia: Carey, Lea, and Blanchard, 1839), pp. 98–99. For additional architectural information, see Elisabeth Donaghy Garrett, "The American Home: Part IV: The Dining Room," *Antiques* 126 (October 1984), p. 912; Edward S. Cooke, Jr., "Domestic Space in the Federal-Period Inventories of Salem Merchants," *Essex Institute Historical Collections* 116 (April 1980), pp. 248–63; Mark R. Wenger, "The Dining Room in Early Virginia" in Thomas Carter and Bernard L. Herman, eds., *Perspectives in Vernacular Architecture III* (Columbia, Mo.: University of Missouri Press for the Vernacular Architecture Forum, 1989), pp. 149–59; and James C. Jordan III, "The Neoclassical Dining Room in Charleston," *Journal of Early Southern Decorative Arts* 14 (November 1988), pp. 1–25.

32. *Etiquette for Ladies* (Philadelphia: Carey, Lea & Blanchard, 1838), pp. 22–23.

33. The appearance of sewing or work tables along with dining tables in one of the inventoried rooms hints that it may have been used daily for dining and for sitting and the other room closed except for special occasions. Rooms in several of the inventoried houses did double duty for dining and office work.

34. A. Hepplewhite, *The Cabinet-Maker and Upholsterer's Guide* (1794; reprint, New York: Dover Publications, Inc., 1969), pp. 23–24. Thomas Sheraton illustrated "a Dining Parlour in imitation of the Prince of Wales's" in *The Cabinet-Maker and Upholsterer's Drawing Book* (1793–1802; reprint, New York: Dover Publications, Inc., 1972), following p. 136. Furnishing practices in early nineteenth century Washington were similar to those in other regions of the United States. See Cooke, Jordan, and Wenger.

35. Orlando Ridout V, *Building the Octagon* (Washington: The AIA Press, 1989), pp. 106–107 and 118–19. By about 1820 other private houses in the city were beginning to have grander public spaces. The most prominent were those of Van Ness and Decatur. See Chapter I, note 22 for a description of the new rooms of John Quincy and Louisa Catherine

Adams. The Wirts also had expansion plans as evidenced in a letter from William Wirt to Mrs. Wirt, 3 December 1817, Wirt Papers.

36. The watercolor plan and section of a dining room that Benjamin Latrobe proposed for a house for John Tayloe hints at what might have been in the house in the early nineteenth century. See Ridout, p. 30.

37. Diary of Harriet Otis, Otis Papers, pp. 24–25.

38. For the visual characteristics of the fashionable taste of the period, see Charles F. Montgomery, *American Furniture: The Federal Period* (New York: The Viking Press, 1966); and Wendy Cooper, "The Classical Impulse," in *In Praise of America* (New York: Alfred A. Knopf, 1980). The best current research about the furnishings of the period is associated with house restoration, for example, work done by Dean Lahikainen at Gardner-Pingree House, Essex Institute, Salem, Massachusetts, and Jane Webb Smith at the Wickham-Valentine House, Valentine Museum, Richmond, Virginia.

39. Frances Byerley Parkes, *Domestic Duties* (New York: Harpers, 1828), pp. 173–74.

40. Although Washington appraisers rarely described anyone's furniture, they did assign values. Higher figures distinguish the furniture of the elite, while relatively lower values suggest that people in the aspiring group did not own impressive pieces. For both groups most mahogany case furniture ranged in value from $25 to $55. Two exceptional sideboards were appraised at $100 and one at $150 (inventories of Chapman and Orr, Barlow). Depending on their size or type, values for mahogany tables ranged from $4 to $60. Although a few decedents owned sets of mahogany chairs, valued from $36 to $60 for a dozen, Windsor and fancy chairs were far more common. Neither settees nor sofas were worth much, about $25. Knife cases, generally appraised at $5, were widely owned in both the aspiring and elite groups.

41. Few inventories listed a center table. The documents are probably a few years too early and the decedent population too old for many tables in this new style to be listed. See Col. Samuel Archer's "2 centre tables" valued at $20. John Graham (elite) and William Prout (aspiring) each owned a sofa table.

The first reference to a center table in Margaret Bayard Smith's published correspondence appears in 1828, and thereafter the tables are mentioned regularly. Smith, *Winter in Washington*, pp. 244, 250, 327, 343, 346, and 385. See Chapter V, note 102.

The center table offered a family a place to sit and share the bright light of the newly invented oil lamp. At large parties it served as a gathering place for the ladies, who began to feel free to leave their seats to examine prints and other curiosities displayed there.

42. There was a single chandelier in the inventories studied (see Decatur). In three estates the combined value of all the lighting fixtures in each was over $150 (Barlow, Decatur, and Wharton). The value of lighting equipment in the other elite inventories clustered close to $50, but even that amount contrasted significantly with the $10 total assigned to the lighting equipment in most of the aspiring inventories.

43. Robert Roberts, *The House Servant's Directory* (1827; facsimile ed., Waltham, Mass.: The Gore Place Society, 1977), pp. 21 and 177.

44. Roberts, p. 52.

45. Ibid., p. 45.

46. The opportunity for historians to determine whether sets were owned in a given household depends upon the early appraisers' ability to perceive the significance of sets and to suggest their presence either with explicit words or in the ways they ordered inventories.

47. Roberts, pp. 46–47.

48. Robert Hamilton, *The Columbian Mirror and Alexandria Gazette*, 2 August 1796. Henry Foxall owned thirty-one tablecloths and only three napkins; Walter Chandler, ten cloths and two napkins.

49. Roberts, p. 47.

50. Ibid., p. 53.

51. The following ceramics were owned in the elite group: A "small set [of] Liverpool" ware was appraised at $8 and something simply called "table china" at $40 (Chandler). "Liverpool" ware was probably transfer printed. Stephen Decatur's "fine French China" was worth twice that amount, but the highest appraisal was $250 for 341 pieces of an "Elegt. Sett [of] India gilt china" (Wharton).

In the aspiring group Dr. James H. Blake's two sets of dinnerware and his glassware were at the upper end of the range. One set with 242 pieces was appraised at $40. The other, with forty-eight pieces of common Queensware, was worth a mere $5. Blake's large assortment of glassware was valued at approximately $32. Another decedent's two sets of dinner china, one blue at $15 and the other "blue and gilt" at $40 were mid-priced (Freeman). More typical of the possessions of the aspiring group were entries like "Common Tea china incomplete and broken" at $1.50 and "Set [of] gilt Tea China incomplete with bowl and 2 cake plates" at $12 in one inventory and a dinner set at $19.25 and a tea set for $14.50 in another (Prout and Moore).

52. Roberts, pp. 47–48.

53. Sarah Carlyle Herbert of Alexandria attended a party and noted $300 worth of glass. Herbert to her daughter, probably 1805, typescript, courtesy, Carlyle House, Alexandria, Virginia.

54. Chandler and Wharton inventories.

55. Diary of Louisa Catherine Adams, 28 December 1822, Adams Papers. In his inventory Decatur's solid silver was not itemized but was assigned a bulk value of $1,200. His plated ware was worth $100.

56. Among the elite the total value for solid plate was usually about $200, mainly invested in tea ware, and $50 to $100 for the cheaper plated material, mainly candlesticks and serving pieces. Ruth Barlow, widow of the poet and mistress of a house called Kalorama, owned more plated ware than the other decedents in this group. She could set out a plated tureen, six covered serving dishes, and two cake baskets.

57. Henri J. Stier to Rosalie Calvert, 1 May 1806, Stier Papers, Maryland Historical Society, Baltimore [to be published in Margaret Law Callcott, ed., *Mistress of Riversdale: The Plantation Letters of Rosalie Stier Calvert, 1795–1821* (Baltimore: The Johns Hopkins University Press, forthcoming)]. Harrison Gray Otis described Mrs. Calvert as "the daughter of a dutch refuge from Antwerp—a man of immense wealth and great respectability—Mrs C a woman of education, and a real lady in manners." Otis to Sally Foster Otis, 9 January 1819, Otis Papers.

58. The *Century Dictionary* (New York: 1889) defines a "cabaret" as a tray or stand with a matching set of dishes and utensils for serving coffee or tea, but because Rosalie Calvert asked for three in two different sizes, she probably used the term interchangeably with waiter or tray.

59. Kathryn C. Buhler, *Mount Vernon Silver* (Mt. Vernon, Virginia: The Mount Vernon Ladies' Association of the Union, 1957), p. 49. Lear was writing to Clement Biddle. For a longer discussion of the ornaments of Washington's presidential table, see Susan Gray Detweiler, *George Washington's Chinaware* (New York: Harry N. Abrams, Inc., 1982), pp. 107–18.

There seems to be little agreement about the term for a mirrored centerpiece. *Surtout-de-table*, plateau, or plateaux (indicating an item of several parts) are all used.

60. Buhler, pp. 50, 53, and 72.

61. Virginia Tayloe Lewis, "Washington Society Before the War," undated typescript in the collection of The Octagon, probably ca. 1900, p. 1.

62. They were Thomas Jefferson, James Madison, James Monroe, Stephen Decatur, the British minister Charles Bagot, and the Spanish minister the Chevl. d'Onis. Jefferson took an unvalued 1809 inventory when he vacated the President's House. It represents official furnishings of the mansion and includes a "plateau in five parts with a set of ornaments." Jefferson Papers. Perhaps this is the same one described at a dinner in the Madison White House. Lord Francis Jeffrey noted "a long table with a tarnished flat plateau in the centre." Typescript, courtesy, the Office of the Curator of the White House. Decatur's plateau, appraised at only $40, apparently was not included with either his solid silver or his plated ware (see his inventory).

63. *Letters of Mary Boardman Crowninshield, 1815–1816*, ed. Francis Boardman Crowninshield (Cambridge: Riverside Press, 1905), p. 20.

64. Jane Shadel Spillman, *White House Glassware* (Washington: White House Historical Association, 1989), figure 24, p. 65.

65. Louis McLane to Catharine McLane, 24 January 1818, McLane Papers.

66. Harrison Gray Otis to Sally Foster Otis, 1 December 1818, Otis Papers.

67. Harry Nimrod, "editor" of *The Fudge Family in Washington* (Boston: Joseph Robinson, 1820), footnotes descriptions of meals in Washington. He said the capital city was probably not so well developed as Philadelphia, where there were both public cooks and public servants. "We recommend to them, if they have not already thought of it, to have publick plates, knives, forks, confectionary, &c." Nimrod, p. 16. Harrison Gray Otis scrambled to secure enough tableware for a dinner party, but he is not clear whether he borrowed them gratis or rented them. Otis to Sally Foster Otis, 21 February 1819, Otis Papers.

68. Smith, *What is Gentility?*, pp. 9–11. If Margaret Bayard Smith had provided readers with a full inventory of the McCartys' house, it certainly would have been in the aspiring category. Readers learn that the family owns knives and forks, p. 59. Later, they give handed teas and dinner parties for about ten people. Although the staff is not listed in detail, readers learn that Mrs. McCarty has little to do except give orders. There is a cook and the activities imply at least one waiter. On the importance of domestic service in conveying information about fashion and behavior, see Neil McKendrick, John Brewer, and J. H.

Plumb, *The Birth of a Consumer Society: The Commercialization of Eighteenth-Century England* (Bloomington and Indianapolis: Indiana University Press, 1982), pp. 56–59.

69. Richard L. and Claudia L. Bushman, "The Early History of Cleanliness in America," *Journal of American History* 74 (March 1988), pp. 1215–38. See Roberts, p. 6, for comments on personal cleanliness of servants. Throughout he mentions details of cleaning a house and its furniture.

70. Smith, *What is Gentility?*, pp. 52–59. At least two Frenchmen traveling in the U.S. in the late eighteenth century commented unfavorably on what they considered an old-fashioned custom of passing a "large china loving-cup" (Ferdinand M. Bayard, 1797) or a "great bowl of punch" (Louis Phillips, Comte de Segur, early 1780s). See Charles H. Sherrill, *French Memories of Eighteenth-Century America* (New York: Charles Scribner's Sons, 1915), pp. 86 and 196–97.

71. Peter L. Berger and Thomas Luckmann, *The Social Construction of Reality: A Treatise in the Sociology of Knowledge* (New York: Anchor Books, 1967); Erving Goffman, *The Presentation of Self in Everyday Life* (Garden City, N.Y.: Doubleday Anchor Books, 1959); Mary Douglas and Baron Isherwood, *The World of Goods* (New York: W.W. Norton & Co., 1979); Ian Hodder, *Reading the Past: Current approaches to interpretation in archaeology* (Cambridge: Cambridge University Press, 1986); and Edward T. Hall, *Beyond Culture* (Garden City, N.Y.: Anchor Books, 1977).

Chapter III

1. Margaret Hall, *The Aristocratic Journey: Being the Outspoken Letters of Mrs. Basil Hall Written during a Fourteen Months' Sojourn in America, 1827–1828*, ed. Una Pope-Hennessy (New York: G. P. Putnam's Sons, 1931), p. 182.

2. George Washington, *Rules of Civility* (Charlottesville, Va.: Lewis Glaser, 1957). Quoted are rules 90, 95 and 96, and 100.

3. In 1688 the Virginia gentleman William Fitzhugh ordered an extensive quantity of plate, including "One dozen silver hafted knives. 1 doz: silver forks One dozen silver spoons large & strong." Richard Beale Davis, ed., *William Fitzhugh and his Chesapeake World, 1676–1701* (Chapel Hill: University of North Carolina Press for the Virginia Historical Society, 1963), p. 244. Even among the plantation elite he set an exceptional table. In late seventeenth century England as well as in Virginia less than 1 percent of the inventoried population owned table knives and forks of any sort. About 1720 the figure on both sides of the Atlantic had risen to approximately 20 percent. Fifty years later, just prior to the Revolution, 53 percent of inventoried households in Massachusetts were so equipped.

When ownership is divided into wealth groups, predictably the rich owned more, but utensils were neither absent from the bottom nor universal at the top. For Virginians the overall percentage was higher than for Massachusetts decedents. Seventy percent of Virginians owned knives and forks, perhaps because they paid greater attention to the way food was eaten, perhaps because of different criteria for probated estates. See Carole Shammas,

"The Domestic Environment in Early Modern England and America," *Journal of Economic History* 43 (March 1983), pp. 12–13; and Lois Green Carr and Lorena S. Walsh, "Consumer Behavior in the Colonial Chesapeake," in C. Carson, R. Hoffman, and T. J. Albert, eds., *Of Consuming Interest: The Style of Life in the Eighteenth Century* (Charlottesville: University Press of Virginia, forthcoming), pp. 10–11, tables 1 a–f.

4. John Hamilton Moore, *The young gentleman and lady's monitor* (New York: Hugh Gaine, 1792), pp. 202–03.

5. Anne W. Shippen to Nancy Shippen, September 1777, quoted in Diane L. Berger, " 'Pray Let Them Be Neat and Fashionable or Send None': Dining in Eighteenth and Early Nineteenth-Century America, An Exploration of Ritual and Equipage with a Case Study of Virginia Probate Inventories," (M.A. thesis, The George Washington University, 1990), p. 53.

6. Christian Cackler, *Recollections of an Old Settler* (1874; reprint, Ravenna, Oh.: The Record Publishing Co., 1964), p. 25. The year was 1804 when Cackler was twelve years old. I am grateful to George Miller for this reference.

7. Margaret Hall, pp. 21 (Catskills); 73 (Albany); 37.

8. Basil Hall, *Travels in North America in the years 1827 and 1828*, vol. 1 (Philadelphia: Carey, Lea & Carey, 1829), p. 141. Conformity was important. In a section on table manners, a manual published in Philadelphia in 1817 advised, "For unforeseen cases, follow the examples of company." V. G., *Elements and Principles of the Art of Dancing* (Philadelphia: 1817), p. 88. See also *The laws of etiquette; or, Short rules and reflections for conduct in society. By a gentleman* (Philadelphia: Carey, Lea, and Blanchard, 1839), p. 27.

9. An exception who remembered to look at the breadth of the English social order when making comparisons with Americans was Charles Augustus Murray, *Travels in North America* (New York: Harper & Brothers, 1839), p. 138. An earlier visitor noted, "Another peculiarity of the country is that in most houses, even in rich ones, you use no napkins at all, and each person wipes himself on the table-cloth, which must be very soiled as a result. Moreover, the people of the country almost all eat (as do the English) with knives (which are rounded at the end) without using forks, which have only *two* points." Evelyn N. Acomb, *The Revolutionary Journal of Baron Ludwig Von Closen, 1780–1783* (Chapel Hill: The University of North Carolina Press, 1958), p. 50.

10. Eliza Ware Farrar, *The Young Lady's Friend, By a Lady* (Boston: American Stationers Company, 1836), pp. 346–47.

11. Esther B. Aresty, *The Best Behavior: the course of good manners from antiquity to the present—as seen through courtesy and etiquette books* (New York: Simon and Schuster, 1970), p. 174.

12. Robert de Valcourt, *The Illustrated Book of Manners, a Manual of Good Behavior and Polite Accomplishments* (New York: Leland, Clay, 1855), p. 135.

13. The best summaries of technological and design changes are Ivor Noel Hume, *A Guide to Artifacts of Colonial America* (New York: Alfred A. Knopf, 1968), pp. 177–84; G. Bernard Hughes, "Evolution of the Silver Table Fork," *Country Life* 126 (24 September 1959), pp. 364–65; and Katherine Pearson, "The Knife, Fork & Spoon: A History," *Metalsmith* 1 (Fall 1981), pp. 30–34. Good illustrations of early examples can be found in Erik Lassen, *Knives Forks & Spoons* (Copenhagen: Host & Son, 1960).

14. For a discussion of the cultural significance of sets, see Edward T. Hall, *The Silent Language* (Garden City, N.Y.: Anchor Books, 1973), pp. 105–12.

Photographs of surviving American-made silver knives, forks, and spoons in the Decorative Arts Photographic Collection at Winterthur indicate roughly the proportion of each utensil originally produced. Compared to the thousands of spoons, only six all silver pre-1800 forks have been photographed. Silver-handled knives are even rarer. Knives and forks dated c. 1825 are more numerous, but not plentiful in relation to spoons. I am grateful to Bert R. Denker, librarian in charge of the Visual Resources Collection, for helping me assess the representativeness of the photographic collection.

15. *A Statement of Prices of Table Knife Hafters* (Sheffield: 1816), a trade journal in the collection of the library at Winterthur.

16. In profile these forks are shaped like spoons for better scooping and lifting.

17. Hume, p. 178; Hughes, pp. 364–65; John Davis, "The Lowry Dale Kirby collection of old Sheffield plate," *Antiques* 136 (October 1989), p. 850; Deborah D. Waters, "From Pure Coin, The Manufacture of American Silver Flatware, 1800–1860," *Winterthur Portfolio* 12 (1977), pp. 19–34. For general background see Noel D. Turner, *American Silver Flatware, 1837–1910* (New York: A. S. Barnes & Co., 1972); and Seymour B. Wyler, *The Book of Sheffield Plate* (New York: Bonanza Books, 1949).

18. Probably for the same reason, the prongs would not have held their shape if they had been curved. The phrase is Margaret Hall's, p. 212.

19. P. G. Marsteller in *Alexandria Advertiser and Commercial Intelligencer*, 30 August 1801.

20. *National Intelligencer*, 1 December 1810, p. 4.

21. Inventory of William Prout, 28 October 1823, vol. H.C.N. 2, pp. 62–63. Although advertisements and inventories of Washington merchants reveal the variety of utensils they sold, they do not connect unit prices to specific types. At the present time basic information about relative cost has to be found outside Washington. The large stock of merchandise owned by Philadelphia merchant Stephen Carmick in 1774 was appraised in sufficient detail for the purpose [Alice Hanson Jones, *American Colonial Wealth*, vol. 1 (New York: Arno Press, 1977), document 13072]. The list of goods he offered for sale included thirty dozen sets of knives and forks, new items in mint condition. Prices for twelve knives and forks to be sold by the set ranged widely as shown in the following chart.

knives with handles made of	price	indexed to cheapest type
wood	2/6	1
sham buck	3/-	1.2
buck	4/6	1.8
ivory	1/16/-	14.4
silver (with case)	4/-/-	32.0
silver (large and with case)	21/-/-	168.0

Prices from two other Philadelphia inventories of 1774 show the relative cost of silver. The appraisers assigned a mere £ 4.00.00 to a "case with a dozen silver handled knives and forks" (Jones, document 13130) and £21.00.00 to a cased set in which the knives were described as "large silver handled" (Jones, document 13048). Perhaps the forks and knife handles were solid silver. Items in the other set may have been smaller in size, the forks may have had steel tines, and the knife handles may have been hollow. If the unknown value of the wooden cases imbedded in the figures for silver is ignored, relative values can be approximated. Taking wooden-handled sets as a base, the price of a dozen ivory-handled knives and forks was fourteen times that of wood. A silver-handled set of the lowest value was a multiple of thirty-two, and the highest 168. The price range was indeed very broad.

In contrast, the cost of the most expensive English transfer printed cups and saucers in 1795 was only seven times the cost of plain creamware. See George L. Miller, "A Revised Set of CC Index Values for Classification and Economic Scaling of English Ceramics from 1787 to 1880," forthcoming in *Historical Archaeology*.

22. Inventory of Daniel Moore, 30 July 1822, vol. H.C.N. 1, pp. 321–22; and inventory of William N. Dernole, 2 November 1819, vol. J.H.B./H.C.N. 1 , pp. 113–15. The preference for silver spoons and knives and forks is conveyed in Thomas Thompson's 1841 description of a meal at a farm in the Hudson River valley where the table was set with "silver spoons, clean knives and forks." Elisabeth Donaghy Garrett, "The American Home: Part IV: The dining room," *Antiques* 126 (October 1984), p. 916.

23. Inventory of Franklin Wharton, 26 March 1818, vol. J.H.B./H.C.N. 1, pp. 115–26.

24. Fragment of 1805 Tayloe ledger or journal, 12 October 1805, uncat. box 2, Tayloe Papers.

25. Estate inventory of Col. John Tayloe III, 8 August 1826, Tayloe Papers. Two silver spoons made by Charles A. Burnett of Georgetown, engraved with Tayloe's initials and marked "Neabsco," are in the possession of descendants (research file 5101, Museum of Early Southern Decorative Arts, Winston-Salem, North Carolina). A hired white manager ran the ironworks called Neabsco, which was outside Dumfries, north of Fredericksburg, Virginia.

26. John Tayloe III inventory book, 1807–26, Tayloe Papers.

27. Inventory of Stephen Decatur, 5 April 1820, vol. J.H.B./H.C.N. 1, pp. 339–42, 2 dozen, valued with other silver; inventory of James R. Wilson, 11 August 1820, vol. J.H.B./H.C.N. 1, pp. 384–88, six valued at $10.07; inventory of Constant Freeman, 26 March 1824, vol. H.C.N. 2, pp. 203–09, 12 old valued at $20; inventory of John Graham, 8 March 1821, vol. J.H.B./H.C.N. 1, pp. 455–59, at least one dozen silver forks valued with spoons at $122.50; inventory of Ruth Barlow, 8 June 1818, vol. J.H.B./H.C.N. 1, pp. 331–37, 34 large table forks valued at $124.80 and "12 pearl handled knives silver" and 12 corresponding forks valued together at $210; and inventory of Thomas Tasker Garett, 1 June 1818, vol. H.C.N. 1, pp. 270–77, six "plated breakfast knives & forks" valued at $5.

28. By the second half of the eighteenth century, the elite in Alexandria and Fairfax County, Virginia, owned silver-handled forks and knives. George Washington ordered "2 Setts best silver handle Knives & Forks best London Blades" in 1757. John Carlyle of Alexandria owned "7 Silver handled Knives & 12 do. forks with a Case" at his death in 1780. The appraisers of the estate of George Johnson of Fairfax County listed "1 doz Sylvr hafted knvs 7 forks" in 1767. Ellen Kirven Donald, Susan A. Borchardt, and Julia B. Claypool, "Carlyle House: Historic Furnishings Plan," prepared for Carlyle House His-

toric Park, Northern Virginia Regional Park Authority (1984), pp. 196–97, 209, and 223.

29. Tayloe bought "1/2 Doz. Buck Handle Knives & Forks" ($3.25) and "1/2 Buck Handle Desert Do" ($2.25). Bill for the purchase of assorted sundries, 4 November 1820, Tayloe in account with H. Carel & Linthicun, Accounts, 1820–24, Tayloe Papers.

30. See Margaret Brown Klapthor, "A First Lady And A New Frontier, 1800," *Historic Preservation* 15 (1963), p. 93; and inventory of President's House, Jefferson Papers.

31. *Letters of Mary Boardman Crowninshield, 1815–1816*, ed. Francis Boardman Crowninshield (Cambridge: Riverside Press, 1905), p. 20. See also Samuel Eliot Morison, "Charles Bagot's Notes on Housekeeping and Entertaining at Washington, 1819," *Publications of the Colonial Society of Massachusetts* 26 (1927), p. 441, which specifies "white handled knives and three pronged steel forks with your crest upon them" for "the use of your household" and not for the ambassador's dinner table.

32. Charles Carroll to his son Charles of Carrollton, 1 June 1772, *Maryland Historical Magazine* 14 (1919), p. 146.

33. Harry Nimrod, "editor," *The Fudge Family in Washington* (Baltimore: Joseph Robinson, 1820), p. 43.

34. Louisa Catherine Adams quoting John Randolph of Roanoke, Diary, 30 March 1820, Adams Papers. The adoption of silver forks by the newly genteel is satirized in an 1835 cartoon in which "The Farmers Son Metamorphosed into a Finished Exquisite" faints at the sight of "that horrible vulgar looking two pronged iron fork." John F. Kasson, *Rudeness and Civility* (New York: Hill and Wang, 1990), pp. 191–92.

35. *Ladies Indispensable Assistant* (New York: F. J. Dow and Co., 1851), p. 125.

36. *Laws of etiquette*, pp. 147–48.

37. B. Faujas de Saint Fond in *Travels in England, Scotland and the Hebrides* (1799), quoted in Hughes, p. 365.

38. Joseph Koenig, quoted in Katie Stuart, *Joy of Eating* (Owings Mills, Md.: Semmes House Publishers, Inc., 1977), p. 120.

39. *Manuel du Bon Ton et de la Politesse*, p. 175, quoted in Esther B. Aresty, *The Best Behavior: the course of good manners from antiquity to the present—as seen through courtesy and etiquette books* (New York: Simon and Schuster, 1970), p. 175. At the present time there is no evidence to support the idea that the timing of the introduction and spread of forks differed significantly in England and America. See James Deetz, *In Small Things Forgotten: The Archaeology of Early American Life* (Garden City, N.Y.: Anchor Press/Doubleday, 1977), p. 123.

40. Aresty, p. 294.

Chapter IV

1. Cutler to his daughter, Mrs. Torrey, 21 February 1805, in William Parker Cutler and Julia Perkins Cutler, *Life Journals and Correspondence of Rev. Manasseh Cutler, LL.D.* (Athens, Oh.: Ohio University Press, 1987), p. 190.

2. "Diary of Edward Hooker," ed. J. Franklin Jameson, *American Historical Association Reports* 1 (1896), pp. 921 and 926. Hooker was in Washington in December 1808.

3. Cutler and Cutler, p. 314; and [Josephine Seaton], *William Winston Seaton of the "National Intelligencer"* (Boston: James R. Osgood and Co., 1871), p. 88. Louisa Catherine Adams noted, "Breakfast at eight oclock: Luncheon at one. Dinner at five and Tea at eight." Louisa Catherine Adams, "Instructions for servants," undated, Adams Papers.

4. Margaret Hall, *The Aristocratic Journey: Being the Outspoken Letters of Mrs. Basil Hall Written during a Fourteen Months' Sojourn in America, 1827–1828*, ed. Una Pope-Hennessy (New York: G. P. Putnam's Sons, 1931), p. 168.

5. Seaton, p. 88. Louisa Catherine Adams remembered "the petit soupers often consisting of little more than Crackers Butter Cake and Wine—which however gave a zest to music, dancing and wit." Louisa Catherine Adams, "The Adventures of Nobody," comment under heading for January 1804, p. 169, Adams Papers.

6. Entries for 21 January 1800 and 5, 8, and 17 May 1800, "Diary of Mrs. William Thornton, 1800–1863," *Records of the Columbia Historical Society* 10 (1907), pp. 97, 137, 139, and 143. Presumably she already owned a tureen and other serving dishes.

7. For biographical information about Thornton, see David Yerkes, *William Thornton: A Renaissance Man in the Federal City* (Washington: AIA Foundation, 1976).

8. The diary from 1800 that contains the fullest comments has been published. "Diary of Mrs. Thornton," pp. 88–226. The following manuscript diaries have been analyzed: 1803, January to June 1804, January to April and November-December 1807, and 1812. The year 1831 has also been studied to gain some insight into Mrs. Thornton's years as a widow. References in the text that can be located by date in the original have not been cited in the notes. Diaries of Anna Maria [Brodeau] Thornton, 1793–1863, Thornton Papers.

9. "Diary of Mrs. Thornton," 1 March 1800.

10. The trip to Mount Vernon lasted a week, 2–6 August 1800. "Diary of Mrs. Thornton," pp. 173–75. The dates of the North Carolina trip were 17 June to 26 August 1805. Travel diary, 1805–06, vol. 2, Thornton Papers.

11. "Diary of Mrs. Thornton," 17 April, 11 and 19 December, 19 December 1800.

12. *Ibid.*, 11 and 25 January, 23 January 1800.

13. Ibid., 27 January 1800.

14. Ibid., 12 January, 13 and 25 January 1800.

15. Ibid., 14 November 1800.

16. Ibid., ladies out alone: 11 and 24 January 1800; visitors to Thorntons: 7, 9, and 28 January 1800.

17. Catharine Mitchill to Margaret Akerly Miller, 8 April 1806, Mitchill Papers.

18. Diary of Anna Maria Thornton, Thornton Papers. Dates during 1812 that Mrs. Thornton went to the "Drawing Room" at the President's House are 12 and 26 February; 18 March; 8, 22, and 29 April; 6, 20, and 27 May; 10, 17, and 24 June; and 1 July; 4 and 18 October; and 9 December. On December 30 she wrote, "Mrs. Tayloe & Forrest wanted me to go to the Drawing Room—but as New Year's day was so near I declined."

19. Orlando Ridout V, *Building the Octagon* (Washington: The AIA Press, 1989), p. 104.

20. Kym S. Rice has analyzed the diary for parts of two social seasons, January to April and November and December of 1807. The references counted are those in which one or both of each couple met each other. During these six months Mrs. Thornton recorded other social occasions. Diary of Anna Maria Thornton, vol. 3 (1807–1818), Thornton Papers.

21. Contrasts between urban and rural living are discussed in Lois Green Carr and Lorena S. Walsh, "Consumer Behavior in the Colonial Chesapeake," in C. Carson, R. Hoffman, and T.J. Albert, eds., *Of Consuming Interest: The Style of Life in the Eighteenth Century* (Charlottesville: University Press of Virginia, forthcoming), pp. 12 and 28; and Ann Smart Martin, "The Urban/Rural Dichotomy of Status Consumption: Tidewater Virginia, 1815" (M.A. thesis, The College of William and Mary, 1986).

22. Entry for 1 June 1819, in *Plantation Life at Rose Hill: The Diaries of Martha Ogle Forman, 1814–1845*, ed. W. Emerson Wilson (Wilmington: The Historical Society of Delaware, 1976), p. 83. The plantation house "Rose Hill" still stands in Cecil County, Maryland. It was worked by approximately fifty slaves. Thomas Forman ended his service in the Continental Army with the rank of major and served as a general in the militia during the War of 1812.

23. Eighteenth century English and American conversation pieces or group portraits and book illustrations frequently show these congenial gatherings. For examples, see Peter Thornton, *Authentic Decor: The Domestic Interior, 1620–1920* (New York: Viking Penguin, Inc., 1984), pp. 120, 121, and 168.

24. Margaret Bayard Smith, *A Winter in Washington, or Memoirs of the Seymour Family* (New York: E. Bliss and E. White, 1824), p. 7. Juliana Seaton also valued William Wirt's company, "He is one of the most elegant *belles lettres* scholars I ever met; . . . a being of the first order." Seaton, p. 114.

25. Margaret Bayard Smith, *The First Forty Years of Washington Society, portrayed by the family letters of Mrs. Samuel Harrison Smith*, ed. Gaillard Hunt (New York: Charles Scribner's Sons, 1906), pp. 244 and 250. For a good discussion of activities and attitudes in a harmonious family circle see Frances Byerly Parkes, *Domestic Duties; or, Instructions to Young Married Ladies, on the Management of Their Households . . .*, (New York: J & J Harper, 1828), pp. 329–32.

26. Catharine Mitchill to Margaret Akerly Miller, 8 April 1806, Mitchill Papers.

27. Harry Nimrod, "editor," *The Fudge Family in Washington* (Baltimore: Joseph Robinson, 1820), p. 26.

28. Diary of Harriet Otis, 30 April 1811, Otis Papers.

29. Mrs. Wirt to her daughter Laura, Richmond, 10 May 1820, Wirt Papers.

30. *The Habits of Good Society* (New York: Carleton, 1864), p. 33.

31. Christina D. Hemphill, "Manners for Americans: Interaction, Ritual and the Social Order, 1620–1860" (Ph.D. dissertation, Brandeis University, 1988), p. 104. Working class women were more independently mobile. They showed deference to their employers, but it is difficult to learn about their demeanor and conversation in the presence of their husbands.

32. [Robert de Valcourt], *The Illustrated Manners Book* (New York: Leland, Clay, 1855), as quoted in Hemphill, p. 471. For more about women's presence in society and the subtleties of sexual attitudes and physical contact, see Hemphill, pp. 492–94.

33. The articles and books listed in the next paragraph discuss women's legal status, the separation of home and work place, family life and loving relationships, women's economic productivity at home and in the work place, and their activities in religious organizations and benevolent associations. The authors use "society" in the general sense and not to refer to a group of equals coming together for conviviality in the polite or fashionable world. See Hemphill, p. 526.

Paula Baker, "The Domestication of Politics: Women and American Political Society, 1780–1920," *The American Historical Review* 89 (June 1984), pp. 620–47; Nancy F. Cott, *The Bonds of Womanhood* (New Haven: Yale University Press, 1977); Linda Kerber, *Women of the Republic* (Chapel Hill: The University of North Carolina Press for the Institute of Early American History and Culture, 1980); Suzanne Lebsock, *The Free Women of Petersburg* (New York: W.W. Norton & Co., 1984); Jan Lewis, *The Pursuit of Happiness* (New York: Cambridge University Press, 1983); Mary Beth Norton, "The Evolution of White Women's Experience in Early America," *The American Historical Review* 89 (June 1984), pp. 593–619; Mary P. Ryan, *Cradle of the Middle Class: The Family in Oneida County New York, 1790–1865* (New York: Cambridge University Press, 1981); Carroll Smith-Rosenberg, "The Female World of Love and Ritual: Relations between Women in Nineteenth-century America" in Michael Gordon, ed., *The American Family in Social Historical Perspective*, 3rd ed., (New York: St. Martin's Press, 1983), pp. 334–58; and Barbara Welter, "The Cult of True Womanhood: 1820–1860," *American Quarterly* 18 (Summer 1966), pp. 151–74.

On the subject of the "social life" of elite women the literature is silent, except for one tantalizing footnote about how the conservative southern domestic ideal differed from the general trend toward individualism and equality. A "code of honor" established women's purity and subordination. This was expressed "in the custom of women coming to the dining table only after men had been served." Steven Mintz and Susan Kellog, *Domestic Revolutions: A Social History of American Family Life* (New York: The Free Press, 1988), p. 267.

34. *Etiquette for Ladies* (Philadelphia: Carey, Lea & Blanchard, 1838), pp. 14, 15, and 70.

35. Ibid., p. 15.

36. Ibid., pp. 54–55.

37. L.G. Moffatt and J.M. Carriere, "A Frenchman [Baron de Montelezun] visits Norfolk, Fredericksburg and Orange County, 1816," *Virginia Historical Magazine* 53 (April 1945), p. 111. Regional practices and age seem to have made a difference. *The laws of etiquette; or, Short rules and reflections for conduct in society. By a gentleman* (Philadelphia: Carey, Lea, and Blanchard, 1839), pp. 113–14, advised male readers to "abstain from grave conversation" with young women but to compliment the intellect of women past twenty-five by raising serious topics. Visiting Washington, Bostonian Harriet Otis was grateful when Mr. Bleecker showed up with "serious ideas on serious subjects that please us the more for being so rare among the gentlemen we meet here." Diary of Harriet Otis, 6 January 1811, Otis Papers.

38. Margaret Hall, p. 186. The "American Colonisation Society" sponsored the lecture.

39. *Daily National Intelligencer* (1831) and other references. When advertising dinners, suppers, oysters, and green turtles in local newspapers, tavernkeepers in the Washington area addressed gentlemen (1798–1809). When promoting tea parties, they mentioned both gentlemen and ladies (1808–1809). See excerpts from Alexandria newspapers on file at Gadsby's Tavern Museum, Alexandria, Virginia.

40. Tonkin's Beef-Steak and Oyster House on Capitol Hill served gentlemen only. *National Daily Advertiser*, 28 December 1800 and 5 January 1801. Drew's advertisement appeared on January 3, 1821. The household of British Minister Bagot, including his wife, dined at Bakers' (presumably a tavern or boardinghouse) on the days they hosted balls. See also notes 40 and 41, chapter vi.

41. *Habits of Good Society*, p. 396. In 1809 several advertisements for tea parties appeared in the *Alexandria Daily Gazette*. The first (April 20) indicated that "Gentlemen's tickets of admittance" cost two dollars; the second (June 13) requested that "those Ladies who have hitherto received tickets to attend the assemblies, will please consider themselves invited." It went on to define the event by saying, "The dancing will commence at 5 o'clock." These advertisement-invitations seem carefully worded to overcome women's reservations about public appearances. Over ten years later in the *Daily National Intelligencer* Mr. Fitzgerald emphasized the select and fashionable character of his "Practicing Ball" or "Cotillion Parties." Gentlemen could obtain "tickets of admission" at the circulating library; "cards of invitation" would be sent to ladies (28 December 1820 and 1 January 1821). The advertisement for the Georgetown subscription cotillion indicated tickets for gentlemen for individual evenings or for the season were available at several locations. Ladies "who, through mistake," had not received invitations were to "have the goodness to make it known."

Mrs. Thornton hesitated to attend balls in public places. Diary of Anna Maria Thornton, February 1800, January 1803, and February 1804, Thornton Papers. Mary Bagot, on the other hand, went to several balls in public places in quick succession: Davis's Tavern, 2 January 1817; Georgetown ball, 9 January 1817; and a "public ball at Alexandria," 20 February 1817. She did not enjoy the last, which was "at least eight miles from this door— never was so bored [?] in my life—& never saw so blackg[uar?]d an assembly. . . ." David Hosford, "Exile in Yankeeland: The Journal of Mary Bagot, 1816–1819," *Records of the Columbia Historical Society* 51 (1984).

42. *Daily National Intelligencer*, 3–15 January 1831.

43. *Etiquette for Ladies*, p. 69.

44. Ibid., p. 71.

45. On the importance of developing conversational skill, see Hemphill, pp. 336, 366–69, and 484–90. Augustus Foster commented on the difficulty he had making general conversation with Americans, whose experience was mostly limited to politics, business, and money: "If they go as far as books of Travels & Magazines it is a vry great deal." Marilyn Kay Parr, "Augustus John Foster and the 'Washington Wilderness': Personal Letters of a British Diplomat" (Ph.D. dissertation, The George Washington University, 1987), pp. 101–102. See also Margaret Hall, p. 69.

46. Seaton, p. 152.

47. William Wirt to Elizabeth Wirt, January [between 4 and 11], 1816, p. 6, Wirt Papers. Elbridge Gerry, Jr., son of Madison's vice president, went out of his way to find female company in Washington. *The Diary of Elbridge Gerry, Jr.*, ed. Claude G. Bowers (New York: Brentano's, 1927), p. 162.

48. Samuel Latham Mitchill, "Dr. Mitchill's Letters from Washington: 1801–1813," *Harper's New Monthly Magazine* (April 1879), pp. 748–49.

49. Catharine Mitchill to Margaret Akerly Miller, 12 February 1809, Mitchill Papers.

50. The best study of American servants is Daniel E. Sutherland, *Americans and their servants: domestic service in the United States from 1800 to 1920* (Baton Rouge: Louisiana State University Press, 1981). See also Karie Diethorn, "Domestic servants in Philadelphia, 1789–1830," report prepared for the National Park Service's Independence National Historical Park, undated; and Fay E. Dudden, *Serving women: household service in 19th century America* (Middletown, Ct.: Wesleyan University Press, 1983).

51. Margaret Hall, p. 67.

52. *Daily National Intelligencer*, 11 August 1819.

53. Smith, *First Forty Years*, pp. 44–45. Other variations in the household are mentioned on pp. 20 and 32.

54. Ibid., pp. 132–33.

55. The information about the Thorntons' servants and slaves has been compiled from diary entries for 1803 and the first half of 1804. No complete inventory has been found. Diary of Anna Maria Thornton, Thornton Papers.

56. Probate Records, Probate Index 1379, Suitland Reference Branch, National Archives and Records Administration. For references to the tutors Samuel Hoare and Samuel Ripley, see Ridout, pp. 105–106, 114. The nurse, "a white woman born in Philadelphia," is discussed in William Henry Tayloe, "[An] Account of the Octagon written by my father at my request 1870 by H. A. Tayloe of Mt. Airy" [William Henry Tayloe (1799–1871) to his son Henry Augustine Tayloe (b. 1836)], typescript copy in the research files, The Octagon, Washington, D.C.

57. Robert Roberts, *The House Servant's Directory* (1827; facsimile ed., Waltham, Massachusetts: The Gore Place Society, 1977), p. v; and Adams, "Instructions for servants," Adams Papers.

58. For more information about the Tayloes' domestic staff, see Ridout, pp. 105–106, and Richard S. Dunn, "A Tale of Two Plantations: Slave Life at Mesopotamia in Jamaica and Mt. Airy in Virginia, 1799 to 1828," *William and Mary Quarterly*, 3rd ser., 34 (January 1977), pp. 32–65. Richard S. Dunn has generously provided additional data from his files.

59. Tayloe, "[An] Account of the Octagon."

60. Receipted bill from Thomas Carpenter, tailor, Jefferson Papers:
    -Decr 1 [1803] To making 4 Livery Coats & all materials, as before 18.27
    To making 4 Waistcoats & Do- 9.60
    To making 4 pr of Pantaloons & Do- 8.80
    8 yds Silver Lace 4.80
    8 yds blue Cloth @ 56 40.- [1804]

2-3/4 yds of Scarlet Do for Waistcoats & facings 13.75

61. British Minister Francis James Jackson noted on 7 October 1809, "Our people are frequently laughed at for wearing a livery." Beckles Willson, *Friendly Relations* (1934; reprint, Freeport, N.Y.: Books for Libraries Press, 1969), p. 67. Even in slaveowning states wealthy Americans had fewer household servants than the British. Nor was it "at all common to have any of the servants in livery except, in rare examples, the coachman, footman, and valet." Thomas Webster, *Encyclopedia of Domestic Economy* (New York: Harper & Bros., 1845), p. 365. Augustus Foster also comments on the impression a servant in livery made on Americans. Parr, p. 270.

62. Harrison Gray Otis to Sally Foster Otis, 21 February 1819, Otis Papers.

63. Seaton, pp. 113–14. When Basil and Margaret Hall returned to England they were delighted once again to see footmen in livery. Margaret Hall, p. 302.

64. Richard Beale Davis, ed., *Jeffersonian America* (San Marino, Ca.: Huntington Library, 1954), p. 152.

65. Tayloe letterbook, 7 June 1801, Tayloe Papers.

66. After a visit to the Tayloes, Harrison Gray Otis wrote, "Yesterday I dined at Tayloes with a small Party—Wormleys and N Amory King Randolph & Self—Pretty well and that's all." Otis to Sally Foster Otis, 20 February 1821, Otis Papers. On February 24, 1820, Louisa Catherine Adams noted in her diary, "a big party at Col. Tayloes the handsomest Ball I have been at this Winter—It was very crowded but I was too ill to take my pleasure in it." Adams Papers.

67. Roberts, pp. 130 and 147.

68. Caroline Howard Gilman, *Recollections of a Housekeeper* (New York: Harper & Bros., 1843), p. 154.

69. Elsewhere Margaret Bayard Smith reports doing her own marketing. Smith, *First Forty Years*, p. 48. There is no gender note in the following description of a visit to the Alexandria market by an English traveler: "Not being able to lie in bed after 5 oClock/a heat We Walk'd into the Market which always begins by day light—It was full of People & many of genteel appearance with their baskets on their arm, it being Customary here for people to make their own market." Journal of Alexander Dick, 9 June 1807, in Alexandria, Dick Papers.

On the other hand, in New Orleans women did not exert themselves. Wrote one visitor, "The ladies of the South seldom make markets or engage in any work that may expose them to any sort of fatigue—a mistaken courtesy, as the morning exercise of market-making could be salutary both to mind and body. The gentlemen, or their coloured servants, make all the markets, and in the crowd I hardly met a single lady." George Lewis, *Impressions of America and the American Churches* (1845; reprint, New York: Negro Universities Press, 1968), p. 203. I am grateful to Kym S. Rice for this reference.

70. Roberts, pp. 138–39.

71. See Stephen Mennell, *All Manners of Food: Eating and Taste in England and France from the Middle Ages to the Present* (Oxford: Blackwell, 1985), pp. 134–35, on the relative status of male chefs and female cooks. Both Thomas Jefferson and John Tayloe III owned expert male cooks.

72. Letters exchanged between William and Elizabeth Wirt, 29 December 1815, 11 and 12 January 1816, Wirt Papers.

73. Wilson J. Cary to Virginia Cary, 9 January and 15 February 1822, quoted in Jan Lewis, *The Pursuit of Happiness* (New York: Cambridge University Press, 1983), p. 142.

74. Alicia Delahunty, "Situation Wanted" (seminar research paper, The George Washington University, May 1990), copy in the files of The Octagon, pp. 6 and 11.

75. *National Intelligencer*, 31 January 1811.

76. *Daily National Intelligencer*, 28 December 1819.

77. Roberts, p. xi.

78. Ibid., p. 45.

79. Ibid., p. 123. See also *Laws of etiquette*, pp. 144–45, and Diane L. Berger, " 'Pray Let Them Be Neat and Fashionable or Send None': Dining in Eighteenth and Early Nineteenth-Century America, An Exploration of Ritual and Equipage with a Case Study of Virginia Probate Inventories" (M.A. thesis, The George Washington University, 1990), pp. 48–51.

80. Roberts, pp. 74–76 and 138.

81. Lydia Maria Child, *The American Frugal Housewife*, 12th ed. (Boston: Carter, Hendee, and Co., 1832). Frugality did not include entertaining at dinner parties.

82. Gilman, pp. 153–54.

83. Roberts, p. 151.

84. George Watterston, *Wanderer in Washington* (Washington: Joseph Elliot, Jr., 1827), p. 45.

85. *National Intelligencer*, 10 January 1810. Other purveyors advertised they would supply families with turtle soup. Several advertisements appear in the *Daily National Intelligencer* between 26 May and 8 July 1820.

86. Elizabeth Wirt to Elizabeth Gamble, 14 February 1819, Wirt Papers.

87. Harrison Gray Otis to Sally Foster Otis, 21 February 1819, Otis Papers. By 1831 at least two French cooks advertised their willingness to prepare special dishes in the *Daily National Intelligencer*, 6 and 21 January 1831. Philadelphians may have had access to more of these services. By 1820 they could hire public cooks and public servants. The "editor" of the Fudge letters noted that strangers, until they were let in on the secret, were surprised to find that servants in different houses were so much alike. He facetiously recommended "publick plates, knives, forks, confectionary, &c" that would allow "a great many to cut a figure in the world and acquire a reputation for hospitality at a small expense." Nimrod, p. 16.

88. Mrs. Smith admired Martineau, but she recognized that few members of Washington society knew why she was celebrated. The gentlemen laughed "at a woman's writing on political economy," even though "not one of them" had "any idea of the nature of her work," she wrote, and "our most fashionable, exclusive Mrs. Tayloe, . . . asked what were the novels she had written and if they were pretty?" Smith, *First Forty Years*, p. 356.

89. Ibid., pp. 359–60; and Charles Day, *Etiquette* (New York: Wilson & Co., 1843), p. 12.

Chapter V

1. Henry Fearon, *Sketches of America* (1818; reprint, New York: Benjamin Blom, 1969), p. 291.

2. E. Cooley, M.D., *A Description of the Etiquette at Washington City, Exhibiting the Habits and Customs that prevail in the intercourse of the most distinguished and fashionable Society at that place, during the session of Congress* (Philadelphia: L. B. Clarke, 1829), p. 62.

3. Ibid., p. 32. Conversations among travelers "in a boat or a coach" did not give "a right to after recognition." *Etiquette for Ladies* (Philadelphia: Carey, Lea & Blanchard, 1838), pp. 11–12.

4. Cooley, p. 37.

5. Ibid., p. 40.

6. Ibid., p. 39.

7. Ibid., p. 36. An excellent account of visiting procedure is found in Margaret Bayard Smith, *What is Gentility?* (Washington: Pishey Thompson, 1828), pp. 117–18 and 122–29. See also Margaret Hall, *The Aristocratic Journey: Being the Outspoken Letters of Mrs. Basil Hall Written during a Fourteen Months' Sojourn in America, 1827–1828*, ed. Una Pope-Hennessy (New York: G. P. Putnam's Sons, 1931), p. 168.

8. Christina D. Hemphill, "Manners for Americans: Interaction, Ritual and the Social Order, 1620–1860" (Ph.D. dissertation, Brandeis University, 1988), pp. 343–45.

9. *Etiquette for Ladies*, p. 55.

10. Cooley, p. 49.

11. Margaret Bayard Smith, *The First Forty Years of Washington Society, portrayed by the family letters of Mrs. Samuel Harrison Smith*, ed. Gaillard Hunt (New York: Charles Scribner's Sons, 1906), pp. 45 and 306–307. See also p. 239.

12. *Letters of Mary Boardman Crowninshield, 1815–1816*, ed. Francis Boardman Crowninshield (Cambridge: Riverside Press, 1905), p. 51. Benjamin Latrobe complained to John Tayloe III in 1811, "My promise to call to see your roof I have performed, altho I was not admitted, and you probably have not heard that I was at your door. Mr & Mrs [?] betrayed your being at home, for he was just leaving you when I rode up." Latrobe to Tayloe, 10 March 1811, Latrobe Papers.

13. Diary of Louisa Catherine Adams, 19 February and 4 March 1819, Adams Papers.

14. *Etiquette at Washington* (Baltimore: Murphy & Co., 1857), p. 31.

15. *New York Evening Post*, 18 November 1801. Reference courtesy of Andrea Kerr. On February 13, 1802, Thomas Jefferson paid William Duane for "1 Ream Invitations 2 on a sheet 4 to post 20—." Jefferson Papers. Margaret Bayard and Harrison Smith had "a general invitation" for Saturday evenings with the Baron and Baroness Hyde de Neuville, although Mrs. Smith does not say whether it was verbal or written. Smith, *First Forty Years*, p. 141.

16. David Baillie Warden, *A Chorographical and Statistical Description of the District of Columbia* (Paris: Smith, 1816), pp. 182–83. Rodris Roth generously provided this reference.

By the 1840s invitations, acceptances, and apologies were written. "If the person invited cannot go, he or she sends a written apology, and these apologies are laid on the centre table or mantlepiece of the drawing room.," observed one contemporary author. George Watterston, *A new guide to Washington* (Washington: Robert Farnham, 1842), p. 140. I am grateful to Dell Upton for this reference.

17. Entry for 2 August 1800, "Diary of Mrs. William Thornton, 1800–1863," *Records of the Columbia Historical Society* 10 (1907).

18. Letter dated 26 February 1809, Smith, *First Forty Years*, pp. 54–55.

19. [George Watterston], *The L. . .Family at Washington* (Washington: Joseph Elliot, 1827), pp. 150–51. See also Thomas Webster, *An Encyclopedia of Domestic Economy* (New York: Harper & Bros., 1845), p. 859.

20. Augustus Foster to Lady Elizabeth Foster, 1 July 1805, in Donald H. Mugridge, "Augustus Foster and His Book," *Records of the Columbia Historical Society* (1953–56), p. 342.

21. By 1815 the salary of the British minister to Washington was 5,500 pounds sterling, with an additional £2,000 for outfit and £500 for house allowance. Marilyn Kay Parr, "Augustus John Foster and the 'Washington Wilderness': Personal Letters of a British Diplomat" (Ph.D. dissertation, The George Washington University, 1987), p. 152. Louisa Catherine Adams, when justifying "not inviting ladies to dinner because my rooms were small" and the expense unsupportable, added that others followed her example, even the "President's family forgetting the difference between a Salary of 25000 and six thousand dollars a year." Diary of Louisa Catherine Adams, 7 January 1821, Adams Papers.

22. Smith, *First Forty Years*, p. 48.

23. William Wirt to his wife, Elizabeth, 4 September 1820; and Robert Wirt to his mother, Elizabeth, 1 October 1820, Wirt Papers.

24. Smith, *First Forty Years*, p. 360.

25. Another congressman wrote on January 21, 1811, about how "a piece of your boiled beef and pork with some squash and potatoes" made a "very good dinner." "Letters of Abijah Bigelow, Member of Congress, to his Wife, 1810–1815," *Proceedings of the American Antiquarian Society* 40 (October 1930), p. 315. See Caroline Howard Gilman, *Recollections of a Housekeeper* (New York: Harper & Bros., 1843), pp. 113 and 130, for two everyday dinner menus in a lawyer's family.

26. See Margaret Bayard Smith, *A Winter in Washington, or Memoirs of the Seymour Family*, vol. 1 (New York: E. Bliss and E. White, 1824), p. 264; and Smith, *First Forty Years*, p. 275. Charles and Mary Bagot picnicked to distance themselves from their servants at a tavern. David Hosford, ed., "Exile in Yankeeland: The Journal of Mary Bagot, 1816–1819," *Records of the Columbia Historical Society* 51 (1984), pp. 46–47. For examples of masters eating with servants, see Margaret Hall, p. 13.

27. Edward C. Carter II, ed., *The Virginia Journal of Benjamin Henry Latrobe, 1795–1798* (New Haven: Yale University Press, 1977), plate 7 following p. 80.

28. Anne Newport Royall, *Letters from Alabama, 1817–1822* (1830; reprint, University, Al.: University of Alabama Press, 1969), p. 169.

29. Smith, *First Forty Years*, pp. 52–53.

30. Jadviga M. da Costa Nunes and Ferris Olin, *Baroness Hyde de Neuville: Sketches of America, 1807–1822* (New Brunswick, N.J.: Rutgers, 1984), p. 25.

31. Louisa Catherine Adams, "The Adventures of Nobody," comment under heading for 1 January 1804–05, p. 190, Adams Papers.

32. Stephen Mennell, *All Manners of Food: Eating and Taste in England and France from the Middle Ages to the Present* (Oxford: Blackwell, 1985), pp. 95–97.

33. Harry Nimrod, "editor," *The Fudge Family in Washington* (Baltimore: Joseph Robinson, 1820), pp. 16 and 41–42.

34. William Parker Cutler and Julia Perkins Cutler, *Life Journals and Correspondence of Rev. Manasseh Cutler, LL.D.* (Athens: Ohio University Press, 1987), p. 154.

35. Cutler and Cutler, p. 71.

36. [Josephine Seaton], *William Winston Seaton of the "National Intelligencer"* (Boston: James R. Osgood and Co., 1871), p. 88. Thomas Jefferson's accounts include wages for someone to help turn ice cream. 5 July 1806, household account book kept by Etienne Lemaire, 12 December 1806–1809, Jefferson Papers. H. Julian on F Street advertised "ice creams on Sunday next, and afterwards every Wednesday and Sunday, dring the season," *National Intelligencer*, 1 June 1810. Articles on the history of ice cream appear in several issues of *Petit Propos Culinaires* 1 (1979); 2 (August 1979); 3 (November 1979); supplement to 3 (November 1979); and 8 (June 1981).

37. Seaton, p. 85.

38. Jeffrey also described the table service, "no plate and no china—ordinary blue English ware," and was equally scornful of the wine and the decanters. Lord Francis Jeffrey, typescript excerpts from a journal of a trip to the United States in 1813, courtesy of the Office of the Curator of the White House.

39. Louise Conway Belden, *The Festive Tradition* (New York: W.W. Norton, 1983), pp. 33–36; and Diane L. Berger, " 'Pray Let Them Be Neat and Fashionable or Send None': Dining in Eighteenth and Early Nineteenth-Century America, An Exploration of Ritual and Equipage with a Case Study of Virginia Probate Inventories" (M.A. thesis, The George Washington University, 1990), pp. 37–38. According to tradition, the Russian ambassador in France in 1810 introduced *service à la russe*. It is not mentioned by name in descriptions of Washington meals, where the distinctions focus on variations in English and French methods.

40. Rosalie Stier Calvert to her brother Charles J. Stier, 1 December 1806, and to her sister Isabelle van Havre, 2 April 1807, quoted in Margaret Law Callcott, ed., *Mistress of Riversdale: The Plantation Letters of Rosalie Stier Calvert, 1795–1821* (Baltimore: The Johns Hopkins University Press, forthcoming). I am grateful to Susan Pearl and Margaret Callcott for sharing this reference.

41. Margaret Hall, p. 188.

42. *The laws of etiquette; or, Short rules and reflections for conduct in society. By a gentleman* (Philadelphia: Carey, Lea, and Blanchard, 1839), p. 139.

43. Louisa Catherine Adams, miscellany, 1 March 1819, Adams Papers.

44. Margaret Hall, p. 180.

45. Charles Day, *Etiquette* (New York: Wilson & Co., 1843), p. 12.

46. Hunter Dickinson Farish, ed., *Journal and Letters of Philip Vickers Fithian, A Plantation Tutor of the Old Dominion, 1773–1774* (Charlottesville: University Press of Virginia, 1957), p. 67.

47. Quoted in Helen Sprackling, *Customs on the Table Top* (Sturbridge, Mass.: Old Sturbridge Village, 1958), p. 20.

48. Diary of Louisa Catherine Adams, 25 March 1819, Adams Papers.

49. Smith, *First Forty Years*, p. 307.

50. Margaret Hall, p. 188.

51. In 1836 *The laws of etiquette* defined a "ladies dinner" as "a dinner at which any women are present, the men after drinking as much wine as they please, join the women in the drawing room when they take coffee. . . . If the company is composed entirely of men, coffee is brought into the dining room." *Laws of etiquette*, p. 167.

52. Caroline Howard King, *When I Lived in Salem, 1822–1866* (Brattleboro, Vt.: Stephen Daye Press, 1937), p. 22, quoted in Elisabeth Donaghy Garrett, "The American Home: Part IV: The dining room," *Antiques* 126 (October 1984), p. 917.

53. Theophilus Bradbury to his daughter, 26 December 1795, quoted in Fritzie and Ben James, *Christmas with George Washington 1776–1799* (Philadelphia: privately printed by Franklin Printing Company, 1954). From the research files, courtesy, the Mount Vernon Ladies' Association of the Union.

54. *Laws of etiquette*, p. 137.

55. Margaret Hall, pp. 162 and 121. Frances Trollope observed, "Mixed dinner parties of ladies and gentlemen, however, are very rare, ..." Frances Trollope, *Domestic Manners of the Americans* (1832; reprint, New York: Vintage Books, 1949), pp. 298–99. In 1833 T. Hamilton noted, "Of the ladies of Boston I did not see much, ... Unfortunately it is still less the fashion, than at New York, to enliven the dinner-table with their presence, and, during my stay, I was only present at one ball." T. Hamilton, *Men and Manners in America* (London: William Blackwood, 1833), p. 240.

56. Journal entry, New Jersey, 28 November 1780 in Marquis de Chastellux, *Travels in North America in the Years 1780, 1781, and 1782*, ed. and trans. Howard C. Rice, Jr. (Chapel Hill: Univeristy of North Carolina Press for the Institute of Early American History and Culture, 1963), p. 119.

57. Ibid., p. 160.

58. Diary of Robert Gilmor, quoted in Raphael Semmes, *Baltimore as seen by visitors, 1783–1860* (Baltimore: Maryland Historical Society, 1953), pp. 94–95.

59. Robert Roberts, *The House Servant's Directory* (1827; facsimile ed., Waltham, Massachusetts: The Gore Place Society, 1977), pp. 60–61. See also Smith, *Winter in Washington*, pp. 16 and 47.

60. *Laws of etiquette*, p. 154.

61. Thomas Pinckney to Harriet Pinckney, January 1777, between Emporia and Williamsburg, Virginia, in *South Carolina Historical Magazine* 58 (April 1957), p. 78. References from the research files of the Museum of Early Southern Decorative Arts.

62. Seaton, p. 89.

63. Harrison Gray Otis to Sally Foster Otis, 1 February 1801, Otis Papers.

64. Journal of Mary Bagot, 20 November 1816, Sir Charles Bagot Manuscripts, Levens Hall, Cumbria, England. David Hosford generously shared the microfilm edition of this journal, from which excerpts were published in Hosford, "Exile in Yankeeland."

65. Diary of Louisa Catherine Adams, 7 January 1821, Adams Papers.

66. Ibid., 25 February 1819.

67. "Diary of Mrs. Thornton," 25 February 1800.

68. Margaret Hall, p. 212.

69. Hosford, "Exile in Yankeeland," p. 46. See also Mary Ellen W. Hern, "Picnicking in the Northeastern United States, 1840–1900," *Winterthur Portfolio* 24 (Summer/Autumn 1989), pp. 139–52. For disagreement about the popularity of picnics elsewhere in the United States, see Trollope, p. 299.

70. *The Diary of Elbridge Gerry, Jr.*, ed. Claude G. Bowers (New York: Brentano's, 1927), pp. 152–76 and 184.

71. Smith, *First Forty Years*, p. 87.

72. Hosford, "Exile in Yankeeland," p. 37. Catharine and Samuel Mitchill rented a horse and gig on the third of May 1812 and drove eighteen miles from Washington to the falls before 10 a.m. They ate breakfast and presumably other meals at a nearby tavern, looked at the falls and canal, and returned to the city the same day. Catharine Mitchill to Margaret Miller, 3 May 1812, Mitchill Papers.

73. George Gibbs Channing, *Early Recollections of Newport, Rhode Island: from the year 1793 to 1811* (Newport, R.I.: A.J. Ward, C.E. Hammet, Jr., 1868), pp. 167–70.

74. Entry refers to Rapalje house, New York City, 8 January 1807, journal of Alexander Dick, Dick Papers.

75. Sophie du Pont to Eleuthera du Pont, Alexandria, 9 May 1831, Letters of Sophie Madeline du Pont, Hagley Museum, Wilmington, Delaware.

76. For two brief but similar descriptions of large tea parties in Salem, see Edward S. Cooke, Jr., "Domestic Space in the Federal-Period Inventories of Salem Merchants," *Essex Institute Historical Collections* 116 (April 1980), p. 252.

In a satirical description of "a sumptuous dinner to twenty gentlemen," the narrator tells that his wife and two daughters were seated while his son "blackened his face a little, and attended at the table." On the same day the couple also gave an evening "jam" for 100 ladies. I am grateful to Andrea Kerr, who gave me this amusing account published in the December 1825 issue of a magazine called *The Ladies Museum*, Providence, Rhode Island.

77. Frances Byerley Parkes, *Domestic Duties* (New York: J & J Harper, 1828), pp. 86–87. According to a French traveler in America, "The principal difference in the expenditure of the two classes [richest merchant and mechanic or farmer], is that the rich man now and then gives a ball, and piques himself on his parade, which the indulgent democracy pardons for one day; this sort of luxury is much more expensive here than with us [U.S. rather than France], and it does not require a very brilliant rout, in small houses in which the company is received in two rooms 20 feet by 25, to cost 700 or 800 dollars." Michael Chevalier, *Society, Manners and Politics in the United States* (1839; reprint, New York: Burt Franklin, 1969), p. 303. I am grateful to Ann Smart Martin for giving me this reference.

78. Harrison Gray Otis to Sally Foster Otis, 20 January 1819, Otis Papers.

79. Smith, *First Forty Years*, p. 268.

80. Margaret Hall, p. 169.

81. Disapproving comments about the Tayloes can be found in the following: William Lee, *A Yankee Jeffersonian*, ed. Mary Lee Mann (Cambridge: Harvard University Press, 1958), pp. 191 and 205; and Smith, *First Forty Years*, p. 356. Further research will undoubtedly turn up others whom the Tayloes saw regularly.

82. For these friends the ratio is about two occasions at the Octagon to one hosted by the Thorntons, Adamses, or Bagots. Kym S. Rice compiled the numbers from Mary Bagot's diary from her arrival in Washington at the end of March 1816 to her departure in the same month of 1819 and from Harrison Gray Otis's correspondence for the seasons of 1818–1819 and 1820–1821. Otis told his wife he entertained John Tayloe III on February 3, 1819. Otis to Elizabeth Otis, 3 February 1819, Otis Papers.

83. Harrison Gray Otis to Sally Foster Otis, 26 November 1818, Otis Papers.

84. Harrison Gray Otis to Sally Foster Otis, 5 January 1819, Otis Papers. Otis undoubtedly used "passe" to mean "gone by" or past her prime. By "secek" he may have meant "séchée" or dry and applied it both to her physical appearance and personality.

85. "Col Tayloe's family were wealthy and their House with his kind and amiable Wife and daughters to grace it was one of the most elegant in the City—Mrs. Ogle of Annapolis was an elegant Woman and greatly admired when she visited at Mrs Tayloes her daughter," from the 1804 section of Adams, "The Adventures of Nobody," p. 190.

"In the Even we all went to Col Tayloe's and being already out of spirits passed the most unpleasant Evening—Col and Mrs Tayloe have always lived upon the most friendly terms with us—The family is of the highest respectability but in the whole though so numerous there is nothing that indicates more than mediocrity—Their wealth [and?] high standing in Virginia gives them great influence and they are ever tendering to us proffers of service and friendship—," from the diary of Louisa Catherine Adams, 10 February 1823, Adams Papers.

86. Diary of Anna Maria Thornton, 29 June 1803 (Laws) and 1 March 1803 (Tayloe), Thornton Papers.

87. Ibid., 21 February, 5 and 30 March, 25 June 1803. On October 18, 1803, Mrs. Thornton noted, "cards for the first time in our house." Mary Crowninshield played loo at the Monroes' and noted she would give her winnings to the orphan asylum, February 1816, *Letters Mary Boardman Crowninshield*, p. 59.

88. Smith, *First Forty Years*, pp. 136–37.

89. Seaton, p. 170.

90. One memoir suggests that all of Salem, Massachusetts, hired "York Morris, the stout colored waiter, who handed with a dexterity peculiar to himself." M.C.D. Silsbee, *A Half Century in Salem* (Boston: Houghton, Mifflin & Co., 1887), p. 21.

91. Entry cites refreshments served at Rapalje house, New York City, January 1807, journal of Alexander Dick, Dick Papers. Catharine Mitchill listed the refreshments, "ice cream, Cordials, Punch, Jelly, Cake, and fruit" of all kinds at a party in 1806. She continued, "The fruit was carried around in small baskets; and strewed amongst the raisons and almonds, were the small pieces of candied sugar, a sample of which I now send to you." Catharine Mitchill to Margaret Akerly Miller, 8 April 1806, Mitchill Papers.

92. Harrison Gray Otis to Sally Foster Otis, 1 February 1801, Otis Papers.

93. Trollope, p. 155. Mrs. Hall endured a ball where similar "peculiar privileges" were granted to the gentlemen. Margaret Hall, p. 100. Others describe variations on the theme or the practice applied at other events like garden parties or suppers following concerts. Semmes, pp. 94–95.

94. *Laws of etiquette*, pp. 98–99.

95. Margaret Hall, p. 62.

96. Ibid., pp. 72 (near Albany), 78 (Stockbridge, Massachusetts), and 198 (Richmond).

97. Ibid., pp. 62–63.

98. Ibid., p. 70.

99. Ibid., p. 75.

100. Ibid., pp. 72, 89, and 90.

101. Ibid., p. 87.

102. Gilman, pp. 60–61. Mrs. Smith refers to center tables as the focal point for evening entertainments. Smith, *First Forty Years*, pp. 250 (1829), 327 (1831), and 343 (1834). A. J. Downing distinguishes the two forms: "As the centre-table is to us the emblem of the family circle, and the sofa-table that of the evening party, we think the former should hold its place in the country, *par excellence*." He explains further, "In towns, they have given place to sofa-tables—as the latter, scattered here and there in a room, afford various gathering-places for little conversation parties—while the centre-table draws all talkers to a single focus." A. J. Downing, *The Architecture of Country Houses* (1850; reprint, New York: Dover Publications, 1969), pp. 428–29. For more about center tables, see footnote 41, chapter II.

103. Smith, *First Forty Years*, p. 268.

104. Smith, *Winter in Washington*, vol. 2, pp. 30–32.

105. Jane C. Nylander, "Henry Sargent's Dinner Party and Tea Party," *Antiques* 121 (May 1982), pp. 1172–83.

106. Nimrod, p. 91.

107. *Etiquette for Ladies*, p. 68.

108. George Watterston, *Wanderer in Washington* (Washington: Joseph Elliot, Jr., 1827), p. 45.

109. Smith, *First Forty Years*, p. 137.

110. "Diary of Mrs. Thornton," 2 July 1800.

111. Laura Wirt, Washington, to her father William Wirt, Baltimore, 23 November 1819, Wirt Papers. The party was at the Decaturs'.

112. Parkes, *Domestic Duties*, p. 86.

Chapter VI

1. William Parker Cutler and Julia Perkins Cutler, *Life Journals and Correspondence of Rev. Manasseh Cutler, LL.D.* (Athens, Oh.: Ohio University Press, 1987), p. 66; and

Samuel Mitchill, "Dr. Mitchill's Letters from Washington: 1801–1813," *Harper's New Monthly Magazine* (April 1879), p. 744.

2. "Leland's *Budget of Scraps* (1810)," *An Occasional Bulletin* of the Virginia Historical Society, 22 (April 1971), p. 8.

3. Cutler and Cutler, p. 66. Peter Lenox was paid for "a frame for the Cheese" (presumably the great cheese) on 29 March 1802 and for "a hoop for the use of the Cheese" on 18 June 1802. Receipted bills, 1800–1818, Jefferson Papers.

4. Everett S. Brown ed., *William Plumer's Memorandum of Proceedings in the United States Senate* (1923; reprint, New York: Da Capo Press, 1969), pp. 212–13. At some time sixty pounds that had spoiled were cut out of the center of the cheese. The last bits were eaten in 1805.

5. Jean Hanrey Hazelton, "Thomas Jefferson Gourmet," *American Heritage* 15 (October 1964), pp. 21–105.

6. Barbara G. Carson, "Abroad in Colonial America," in C. Carson, R. Hoffman, and P. J. Albert, eds., *Of Consuming Interest: The Style of Life in the Eighteenth Century* (Charlottesville: University Press of Virginia, forthcoming); Jane Boyle Knowles, *Luxury Hotels in American Cities, 1810–1860* (Ph.D. dissertation, University of Pennsylvania, 1972); and Kym S. Rice, *Taverns: For the Entertainment of Friends and Strangers* (Chicago: Regnery Gateway, 1983). For the story of the Union Public Hotel, also known as Blodgett's Hotel, see Doris Elizabeth King, "Early Hotel Entrepreneurs and Promoters, 1793–1860," *Explorations in Entrepreneurial History* 8 (February 1956), pp. 148–50.

7. Barbara G. Carson, "Housing Travelers: Accommodations for Americans on the Road," in Catherine E. Hutchins, ed., *Everyday Life in the Early Republic, 1789–1828* (New York: W. W. Norton & Co. for Winterthur, forthcoming).

8. The generalization made by E. Cooley, *A Description of the Etiquette at Washington City* (Philadelphia: L. B. Clarke, 1829), p. 59, is supported by specific comments quoted in the text. Henry Fearon, who considered Washington accommodations inferior to those of other American cities, wrote, "I first applied at. . .Davis's Indian queen tavern: most of the door handles are broken; the floor of the coffee room is strewed with bricks and mortar, caused by the crumbling of the walls and ceiling; and the character of the accommodations is in unison with this unorganised state of things: the charges are as high as at the very first London hotel." Henry Fearon, *Sketches of America* (1818; reprint, New York: Benjamin Blom, Inc., 1969), p. 292.

9. Cutler and Cutler, pp. 50–51.

10. Albert Gallatin to Hannah Nicholson Gallatin, 15 January 1801, Papers of Albert Gallatin, sponsored by New York University, New York City, and the National Historical Publications Commission; microfilm ed., Manuscript Division, Library of Congress. Oliver Wolcott, Jr., secretary of the treasury in 1800, also used the phrase about monks. See Thomas Froneek, ed., *The City of Washington, An Illustrated History* (New York: Alfred A. Knopf, 1985), p. 71.

11. Margaret Bayard Smith, *The First Forty Years of Washington Society, portrayed by the family letters of Mrs. Samuel Harrison Smith*, Gaillard Hunt, ed. (New York: Charles Scribner's Sons, 1906), p. 48. Later the Barlows moved to their house, Kalorama, which was then in the country north of the developed areas of the city. See Mrs. Barlow's inven-

tory (8 June 1818, vol. J.H.B./H.C.N. 1, p. 331–37). Boarders often agreed to supply their own fuel and candles. See Carson, "Housing Travelers."

12. Journal of Alexander Dick, 20 and 26 June 1807 (in Alexandria), Dick Papers. Mary Thomson's probate inventory taken in 1819 provides a good glimpse of the interior appointments of her establishment. Probably she purchased some of the furnishings in the twelve years after Dick boarded with her. Although the appraisers did not label the rooms, the order of the objects conforms to those likely to have been in a house of Dick's description. One of the ground floor rooms, probably the parlor, was furnished with a carpet, sofa, twelve rush bottom chairs, a pair of card tables, fireplace equipment, and a hearth rug. A looking glass and two prints were gilt framed. The three pairs of window curtains were held in place with curtain pins. The dining room can be distinguished by a mahogany sideboard, two walnut dining tables, three other tables, fourteen Windsor chairs, and possibly a bureau. Its carpet valued at fifteen dollars was protected with a "green bays carpet" valued at two dollars. The windows were inexpensively curtained, and the low value of the looking glass that was itemized after the "Wash Stand bowl & pitcher" suggests it was more practical than decorative. Knives and forks, casters, salts, decanters, tumblers, wineglasses, and waiters or trays were grouped with the furniture. The passage and stairs leading to the adequately furnished bedrooms were carpeted. More tables and tea and coffee ware, including "1 Set of Dining china" valued at $32.50, follow. There were seven tablecloths but neither napkins nor towels. Inventory of Mary Thomson, 4 February 1819, vol. J.H.B/H.C.N. 1, pp. 268–70.

13. "Letters of Abijah Bigelow, Member of Congress, to his Wife, 1810–1815," *Proceedings of the American Antiquarian Society* 40, new ser. (October 1930), pp. 311–12.

14. William Wirt to Elizabeth Wirt, 15 November 1817, Wirt Papers. Perhaps the arrangement explains an ambiguous note in Alexander Dick's correspondence that Mrs. Thomson had "two of these Houses at $200 each = £45 5s." Journal of Alexander Dick, 26 June 1807, Dick Papers.

15. *Daily National Intelligencer*, 15 January 1821; 8 January 1831; and 2 December 1830.

16. Cooley, pp. 58–59.

17. Smith, *First Forty Years*, p. 12. The reminiscences were written in 1837.

18. J. Franklin Jameson, ed., "Diary of Edward Hooker," *American Historical Association Reports* 1 (1896), pp. 921, 926, and 928.

19. Hooker, p. 921.

20. Bigelow, p. 313.

21. Cutler and Cutler, pp. 51–52 and 132.

22. *The Diary of Elbridge Gerry, Jr.*, ed. Claude G. Bowers (New York: Brentano's, 1927), pp. 196 and 200. On one occasion Gerry and a friend "pitched a tent" in his lodgings "and drank port wine and ate cake untill day light." Another boarder, Mary B. Crowninshield, noted in 1815 that after dinner and tea "we can play whist, chess or [back]gammon, for there are always enought to make up a party. I generally return to my own room till the girls tease me so to go visiting in some of the other parlours." *Letters of Mary Boardman Crowninshield, 1815–1816*, ed. Francis Boardman Crowninshield (Cambridge: Riverside Press, 1905), p. 19.

In January 1822 Louis McLane was preparing for his wife and children to come to Washington. He proposed that they stay in Georgetown, where accommodations would be ten dollars cheaper than those in a Washington hotel. There they would have a private parlor, which he thought necessary for the size of their party, where they would take breakfast and tea. They would dine with the mess. Louis McLane to Catharine McLane, 10 January 1822, McLane Papers.

23. Albert Gallatin to Hannah Nicholson Gallatin, 15 January 1801, Papers of Albert Gallatin.

24. Harrison Gray Otis, Boston, to Sally Foster Otis, New York, 30 May 1815, Otis Papers.

25. Harrison Gray Otis to Sally Foster Otis, 3 and 5 February 1819, Otis Papers.

26. Harrison Gray Otis to Sally Foster Otis, 21 February 1919, Otis Papers.

27. Harrison Gray Otis to Sophia Otis, Philadelphia, 30 January 1818, Otis Papers.

28. Diary of Louisa Catherine Adams, 16 February 1821, Adams Papers.

29. Louisa Catherine Adams, "The Adventures of Nobody," 1805, p. 179, Adams Papers.

30. Diary of Harriet Otis, 5 February 1811, Otis Papers.

31. Bagot summarized his "kit" and advised his successor, Stratford Canning, what to bring to the United States. Samuel Eliot Morison, "Charles Bagot's Notes on Housekeeping and Entertaining at Washington, 1819," *Publications of the Colonial Society of Massachusetts* 26 (1927), p. 443.

32. Richard Beale Davis, ed., *Jeffersonian America, Notes on the United States of America Collected in the Years 1805–6–7 and 11–12 by Sir Augustus John Foster, Bart.* (San Marino, Ca.: The Huntington Library, 1954), p. 253.

33. *Diary of Elbridge Gerry*, p. 202. The minister was Louis Sérurier.

34. Harrison Gray Otis to Sally Foster Otis, 15 December 1818, Otis Papers. The minister was Hyde de Neuville.

35. David Hosford, "Exile in Yankeeland: The Journal of Mary Bagot, 1816–1819," *Records of the Columbia Historical Society* 52 (1984), p. 45.

36. John Quincy Adams quoted in Jadviga M. da Costa Nunes and Ferris Olin, *Baroness Hyde de Neuville: Sketches of America, 1807–1822* (New Brunswick, N.J.: Rutgers, 1984), p. 25.

37. Cutler and Cutler, 12 and 19 February and 2 March 1805, pp. 183 and 185. Louis McLane noted the abundance of silver on Bagot's table, "Our entertainment magnificent—We literally eat off of plate, and of the most splendid kind." He then described the plateau, the liveried servants, and the guests. Bagot's successor set a table where "gold and silver were in a profusion to dazzle the eyes." Louis McLane to Kitty McLane, 24 January 1818, December 1821, and February 1822, McLane Papers.

38. Cutler and Cutler, 26 February 1805, p. 184.

39. Augustus Foster to his mother, Lady Elizabeth Foster, 2 January 1812, in Marilyn Kay Parr, "Augustus John Foster and the 'Washington Wilderness': Personal Letters of a British Diplomat" (Ph.D. dissertation, The George Washington University, 1987), p. 325.

40. Journal of Mary Bagot, 13–27 January 1817, Sir Charles Bagot Manuscripts, Levens Hall, Cumbria, England; microfilm copy.

41. Ibid., 10 September 1817.

42. Harrison Gray Otis to Sally Foster Otis, 28 November 1818, Otis Papers. A ball hosted by Stratford Canning in February 1821 impressed Juliana Seaton. [Josephine Seaton], *William Winston Seaton of the "National Intelligencer"* (Boston: James R. Osgood and Co., 1871), p. 152. Margaret Hall described a ball at the residence of Charles Richard Vaughan where the floor was chalked and other details met the expectations of her British eyes. 29 January 1828 in Margaret Hall, *The Aristocratic Journey*, ed. Una Pope-Hennessy (New York: G. P. Putnam's Sons, 1931), p. 193.

43. Harrison Gray Otis to Sally Foster Otis, 19 January 1819, Otis Papers.

44. Journal of Mary Bagot, 6 April 1818.

45. Hosford "Exile in Yankeeland," p. 49. For the earlier descriptions, see Diary of Louisa Catherine Adams, 26 February 1819, Adams Papers; and Beckles Willson, *Friendly Relations: A Narrative of Britain's Ministers and Ambassadors to America, 1791–1830* (1934; reprint, Freeport, N.Y.: Books for Libraries Press, 1969), p. 107. If the secretary of state had been a subscriber, the ball would have carried a political message. Louisa Catherine Adams makes it clear she and John Quincy Adams went as guests.

46. Hosford, "Exile in Yankeeland," p. 36.

47. *Letters of Mary Boardman Crowninshield*, p. 20.

48. Cooley, pp. 25–30 and 59–60.

49. Mary Bagot reports pieces of wedding cake wrapped in paper in her journal, 8 April 1816. Hosford, "Exile in Yankeeland," p. 44.

50. Seaton, pp. 90–91. The reference is dated 2 January 1813.

51. Harrison Gray Otis to Sally Foster Otis, 6 December 1818, Otis Papers.

52. Harrison Gray Otis to Sally Foster Otis, 19 February 1819, Otis Papers.

53. Cooley, p. 30.

54. Mitchill, "Dr. Mitchill's Letters," p. 752. For a good assessment of the architecture and furnishings and some lively sketches of entertaining during all administrations, see William Seale, *The President's House, a History* (Washington: White House Historical Association, 1986). For a superficial account of presidential entertaining, see Marie D. Smith, *Entertaining in the White House* (Washington: Acropolis Books, 1967).

55. Mitchill, "Dr. Mitchill's Letters," p. 743. The practice of introducing young ladies to society persisted into the 1820s and is confirmed in Margaret Bayard Smith, *A Winter in Washington, or Memoirs of the Seymour Family*, vol. 1 (New York: E. Bliss and E. White, 1824), p. 12.

56. Cutler and Cutler, pp. 114–15 and 180.

57. Catharine Mitchill to Margaret Akerly Miller, 11 January 1809, Mitchill Papers.

58. *Letters of Mary Boardman Crowninshield*, pp. 35–36. See also Seaton, p. 112–13; and Hosford, "Exile in Yankeeland," p. 44.

59. W. W. Abbot, ed., *The Papers of George Washington, April-June 1789*, Presidential Series, vol. 2 (Charlottesville: University Press of Virginia, 1987), p. 248.

60. Stewart Mitchill, ed., *New Letters of Abigail Adams, 1788–1801* (Boston: Houghton Mifflin Co., 1947), p. 19.

61. Kathryn C. Buhler, *Mount Vernon Silver* (Mt. Vernon, Va.: The Mount Vernon Ladies' Association of the Union, 1957), p. 58.

62. Somewhat like the extension of the time for morning visits into the afternoon, the term "levee," when first used in the United States, indicated a presidential reception in midday for men. Later it was used with less discrimination and became a substitute term for evening tea or "drawing room," as in "night levee." Elbridge Gerry, Jr. used the phrase; see Bowers, p. 181.

63. Dumas Malone, "Without Benefit of Protocol: The Merry Affair," in *Jefferson the President, First Term, 1801–1805* (Boston: Little, Brown & Co., 1970), pp. 367–92.

64. Mitchill, "Dr. Mitchill's Letters," 1802, p. 744.

65. Cutler and Cutler, February 1803, p. 132.

66. Catharine Mitchill to Margaret Akerly Miller, 8 April 1806, Mitchill Papers. In later letters to her sister Mrs. Mitchill described dinner at the Madisons' (11 December 1808) and another at the White House (21 November 1811).

67. Journal of Alexander Dick, 7 June 1809, Dick Papers. Dick had just returned to Washington after an extensive southern trip.

68. Journal entries for 27 March and 3 April 1816 in Hosford, "Exile in Yankeeland," p. 35.

69. Catharine Mitchill to Margaret Akerly Miller, 11 January 1811, Mitchill Papers. Irving also tells the story; see Conover Hunt-Jones, *Dolley and the "great little Madison"* (Washington: The AIA Foundation, 1977), p. 31.

70. Catharine Mitchill to Margaret Akerly Miller, 21 February 1812, Mitchill Papers.

71. Smith, *First Forty Years*, p. 131.

72. William Wirt to Elizabeth Wirt, 27 December 1815, Wirt Papers. After the Wirts had moved to Washington, Mrs. Wirt commented on the dwindling of the 1820 social season because of Mrs. Monroe's health and "the death of our hero Decatur." Elizabeth Wirt to her daughter Laura, Richmond, 10 May 1820.

73. Smith, *First Forty Years*, p. 141.

74. Seaton, p. 136.

75. John Quincy Adams denied any knowledge that "visiting of form" was a part either "of official right, or official duty." He claimed, in spite of many seasons in Washington, that neither he nor Mrs. Adams had ever received first visits from heads of departments or their wives. He then established presidential policy for practical reasons and extended it to the president's wife and the wives of the heads of departments. He closed the letter by stating that while the Adamses were "happy to receive any respectable stranger who pleases to call upon us, we have no claim or pretension to claim it of any one." Cooley, pp. 84–99.

By 1821 Harrison Gray Otis reported that Mrs. Adams was "advancing in public favor—Mrs Tayloe Says there has never been any collisions between her and the Washington ladies, but only with the Congressional cortege—I think too on the whole that John's chance for the Presidency brightens, but it is yet too early to begin our calculations." Otis to Sally Foster Otis, 2 January 1821, Otis Papers. Mrs. Adams understood what had been going on. She told a story of one man's long resentment when a visit had not been returned and he did not receive a card sent to invite him to dinner because he had changed lodgings. Diary of Louisa Catherine Adams, 20 January 1822, Adams Papers.

The matter was not entirely settled by 1829. Cooley reprints Adams's letter with a heading that explains his remarks "have been confined to such ceremonies as have from time and practice become established; but there are a few other points of etiquette . . . which yet remains to be determined, before they can, with certainty, be included in the established etiquette of that place." Cooley, p. 84.

76. Cooley, pp. 5–14.

77. Ibid., p. 77.

78. Smith, *First Forty Years*, p. 154.

79. Harrison Gray Otis to Sally Foster Otis, 6 April 1820, Otis Papers.

80. Harrison Gray Otis to Sally Foster Otis, 23 December 1818, Otis Papers.

81. Smith, *First Forty Years*, p. 97.

82. *How to Behave* (New York: 1856), p. 124.

Index

References to illustrations are in italics.